Philosophical and Empirical Approaches to Psychology

Philosophical and Empirical Approaches to Psychology

Mentalism vs. Antimentalism

Giuseppe Lo Dico

LEXINGTON BOOKS
Lanham • Boulder • New York • London

Published by Rowman & Littlefield
A wholly owned subsidiary of The Rowman & Littlefield Publishing Group, Inc.
4501 Forbes Boulevard, Suite 200, Lanham, Maryland 20706
www.rowman.com

Unit A, Whitacre Mews, 26-34 Stannary Street, London SE11 4AB

British Library Cataloguing in Publication Information Available

Library of Congress Cataloging-in-Publication Data Available

ISBN 978-1-4985-1660-0 (cloth : alk. paper)
ISBN 978-1-4985-1661-7 (electronic)

™ The paper used in this publication meets the minimum requirements of American National Standard for Information Sciences—Permanence of Paper for Printed Library Materials, ANSI/NISO Z39.48-1992.

Printed in the United States of America

Dedicated to Stefania

Contents

Introduction

Why should you read this book even though I cover some of the same ground—Wundt, behaviorism, cognitivism, James, the mind-body problem—as other more notable authors? It is a truly interdisciplinary work between philosophy (more precisely, philosophy of mind, science, and psychology) and experimental psychology. The *philosophical* part of this book cannot set aside from the *experimental* part (and vice versa) because they are strictly intertwined and complementary. I believe the former can lose much (if not all) of its strength without the latter (and vice versa) so that they must be considered together.

Philosophical and Empirical Approaches to Psychology: Mentalism versus Antimentalism shows how certain philosophical stances toward the mind can have a strong influence on the methods used by psychologists and, more in general, on the practice of scientific research. In my experience as a scholar in psychology I realized that psychologists (me included, of course) are continuously influenced by these stances and are often unaware of them. Psychologists often do not have explicit views about methodological issues (such as theory construction, explanation, confirmation, evidence, etc.) and ignore that they are based upon certain philosophical arguments and positions. As clearly stated by the philosopher Thagard (2009, 240), this "is not because they do not have any views, just that the views they hold are usually implicit and unreflective."[1] Thus, for making these views more explicit and clear, psychologists must consider philosophy as a basic support to their discipline. More precisely, as I show in this volume, I think that philosophy can play a crucial role in psychology. I believe the role of philosophy is the critical assessment of many of psychology's methodological and theoretical underpinnings.[2]

I want to clarify that *Philosophical and Empirical Approaches to Psychology: Mentalism versus Antimentalism is not* two sorts of book. First, *it is not* a textbook for graduate students, because it requires some background knowledge of philosophy of mind and science and research methodology in social sciences. Second, *it is not* a history of psychology, because it does not aim at historically reconstructing the different positions exposed but at critically assessing and discussing them.

So, what *is* this book? *Philosophical and Empirical Approaches to Psychology: Mentalism versus Antimentalism is* a balanced integration between a research monograph and a reference work. It offers an exploration of the idea of mind from the late nineteenth and early twentieth centuries to its role in contemporary psychology. Throughout this period, differing and often incompatible ideas of mind have been proposed. Thus, for simplicity, I will divide these ideas into two big groups: mentalism (whose supporters assume that the mind is not reducible to something else) and antimentalism (whose supporters assume that the mind is indeed reducible to something else). I argue that the adoption of one of these ideas over the others can have a profound influence in research practice, especially in determining the researchers' choice of methods and their interpretation of data. Further, I show that some controversial psychological notions such as *consciousness* or *introspection* pertain to a peculiar mentalistic approach (that is, introspectionism). Moreover, the fact that many psychologists consider these notions nonscientific depends upon their adherence to a certain antimentalistic approach (that is, behaviorism or cognitive neuroscience) or to a specific mentalistic perspective (that is, cognitive psychology). I consider these issues by assessing experimental psychology in relation to neurobiology (whose vocabulary has recently colonized psychology) and philosophy (providing arguments in favor or against a certain form of mentalism or antimentalism). I integrate a series of *philosophical and theoretical* chapters with a series of *empirical and experimental* chapters by using an interdisciplinary perspective from philosophy of psychology and experimental psychology; I believe this is the most innovative aspect of the book that differentiates it from others on the subject. I show the strong and the controversial points of the various mentalistic and antimentalistic approaches to psychology by integrating a philosophical analysis and an empirical research.

Philosophical and Empirical Approaches to Psychology: Mentalism versus Antimentalism begins with a philosophical (I mean, epistemological, methodological, and metaphysical) analysis of four different approaches to psychology in chapters 1–4: introspectionism, behaviorism, cognitive psychology, and cognitive neuroscience. These approaches will be treated not from a historical perspective but from a conceptual, logical, and theoretical one. I deal with these approaches more or less as Kuhnian paradigms; that is to say, I examine them on the basis of their empirical, methodological, and metaphysical assumptions.

Subsequently, I use empirical research to examine the role that these four psychological paradigms play in a specific experimental setting in chapter 5–7. I base this on a replication and two new trials of the experiments carried out by the neurologist Antonio Damasio for testing his somatic marker hypothesis.

In the third and final part of the manuscript, I offer an integration of the first two sections with an evaluation of Damasio's experiments in chapter 8. I critically consider the results of my experiments and theoretical considerations compared to Damasio's and his idea of the mental. Furthermore, I criticize Damasio's rebuttal of introspective verbal reporting as a reliable method for dealing with emotions and cognition. In this context, I argue that, along with behavioral and neurological measures, verbal reporting must be considered as a reliable method for experimental psychology.

I hope the reader will find this book interesting and enjoyable. That does not mean that the reader must accept all of the philosophical positions taken and the empirical results reported uncritically: I am fully aware that my ideas are controversial. What I would like above all is that the contents of this volume be thought-provoking and contribute to the discussion about the role of philosophy in psychology and cognitive science.[3]

NOTES

1. At the beginning of this 2009 article, Thagard is even much more explicit in this sense: "Those who believe themselves to be exempt from philosophical influence are usually the slaves of some defunct philosopher" (238).
2. See Dennett 2009.
3. See, for example, Dennett 2009, Thagard 2009, Bechtel 2010, Castiglioni and Corradini 2011, and Gaj 2016.

Chapter One

Mentalism

In the late nineteenth and early twentieth century scientific psychology, the orthodox view considers the *conscious mind* as the proper object of study (rather than, for example, the patterns of behavior or the subdoxastic processes or the *unconscious mind*) (Manson 2000, 150). According to this view, the mind is conceived as something accessible and understandable only from a *subjective* or *first-person perspective* and not accessible from an (almost) *objective* or *third-person perspective* as the natural phenomena are. This means that the properties and the laws of the mental realm must be considered irreducible to those of the physical realm and thus also the ways for studying them.

In this chapter, I will provide an examination of this perspective by considering the works of two representative authors of the late nineteenth and early twentieth century psychology (Wilhelm Wundt's *Outlines of Psychology* [1897] and William James's *Principles of Psychology* [1890–1918)]) and I will propose a comparison between them. I choose to deal with Wundt and James for two reasons. First, both were among the first to propose a mentalistic psychology autonomous and detached from philosophy (Mandler 2007, XV and 7). Second, and perhaps more substantial, although both of their positions are usually classified as introspectionist and dualist (of some sort), they endorse two different and often conflicting approaches to the mental resulting in two different and conflicting methodologies for inquiring into it.

WILHELM WUNDT'S POSITION

In his fundamental book on the history of experimental psychology, the psychologist and historian Boring (1929) starts discussing Wundt's work by calling him "the senior psychologist in the history of psychology" and "the first man who without reservation is properly called a psychologist" (310). Although Boring's definition of Wundt as the first psychologist in the history of psychology is probably exaggerated and based upon a controversial historical reconstruction,[1] Wilhelm Wundt is undoubtedly a central figure in psychology.[2]

Wundt's intellectual activity spans many disciplines such as physiology, psychology, and philosophy. Because of this eclecticism, his discourse does not appear always coherent and well defined. Nevertheless, Wundt considers himself as a foundationalist, whose great ambition is to establish a philosophic and scientific system of knowledge (A. Kim 2006). His *Outlines of Psychology* (1897) is probably the clearest attempt to show his systematic position (Lundin 1996, 81). In this chapter I'll discuss this position by considering three aspects:

1. Wundt's idea about the relation between mind and body
2. His idea of psychology as a science
3. His notion of mind

Wundt on the Mind-Body Relation

Wundt's position about the relation between mind and body is known as *psychophysical parallelism* (PPP). He argues that every mental process, from the simplest to the most complex one, runs in parallel with a bodily process. He points out that "there must be a necessary relation between all the facts that belong at the same time to both kinds of experience . . . for they are nothing but component of a single experience which is merely regarded in the two cases from different points of view. Since these facts belong to both spheres, there must be an elementary process on the physical side, corresponding to every process on the psychical side" (Wundt 1897, 317).

A common but useful image for this proposal is the following one: mental and bodily processes are as two parallel and separate railway lines that do not interconnect in any point but every mental process or event has a corresponding bodily process, and vice versa (Reber and Reber 2001, 507). This means that both mental and bodily processes must be understood in terms of their own laws, so psychological states cannot be explained in terms of physical or biological states in any way. Wundt argues that studying both psychological and physiological processes is important for comprehending the person in its totality. But, according to the PPP, physiology deals with the person as a physical object that must be understood in the same way as other physical objects.

Psychology, on the contrary, is about the person as an experiencing subject whose principal characteristic is her subjectivity or first-person perspective. Psychological and physiological explanations are thus independent and incommensurable because they pertain to two different domains of inquiry (Boring 1929, 328). For Wundt, psychologists must not be interested in finding the psychophysical connections between the nervous system's mechanisms and the mind's processes but only in describing and measuring the psychological regularities that can be found in psychological experiments (A. Kim 2006).

As we can see, Wundt makes a distinction between experimental psychology and physiology (and natural sciences in general), although he maintains that both must be considered as empirical sciences. The reason for such a distinction is that psychology and natural sciences use two different *supplementary concepts*: concepts that are not contained in experience but that are gained through a process of induction from it. The supplementary concept of psychology is the term mind, which is used for comprehending all of the psychological experiences taking place in an individual consciousness (Wundt 1897, 312). Instead, the supplementary concept of natural sciences is the term matter, which refers to the permanent substratum assumed to exist in the universal space and to whose activities we must attribute all natural phenomena (311).

Thus, for Wundt the concepts of mind and matter are indispensable for explanation respectively in psychology and in natural sciences. However, if the concept of matter is "used as a general supplementary concept that serves primarily to cluster the phenomena of natural sciences and secondarily to give a causal interpretation of them . . . ," the use of the concept of mind is not defined as well as that of matter. In other words, Wundt points out that psychologists collectively do not have a clear and shared definition of the notion of mind. This is because, unlike natural sciences (that have reached a strict *methodical definition*) of their concepts, psychology is still trying to come out from the *mythological stage of speculative definition* of them (312).

The appeal to the PPP leads Wundt to oppose the *psychophysical materialism* (PM), a doctrine that "does away with psychology entirely and puts in its place an imaginary brain" (313). According to this view, all mental experience must be considered identical to the body. Wundt points out that the PM is epistemologically untenable and psychologically unproductive. It is epistemologically untenable because a psychology that starts with a purely physiological definition of its concepts depends not upon experience but, similar to the older materialistic psychology, on a metaphysical unfounded presupposition (17). Yet, it is also psychologically unproductive because it allows interpreting only the physiological processes and not the mental ones as having causal powers. For Wundt, PM is flawed because it is based upon *a sort of faith* in the future physiological discoveries: "physiology has not yet furnished such an interpretation and never will be able to do so, because of the difference between the manner of regarding phenomena in natural science and in psychology. It is obvious; too, that such a form of psychology, which has been turned into hypothetical brain-mechanisms, can never be of any service as a basis for the mental science" (17–18).

As the psychologist Boring (1929, 328) and the philosopher Alan Kim (2006) pointed out, Wundt does not conceive the PPP as a universal and general metaphysical principle for solving the mind-body problem but as an empirical postulate necessary for giving an account of two different explanations of natural and psychological phenomena. He points out that such a postulate is necessary because it permits a clear definition of the fundamental laws of natural phenomena, on the one hand, and the fundamental laws of psychological phenomena, on the other (Wundt 1897, 320). In this sense, Wundt seems to refuse to adopt not only monism and materialism as ontological and metaphysical perspectives but also dualism. He explicitly rebuts substance dualism according to which mind and body must be conceived as two different and distinct realms whose events unfold upon separate but parallel causal tracks (A. Kim 2006; Robinson 2011). In fact, he points out, if mind and body were conceived as different substances, their connection would be nothing but a continual miracle (Wundt 1897, 316).

Thus, Wundt's PPP is not to be confounded with an ontological dualism similar to Descartes's, very roughly, postulating a neat division of the world in matter (or *res extensa*) and mind (or *res cogitans*) (Heidelberger 2003, 237; Robinson 2011). Nonetheless, Wundt's proposal does not seem to fit with a property dualistic position according to which a single substance is conceived as having two essentially different kinds of properties, the physical and the mental ones (Robinson 2011).

Thus, we can say that PPP appears to be better conceived as a form of explanatory or methodological dualism according to which natural sciences and psychology do not deal with different objects but with different points of view from which we take up the consideration and scientific treatment of a unitary experience (Wundt 1897, 2). In other words, Wundt points out that although natural scientists and psychologists study one and the same organism,[3] they deal with different kinds of experience derived from different perspectives. This means that natural scientists and psychologists deal with the same object of inquiry by appealing to different but incompatible "*methodologies*, in the sense of separate types of observations, that . . . run in parallel" (Blumenthal 1975, 1082). Thus, according to Wundt, transferring the point of view of natural sciences to the study of psychological phenomena in order to individuate their laws or their mechanical functioning can be a source of mistakes and errors (Mischel 1970, 8).

To sum up Wundt's position on this point, we can say that, for mental sciences, the contents of experience are considered directly related to the subject and they do not need to be abstracted away to be grasped. In this sense, the subject matter of psychology is the *immediate experience*. Rather, for natural sciences, the objects of experience are considered to be independent from the subject who has experience of them. But, because natural scientists can approach these objects first through immediate experience, they must abstract these objects from subjectivity to define them objectively. In this way, the subject matter of natural sciences is the *mediate experience*. Wundt adds: "The point of view of natural science may . . . be designated as that of mediate experience, since it is possible only after abstracting from the subjective factor present in all actual experience; the point of view of psychology, on the other hand, may be designated as that of immediate experience, since it purposely does away with this abstraction and all its consequences" (1897, 3).

Wundt on the Methods of Psychology

At this point, it is clear that if the subject matter of psychology is the immediate experience,[4] the best way to deal with it is to ask experimental subjects to report verbally what they are immediately experiencing (Boring 1929, 327). In other words, it is to ask experimental subjects to make introspection in their minds. But what does introspection exactly mean for Wundt? In general terms, introspection can be defined as a mental process or activity through which a person becomes aware of properties or aspects of her conscious experience (Hatfield 2005, 260; Schwitzgebel 2014). Examples of introspection can be the feeling of a cold or the perception of a certain color or the fact of being in a particular mood. It is clear that all of these feelings, perceptions, or states of being are based upon subjective (or in a first person) reports of experience that appear to contrast with the objective (or in a third person) reports of natural sciences. In this sense, for Wundt the problem for a scientific psychology is to create the conditions under which introspective observations can be transformed into something like scientific observations (Danziger 1990, 30).

In Wundt's experimental design, such conditions deal first with the role of the experimental subject and of the experimenter. During the experiment, the subject is asked to maintain a state of *readiness* or *strained attention* toward a series of physical stimuli presented and manipulated by the experimenter and to verbally report about how these stimuli are consciously perceived or felt (Lundin 1996, 79 and 83–84; Lyons 1986, chap. 1). It is assumed that the variations in the stimuli due to the experimenter's manipulations should result in the experimental subject's conscious experience (Lundin 1996, 83; Schultz and Schultz 1996, 78).

It is important to note that Wundt's conditions are very strict and demanding: first, experimental subjects are required to pass a long period of apprenticeship for gaining readiness or strained attention and are informed about what they are supposed to be experiencing before performing the task (Benjafield 1996, 69–71). Second, the aim of introspective experiments is narrow: for Wundt, the introspection is not a matter of uncontrolled retrospective and discursive description of the phases of a person's mental life (Davies 2005). Rather, his experiments principally regard sensations, perceptions, and feelings. Subjects are asked to make simple sensory judgments; I mean, to assess the brightness or size of two presented physical stimuli (Danziger 1990, 30). This is because Wundt assumes sensations, perceptions, and feelings are something simple and experimentally controllable. In this sense, experiments can be easily repeated and experimental observations checked by other investigators (Mischel 1970, 12; Benjafield 1996, 70).[5] It is important to say that for Wundt sensations and perceptions must be considered as the objective contents of the mind, whereas feelings are the subjective ones. He defines sensations, perceptions, and feelings as the elementary contents of the mind and argues that a single mental content can also consist of a combination of them (Schultz and Schultz 1996, 78–79).

As we have see above, for Wundt the condition for studying and observing sensations, perceptions, or feelings is when they are caused by an external physical stimulation as, for example, an external tone-vibration or an external light-impression (Wundt 1897, 21). In this sense, experimental psychology appears as an empirical science combining the experimentation typical of natural sciences (such as physics and physiology) and the self-observation and self-reporting of an experiencing subject (Wolman 1960, 12–13; Hatfield 1997, 358). In this view, we can see an application of the PPP according to which natural sciences and psychology do not have two different objects of inquiry, but they deal with the same object from two different points of view. In fact, once an external physical object provokes the rise of a sensation or a feeling, it is no more an object of natural sciences but has become an object of psychology (Danziger 1990, 30). This means that objects such as stones, plants, flowers, and so on can be seen as objects of both natural sciences and psychology depending upon the point of view assumed.

From the point of view of psychology, they must be considered as ideas, and the psychologist's aim is to give an account of "the genesis of these ideas, and for their relations, both to other ideas and to those psychical processes, such as feeling, volitions, etc. . . ." (Wundt 1897, 2). For example, the idea of a rose must be considered as a psychical compound; I mean, a cluster of sensations and perceptions (for example, the objective sensation of the rose's colors, shape, etc.) and feelings (the subjective sensation of pleasantness of seeing a rose). The psychologist has to explain through which laws and processes the concept of rose appears in a person's mind. Instead, from the point of view of natural sciences, the rose must be considered as an object classified in terms of the laws of chemistry, botany, physics, and so forth. The distinction between these two points of view has consequences for the methods used in natural sciences and psychology.

Wundt argues that natural sciences use experimentation and observation as methods of inquiry. He defines experimentation as an observation of a certain phenomenon linked to an *intentional interference* or manipulation of this phenomenon coming from an experimenter and observation as an investigation of certain phenomenon without such interference or manipulation but just as they are presented to the observer (19). For Wundt, *pure observation* has no room in psychology because it would mean using a form of uncontrolled introspection. As just shown, only *controlled introspection* can be empirically tenable. This is because the objects of psychology are conceived as subjective processes that vary according to different conditions and, without any form of control, can lead to false and unreliable experimental results. More precisely, a strict control by the experimenter is important because the objects of psychology are not permanent (they change continuously because of our observation of them) as the objects of natural sciences are. For these reasons, because of the subjective character and variability of the objects of the conscious mind, only controlled experimentation is conceivable in psychology (20).

It is important to note that, in his *Outlines of Psychology*, Wundt seems to assume that, because psychology and natural sciences have different methods of inquiry, they also have two distinct ways of measurement. Wundt points out that physical measurement deals with objects such as objective masses, forces, and energies. These objects are supplementary concepts that we must use for assessing the natural world and discovering the laws governing it. Instead, psychical measurement is concerned with the comparison of psychical components and their resultants and has to do with subjective values and ends (322).

For Wundt, the principle of PPP is relevant in this case, too, because it allows us, at the same time, to distinguish and put together these two kinds of measurement. For example, if we consider the muscular movements required for an external volitional act, the physical processes accompanying such an act invariably will follow the laws of physics and thus can refer to explanatory concepts such as masses, forces, and energies. But the mental values and ends that accompany the muscular movements can be qualitatively (subjectively) different even if the quantity of masses, forces, and energies remains the same (322–23). As we can see, the physical and the psychological measurements are considered as different but parallel as predicted by the PPP. As Wundt pointed out, "physical measurement deals with quantitative values, that is, with quantities that admit of a variation only in the relation of the quantity of the phenomena measured. Psychical measurement, on the other hand, deals in the last instance in every case with qualitative values, that is, values that vary in degree only in respect to their qualitative character" (323).

However, it is important to stress that, in spite of the distinction between *qualitative values* (typical of the psychical measurement) and *quantitative values* (typical of the physical measurement), Wundt does not renounce anchoring the empirical method of psychology to that of natural sciences. More precisely, the experimental method he promotes for psychology is directly derived from that of physics (with particular emphasis upon the study of light and sound) and physiology (Wundt 1897, 320; Danziger 1990, 24 and 27; Schultz and Schultz 1996, 77). This suggests that Wundt's psychology aims to provide a *metrization* or an objective quantification of the qualitative values expressed by the experimental subjects. In fact, only a small number of his studies involve reports about feelings (such as the pleasantness of a certain sensation): Most of them deal primarily with sensations and perceptions (in the form of judgments about size or temporal duration of a certain physical stimulus) (Danziger 1990, 35; Schultz and Schultz 1996, 78); in other words, with reports translatable in an objective and quantifiable language.

Wundt's Notion of Mind

To sum up, the appeal to the PPP leads Wundt to assume that natural sciences and psychology have two different objects of inquiry, the mediate experience and the immediate experience, respectively. An example of the first is when we look at a rose and we say that it is red. In this case, with the statement *the rose is red*, we give an objective and biased by interpretation description of an experience we have. An example of the second is when we look at a rose and we say something about its color intensity. In such a case, with the statement *the red of this rose is very intense*, we give a subjective and unbiased by interpretation description of an experience we have (Schultz and Schultz 1996, 77).

It is clear that, for studying the immediate experience experimentally, it is necessary to postulate that the experimental subject having this experience is conscious and able verbally to report sensations, perceptions, and feelings provoked by an external (physical) sense stimulus. In other words, this means using the term *mind* to indicate *consciousness* (Lundin 1996, 81). As Wundt clearly stated: "All that is necessary to presuppose is the consciousness which accompanies all experience, that in this experience objects are being presented to a subject" (1897, 5). It is important to note that Wundt identifies the consciousness of the mental with its subjective character. This is clear because, in psychological experiments, the researcher cannot avoid investigating "the whole content of experience in its relation to the subject and also in regard to the attributes which this content derives directly from the subject" (3). In a few words, the whole content of experience is not knowable or (introspectively) accessible to anyone except the experiencing subject (Reber and Reber 2001, 720). For Wundt, this means identifying the subject matter of psychology only with the person's subjectivity (Danziger 1990, 17–18) and thus completely excluding her observable behavior, conceived merely as a series of movements that can be explained by natural sciences (Mischel 1970, 11).

Wundt's choice to focus on sensations, perceptions, and feelings emphasizes a further aspect of how he conceives the mental: its divisibility into simple elements and compounds having attributes of their own that can be connected by the principles of association (Boring 1929, 324; Lundin 1996, 76). In other terms, Wundt assumes it is possible, through an introspective analysis with trained experimental subjects, to arrive at describing the elementary parts of the mind as the basis of the higher mental functions. It is important to stress that introspective analysis cannot study these functions. In fact, they appear to resist the distinction into elements and compounds. This seems to be due to a practical difficulty in experimentation: In the study of higher mental functions it is not possible to achieve a reliable coordination between external experimental conditions and internal changes in the experimental subject's consciousness (Danziger 1990, 36). As a consequence, Wundt argues that these functions can be studied only by appealing to non-experimental (laboratorial) research methods; that is to say, by looking at the *mental products* in philology, ethnology, and mythology (Hatfield 1997, 359).

A final feature of Wundt's notion of mind is that it is postulated as having proper causal powers. Wundt points out that this follows directly from the PPP, which recognizes "an independent psychical causality, which is related at all points with physical causality . . . but it is just as different from it as the point of view adopted in psychology, or that of immediate, subjective experience, is different from the point of view taken in the natural sciences, or that of mediate, objective experience due to abstraction" (Wundt 1897, 320). It is evident from this quotation how Wundt refuses to consider the PPP as a metaphysical principle and prefers to assume it as an empirical postulate for distinguishing the objects and the methods of study of psychology and natural sciences. Thus, by following his line of thought, we can assess whether the causal power of a certain thing pertains to the mental or to the physical realm only on the basis of the point of view we adopt (Mischel 1970, 11).

For example, my perception of a flower can be assessed both in terms of physical causality if we take the point of view of natural sciences (by giving an account of my perceiving behavior) and in terms of psychical causality if we take the point of view of psychology (by giving an introspective report of what I am perceiving). This position appears quite puzzling because it does not seem to allow distinguishing between a case of genuine physical causality and a case of genuine psychical causality. In fact, every example we can make of physical causality can be seen also as an example of psychical causality (and vice versa). In my opinion, the puzzle with Wundt's position relies upon its definition of his PPP at the explanatory and methodological level but not at the metaphysical one. In fact, assuming that a certain (physical or psychical) entity has a genuine causal power means taking a metaphysical stance regarding it. Thus, the definition of the PPP only in explanatory terms as Wundt proposed does not seem to allow for providing an exhaustive account of the problem of mental causality in general.

WILLIAM JAMES'S POSITION

James was without a doubt a central figure in the history of psychology; the influence of his *Principles of Psychology* can be found in the theories and terminology of many contemporary authors.[6] It is quite curious that, in spite of his importance and its pioneering work in America, James was not an experimentalist (Boring 1929, 493 and 494) and always preferred the philosophical and theoretical work.

Similar to Wundt's *Outlines of Psychology*, James's *Principles* (1890/1918) touches many topics, such as physiology, philosophy, and psychology and does not appear to be always coherent and clear in the positions assumed and defended. As pointed out by the philosopher Goodman (2006), James appears in different moments to be a monist, a dualist, or a neutral psychologist who does not want to consider philosophical or metaphysical questions. It must be pointed out that, in comparison to Wundt's *Outlines*, the *Principles* appears quite unsystematic and not aimed at founding a science of psychology (Lundin 1996, 104). Rather, its aim seems to discuss critically a certain number of topics in psychology.

Shifting from Wundt, in the next paragraphs I will discuss James's position by considering three aspects:

1. His idea about the relation between mind and body
2. His idea of psychology as a science
3. His notion of mind

James on the Mind-Body Relation

In the *Principles* James argues that knowing how the brain works is fundamental for psychology. In fact, "the brain is the one immediate bodily condition of the mental operations" and thus "a certain amount of brain physiology must be presupposed or included in psychology" (1890/1918, 4–5). In spite of the importance of brain processes for psychology, James seems to find unacceptable that the mind could be studied scientifically only through physiological and neurological methods. He argues that a focus only upon the mechanical functions of the brain would reduce mind to a mere *epiphenomenon*, an entity without any causal power (129). James calls the *automaton theory* the doctrine according to which the mental and its expressions (such as feelings, desires, sensations, perceptions, etc.) are nothing but products of the cerebral functioning and thus they can be reduced to them. Such a position is well exposed by the biologist Thomas Huxley, quoted at 130 of the *Principles*: "The consciousness . . . would appear to be related to the mechanism of the body simply as a collateral product of its working and to be as completely without any power of modifying that working as the steam-whistle which accompanies the work of a locomotive engine is without influence on its machinery." James refuses this theory because of its reductionistic and epiphenomenalistic outlook. He argues that even if we knew everything about the nervous system of a certain person (for example, of William Shakespeare), we could not give any account of its mental and behavioral activities (for example, of Shakespeare's thoughts about the plot of *Hamlet* and of the way he wrote it in a manuscript) (132).[7]

Another position about the mind-brain relation James opposed is the psychophysical parallelism (PPP). James interprets such a doctrine as a variety of substance dualism assuming both the absolute separateness of mind and matter and the invariable concomitance of a single mental change with a single bodily change, and vice versa (136). For James, such a position aims to preserve both physical science (and physical world) and psychological science (and psychological world). Sometimes mind and body seem to behave as if they interact, which can be considered only a bizarre coincidence (Robinson 2011). James finds PPP unacceptable because it implies that the mental, in virtue of its separateness from the physical world, cannot have any causal efficacy.

It is interesting to note that James levels more or less the same criticisms at the PPP and the automaton theory. In fact, he accuses both of these doctrines of not being able, on the one hand, to offer any satisfying solution to the problem of connecting mind and brain and, on the other, to give an account of the causal efficacy of the mental. Regarding the problem of the relation between mind and brain, in the *Principles* James seems to cast doubts about the possibility of solving this problem. He argues that a solution to such a problem should provide at least an example of an *elementary form* of causal and nomological connection between the mind and the brain. In James's words,

> one must reduce it to its lowest terms and know which mental fact and which cerebral fact are, so to speak, immediate juxtaposition. We must find the minimal mental fact whose being reposes directly on a brain-fact; and we must similarly find the minimal brain-event which will have a mental counterpart at all. Between the mental and the physical minima thus found there will be an immediate relation, the expression of which, if we had it, would be the elementary psycho-physic law. (1890/1918, 177)

However, James seems to be quite skeptical about the possibility of finding such an elementary form of connection. In this sense, it can be said that for James, although he has few doubts that a connection between mind and brain exists, the way in which this is possible seems quite mysterious. We can also say that an *elementary law* explaining such a connection at the ontological level probably exists, but it appears quite impossible to unravel it at the methodological and epistemological level.

In spite of James's skepticism about the possibility of finding a plausible solution to the mind-brain relation at the ontological, epistemological, and methodological levels, the view he seems to assume in the *Principles* is a form of *interactionistic dualism*. According to this view, mind and body are conceived as two separate realms, each owning its specific properties and characters but interacting between them (Reber and Reber 2001, 219; Robinson 2011). In other words, this position assumes that sometimes the mind operates to serve the physical and sometimes the body operates automatically, leaving the mind free of performing more complex functions than the bodily ones (Lundin 1996, 105). In this sense, we can say that for James the physiology of the nervous system provides necessary but not sufficient conditions for mental life. This is the reason why psychology must be conceived as the science of the mental, but simultaneously it must take into account the study of the nervous system's physiology (Lehaey 1992, 261). In the next paragraph, we will see how mind and brain are postulated to have different but complementary functions and why a psychological science is necessary to explain both their functioning and their interaction.

JAMES ON THE METHODS OF PSYCHOLOGY

In chapter 7 of the *Principles*, James argues that psychology must be considered as a natural science because, from the point of view of the psychologist, the mind is nothing but an object in a world of other objects. In fact, when a psychologist makes introspection upon her thoughts and she verbally reports them, she talks about them in an objective way. For example, she says that, under certain conditions, the color gray appears to her as green, and she calls such an appearance an illusion. This means that the psychologist compares two different objects (a real perception [gray] and an illusory perception [green]), and she says there must be a sort of relation between them (James 1890/1918, 183). James assumes both of these kinds of perception as the objects of psychological inquiry that psychologists must approach through a third-person perspective. Although the psychologists' point of view must be objective, it is clear that James conceives their subject matter to be subjective—that is to say, the immediate experience (Schultz and Schultz 1996, 156). For this reason he states that "introspective observation is what we have to rely on first and foremost and always" (James 1890/1918, 185).

However, it must be said that James does not conceive the introspective method as Wundt does. In fact, he argues that Wundt's experimental results are too narrow and artificial and have brought very small contributions to psychology (James 1890/1918, 192–93; Marx and Hillix 1963, 87–88). More precisely, James accuses Wundt of commiting the so-called *psychologist's fallacy*. Such a fallacy can be clearly exemplified in this way: Let us consider two food tasters, one trained and one untrained. The former is able to discriminate the different single elements of a certain flavor. But the latter does not have this ability, so she experiences a total blend of different flavor elements. Similarly, the fact that trained subjects can analyze their conscious sensations and feelings does not mean that the discrete elementary contents they report are present in the consciousness of all people exposed to the same experience (Schultz and Schultz 1996, 156). As we will see, the target of James's attack is not only Wundt's introspective method but also his idea of mind. In fact, as we will see, for James mental experience must be conceived as something transitive, fluid, unitary, and relational (a *stream of thought*) (Reed 1997, 202; Mandler 2007, 66). Thus, because of this character, it is an error to divide this experience into simple elements (Lundin 1996, 108).

This means that the units of analysis of psychological research James postulated are much larger than those Wundt postulated. This can cause some problems to the reliability of the introspective method. In fact, because the introspective method must not be limited to simple sensations or feelings but it must deal with complex mental contents, a psychologist could be very prone to confound her own standpoint with that of the mental facts about which she is making her introspective report. In this way, introspective data could bring confusion between the vocabulary used in a first-person perspective (that used by every person in everyday life) and that used in a third-person perspective (that used by the psychologist) (James 1890/1918, 196).

In summary, we can say that for James, on the one hand, narrow introspection (as Wundt and other supporters of elementarism proposed) is hopeless for scientific psychology because the mind cannot be divided into small and single elements. But, on the other hand, he argues that wide introspection (the verbal reports of subjective stream of thoughts) is necessary for scientific psychology but cannot be completely reliable because it cannot be put under strict experimental control. Thus, how is it possible to give an account of the validity and veridicality of introspective data?

On the one hand, James's proposal is clear because he argues that introspective results have to be supplemented and compared with other sources of data, in particular those coming from the experimental (psychophysical and physiological) and comparative methods (James 1890/1918, 192–94.)[8] In James's words,

> psychology assumes that thoughts successively occur, and that they know objects in a world which the psychologist also knows. These thoughts are the subjective data of which he treats, and their relations to their objects, to the brain, and to the rest of the world constitute the subject matter of psychological science. Its methods are introspection, experimentation and comparison. (1890/1918, 197)

However, on the other hand, his proposal in favor of the adoption of a plurality of methods in psychology seems to be quite vague and undefined. In fact, all through the *Principles*, James does not provide any methodological guideline for integrating the results coming from many different sources. In this sense, his proposal seems to be spurious and to remain at a programmatic level.

James's Notion of Mind

As I said above, in the *Principles* (especially in chapter 5) James seems to support and defend a variety of interactionistic dualism about the relation between mind and brain (Gale 1997, 55–56). To put it simply, according to this sort of position about the mind-body problem, mind and brain are conceived as causally influencing each other (Robinson 2011). Thus, although mind and brain must be considered as two separate realms (no matters if defined in terms of substances or properties), they are strictly connected and cannot be considered separately at the ontological and methodological levels. For this reason, in the *Principles* James starts to discuss his idea of mind by examining the human brain, its features and functions. He argues that the brain has to be considered as a quite instable biological mechanism potentially adapted to respond to an infinite variety of minute stimuli and features of a certain situation but whose fallibility is as great as its elaboration power. So, James seems to consider the brain as an organ able to process a lot of information useful for living in a certain environment. He argues that, due to its complex structure, the performances of a human brain are quite unstable, that is, similar to a die rolling forever on a table. Obviously, this instability cannot guarantee any certainty in the choices of the human being. In this sense, the brain seems to need a sort of *external support* able to increase its efficiency and thus guarantee a certain level of certainty in the person's choices. This would mean bringing "a more or less constant pressure to bear in favor of those of its performances which make for the most permanent interests of brain's owner; it would mean a constant inhibition of the tendencies to stray aside" (James 1890/1918, 140).

What can bring this pressure is the mind, which can be defined in terms of its functions. That is to say, James aims at defining the mental in terms of what it does (rather than in terms of what it is) (Lehaey 1992, 261); or, in other words, as "an organ with a function in the psychophysical economy" (Boring 1929, 501), a *selective agency* (James 1890/1918, 149) possessing a sort of *eye view* that can plan future ends and choose the means for their attainment. As James clearly pointed out: "no actions but such as are done for an end, and show a choice of means, can be called indubitable expressions of mind" (11). This function is what allows discriminating between an intelligent performance (as that performed by the mind) and a mechanical performance (as that performed by the brain) (8). Such an idea of mind clearly shows how James conceives the interaction between the mind and the brain and how their functions must be distinguished. In fact, the brain seems to be characterized as a sort of *instrument of possibilities* that gives no certainties and the mind as an entity that can select or refuse the options offered by the brain (141–42).

It is worth noting that James assumes that a necessary condition for mind's functioning is its conscious character. For this reason, in the *Principles* he uses interchangeably the terms consciousness and mind. As I said above, for James as well as for the other late nineteenth and early twentieth century mentalists, consciousness is the mark of mentality. In chapter 6 of the *Principles* he emphasizes this point and argues that the unconscious mind does not exist and so cannot be postulated in the psychological explanations. He points out that postulating unconscious mental states or operations is "the sovereign means for believing what one likes in psychology, and of turning what might become a science into a tumbling-ground for whimsies" (163). This means that, if we want to give an exhaustive description or explanation of mental phenomena, we must describe only the processes and contents of consciousness without making any appeal to unconscious phenomena of any sort (Manson 2000, 151).

In pages 164–76 of volume 1, James outlines ten proofs in favor of the existence of the unconscious mental states and refuses all of them. His way of replying can be resumed in this way: The postulation of an unconscious mental state in a psychological explanation is wrong because it is redundant. In fact, because of the neat distinction between the brain as the entity in which the functions of storing and analyzing information coming from the environment take place and the conscious mind as the entity that has to choose and select among the different options elaborated by the brain, there is no room for an unconscious mind. That is to say, for giving an exhaustive account of a certain mental phenomenon, it is sufficient to appeal to an explanation making reference either to the functions of the brain or to those of the conscious mind. Adding something more as an unconscious mind would lead to confusion and misunderstandings.

For example, we can clearly explain all our perceptual judgments about the size or the shape of an object with the principles of cerebral association (and thus reduce the former to the latter ones) without any appeal to an unconscious mental activity (169). Or, when we go to bed having some problems unsolved and we find their solutions when we awake in the morning, we can easily explain this situation as a case of consciousness forgotten (more or less as in the hypnotic trance) without any appeal to an unconscious mental activity (166). We can say that, for James, appealing to the unconscious processes is an error, because they are reducible either to brain functions or to consciousness functions. As we can see, by attacking the idea of an unconscious mind James defines what he thinks are the features of mentality: consciousness, personality, individuality, accessibility to an examination in a first-person perspective, definability in functional terms, ability to act selectively and thus to choose means for reaching certain ends (Marx and Hillix 1963, 89; Lundin 1996, 107). This is probably the main reason why James considers introspection as an indispensable source of data for psychology, although he realizes that it shows many methodological difficulties and that it is prone to error.

CONCLUDING REMARKS

As we have seen throughout the chapter, Wundt's and James's positions differ in many respects. First, they have different and incompatible ideas about how to define the relation between mind and body. Wundt defends a position called PPP, according to which mind and body are conceived to run in parallel and every mental event must be correlated with a bodily event and vice versa. Wundt interprets such a claim as an empirical postulate that permits contemporarily making psychology autonomous from natural sciences and avoids distinguishing between mind and matter in metaphysical terms. So conceived, it seems that the PPP can be compatible with some form of physicalism, because the mental and the physical are conceived as two different parts of the same unitary experience. Unfortunately, Wundt's refusal to give a metaphysical foundation to the PPP obfuscates its intelligibility, in particular about the issue of causality. In fact, it seems to be quite difficult to understand how the mental can have a genuine and autonomous causal power. According to James, Wundt's position about this issue is untenable and, in opposition, he proposes an interactionistic dualism postulating the mental as strictly entrenched in the physical but at the same time autonomous from it. In this sense, mind and brain are conceived as having distinct but complementary functions; and the former seems to be able to exert its causal powers on the latter. So defined, James's position seems incompatible with any form of physicalism, because the mental and the physical are conceived as separate and distinct realms with their proper features.

However, in spite of their differences, both Wundt and James refuse to reduce the mental to the physical (by rebutting the PM and the automaton theory, respectively) and support a dualistic idea of the relation between mind and body. Further, both admit a separation between psychology and natural sciences. This means that for both the mind is a phenomenon distinguishable from the biological and the physical ones in general and requiring proper methods for being studied. In fact, both Wundt and James look at introspection as the fundamental method for psychology and both assume that it needs strict controls to be considered reliable. Such an emphasis upon the introspective method indicates that they conceive the mental as *conscious in principle*, that is to say, as accessible to the subject's point of view. In other words, consciousness must be considered as the mark of mentality and what really distinguishes the mental from natural phenomena.

NOTES

1. See Danziger 1990, chaps. 2 and 3, and Hatfield 1997 for alternative proposals.
2. The traces of his influence can be found, for example, in the positions of the founders of that important movement known as Phenomenology (A. Kim 2006; Käufer and Chemero 2015, 7).
3. I mean the person and all of her aspects.

4. In fact, according to Wundt's proposal, only the person from her own point of view is able to give an account of her mental states (no other person can tell by observing her what happens in her mind) (Mischel 1970, 13).

5. In this sense, we can say that Wundt's experimental psychology is definable as a *sensory psychology* that does not consider many topics such as thought and affective processes (Danziger 1990, 36; Mandler 2007, 56–57).

6. See, for example, the work on emotion of an important researcher we will meet later in this book, the neurobiologist Damasio.

7. It is worth noting here a difference between Wundt's and James's ideas of psychology. For the former, behavior does not seem to be the focus of psychology because it is reducible to something physical and thus open to observation. For the latter, behavior seems to be understandable as a consequence of the mental activity and thus not completely reducible to something physical.

8. See also Lundin 1996, 100; Hatfield 1997, 367.

Chapter Two

Antimentalism

Wundt and James define psychology as the science of mental phenomena, and they consider the study of consciousness its core (J. Kim 1998, 25). However, given that consciousness must be the subject matter of psychology and must be defined on the basis of its subjective and private character, a shared definition of it among mentalistic psychologists does not seem to exist (Wozniak 1997). Further, mentalistic positions are open to criticisms on empirical and methodological grounds. These criticisms mainly regard the fact that introspection does not appear to be a completely trustworthy and reliable method, even if put under strict experimental control.

Behaviorism arises as an answer to these problems. It is often argued that its birth was in 1913 when the animal psychologist Watson's paper "Psychology as the Behaviourist Views it" was published (Marx and Hillix 1963, 137–38; Benjafield 1996, 154). This paper is considered to be the manifesto of behaviorism, and it is commonly viewed as something revolutionary for psychology. However, according to most historians of psychology, such a paper does not create anything new but simply points out an emerging and widespread (although implicit) trend; that is, psychology no longer has to be considered the science of consciousness but the science of behavior (Wozniak 1997). The publication of the manifesto marks only the moment when most psychologists become aware of it and provides for them a justification for abandoning the method of introspection considered unreliable and sterile (Leahey 1992, 312).[1]

In this chapter, I will consider two versions of behaviorism, that of Watson and that of Tolman. Although both are generally classified as behavioristic psychologies, we will see that they show some important differences.

WATSONIAN BEHAVIORISM

I believe the best way to start with Watsonian behaviorism is to quote the opening of his manifesto (my italics):

> Psychology as the behaviourist views it is a *purely objective experimental branch of natural science*. Its theoretical goal is the prediction and control of behaviour. *Introspection forms no essential part of its methods*, nor is the scientific value of its data dependent upon the readiness with which they lend themselves to interpretation in terms of consciousness. *The behaviourist*, in his efforts to get a unitary scheme of animal response, *recognizes a non dividing line between man and brute.* The behaviour of man, with all of its refinement and complexity, form only a part of the behaviourist's total scheme of investigation." (1913, 158)

Having been trained in animal psychology, Watson aims to apply its methods and theories to the study of the human being (Boring 1929, 582–83). This point is important, because in animal psychology the golden rule is to avoid the risk of anthropomorphizing animals. This means that animal psychologists consider it a mistake to describe and explain animals' behavior by using terms typical of the human realm, such as mental content or consciousness. This assumption is known as *Lloyd Morgan's Canon*, because the psychologist and zoologist Lloyd Morgan first proposed and articulated it (Reber and Reber 2001, 400).

The canon is a warning against the explanatory excesses in animal and comparative psychology and states that in no case may we interpret an action as the outcome of a higher psychological capacity if we can interpret it as the outcome of one that stands at a lower level on the psychological scale. In other terms, before appealing to higher psychological faculties (implying necessarily mentalistic terms), we must try to appeal to lower level faculties (not implying mentalistic terms) (Marx and Hillix 1963, 132–33). Lloyd Morgan's canon is crucial for Watson's behaviorism, because it suggests that if we can have an exhaustive account of human psychology without referring to higher-level capacities, we do not need to introduce mental terms in our explanations. It must be said that the appeal to the canon does not imply per se an elimination of the mentalistic vocabulary or the denial of consciousness. In fact, it was originally conceived as a caution against overestimating the application of mentalistic (or *high level*) vocabulary to the animal kingdom (Greenwood 1999, 3 and 14). For this reason, we can say that Watson's interpretation of the canon appears to be quite radical. In fact, he assumes that the appeal to consciousness or mind must be considered always a mistake, and so he aims to eliminate it from experimental psychology.

The main reason for such a radical position for Watson is the fact that the definition of the mentalistic terms is too confusing and speculative (Watson 1913)—that is, mentalistic experimental psychology does not agree on the psychological vocabulary. The concept of consciousness and the terms used to describe it (such as quality, extension, duration, and intensity) vary too much from author to author. Despite this situation, psychologists use these concepts in their descriptions and explanations as if they were justified to do so. He argues that no justification exists because consciousness, the core concept of mentalistic psychology, is as unapproachable as the old concept of soul, and it is put into psychology as a preliminary assumption that does not need either to be proved or defined (Watson 1925, 5). In other terms, he refuses to consider consciousness as a *primitive concept* or as a *basic assumption* of psychological science and to use it as the fundamental interpretative standard of the experiments (Marx and Hillix 1963, 139; Wozniak 1997).

Watson argues that consciousness cannot be the proper subject matter of psychology, mainly because of the unreliability of the introspective method. He points out that introspection can be neither objective nor comparable with to methods of the natural sciences and thus, as long as psychology is based on it, it cannot be defined as an empirical discipline. In other words, psychology

> has failed signally, I believe, during the fifty-odd years of its existence as an experimental discipline to make its place in the world as an undisputed natural science. Psychology, as it is generally thought of, has something esoteric in its methods. If you fail to reproduce my finding, it is not due to some fault in your apparatus or in the control of your stimulus, but it is due to the fact that your introspection is untrained. The attack is made upon the observer and not upon the experimental setting. In physics, the attack is made upon the experimental conditions. (Watson 1913)

Certainly, Watson's arguments touch a very controversial point of the introspective method and of the idea of conscious mind at its basis: the fact that it is strictly connected to the subjective (or first-person) point of view, whereas the objects of the natural sciences must be studied only from an objective (or third-person) perspective (Marx and Hillix 1963, 140). However, it must be pointed out that Watson seems to take his position for granted without really discussing these issues. In fact, in his writings he says nothing about how mentalists try to solve such problems both theoretically and experimentally. For example, he does not consider at all Wundt's attempts to provide a metrization of conscious subjective phenomena and so a natural science-based foundation of the introspective method.[2] We can say that instead of answering the question of why consciousness cannot be assessed objectively through introspection, Watson neutralizes it by a priori sanctioning the impossibility of studying the mental by introspecting it. The consequence of such a (radical) move is the elimination of mind from psychology and the adoption of a subject matter different from consciousness (Boring 1929, 581). This new subject matter is the *observable behavior* (Marx and Hillix 1963, 168). How exactly does Watson define it?

A Stimulus-Response Psychology

Someone could correctly argue that, in general, the focus on the behavioral data is something important for all psychologies (*folk psychology* included), and it is not peculiar to behaviorism. Every psychologist is interested in how people behave, and most of her work is to provide descriptions and explanations of it. Further, most of her inferences start from the observation of persons acting in different contexts and environments. Thus, this means that, at last, behaviorism does not offer anything different or new in comparison with the rest of psychology or psychologies.

A reply to this point could be that behaviorism does not deny that all psychologies focus on behavior in their analyses. Rather, it stresses that their perspective is wrong because of a lack of objectivity. That is, for mentalists behavioral data have no value per se: They are significant only insofar as they can shed some light upon consciousness (Watson 1913). For Watson, both James's and Wundt's psychologies use behavioral data from a wrong point of view—that is, personal and subjective. But if psychology aims at being part of natural sciences, it must assume a third-person (not first-person) and objective (not subjective) perspective. In this case, objective means observable and empirically testable. In Watson's words:

> why don't we make what we can observe the real field of psychology? Let us limit ourselves to things that can be observed and formulate laws concerning all those things. Now what can we observe? Well, we can observe behaviour—what the organism does or says. And let me make this fundamental point at once: that saying is doing—that is, behaving. Speaking overtly or to ourselves (thinking) is just as objective a type of behaviour as baseball. (1925, 6)

This quotation does not only define what should be the field of a behavioristic psychology, but it is a further attack on introspection. In fact, Watson does not deny the importance of verbal reports for psychology per se. Rather, he argues that they must be relevant only if considered objectively (and thus as kinds of behavior) and not subjectively. He argues that verbal reports can potentially be useful data, under the condition that they can be interpreted (or translated) in observable and behavioral terms. In brief, we can say that Watson's main point is that psychology must be concerned with observables to be defined as a science (Boring 1929, 586; Mandler 2002, 586; Mandler 2007, 103).

But how can a psychologist make his observations objectively? How can he describe behavior? Watson argues that behavior is based upon two features: stimulus (S) and response (R). He defines the former as a certain object in the environment or any change in the tissues due to the physiological condition of the animal—for example, the change we get when we keep an animal from sexual activity or from feeding or from building a nest. He defines the latter as anything that is animal activity or behavior—for example, jumping to a sound or performing a far more complex task like building a skyscraper (Watson 1925, 6–7; Marx and Hillix 1963, 140).

Through the analysis of the chains of Ss and Rs, a psychologist will be able to describe, predict, and control all of the behaviors, from the simplest one to the most complex.

> We can throw our psychological problems and their solutions into terms of stimulus and response. Let us use the abbreviation S for stimulus (or the more complex 'situation') and R for response. We may schematize our psychological problems as follows:
>
> S..R
> Given ?(to be determined)
> S..R
> ?(to be determined) Given
> Your problem reaches its explanation always when:
> S..R
> Have been determined have been determined. (Watson 1925, 20–21)

The major and most successful area of application of the S-R formula probably is learning. According to behaviorists, the capacity to learn in animals and human beings is governed by the formation of certain links between particular stimuli and specific responses. For Watson, this is plausible for every kind of learning, from the acquisition of fear responses by children to the reaction of a mother to the cry of her babies (Watson 1925, 8 and 19). The reconstruction of the chains of stimuli and responses allows the psychologist to give an exhaustive account of those phenomena without any appeal to consciousness or any other kind of unobservable mental states (conscious or unconscious).

For Watson, the avoidance of terms referring to the mental is what makes scientific the behavioristic explanatory strategy compared to the mentalistic one. An example of how behavioristic theories are preferable to mentalistic ones can be seen in a study of vision in animals. An experimenter puts an animal in a certain situation in which it has to respond (or to learn to respond) to one of two monochromatic lights. Then, the animal is fed at the one light (positive) and punished at the other one (negative). In brief, the animal learns to go to the *positive light* where he can be fed. At this point, a certain number of questions arise, and the experimenter can phrase them in two ways, one mentalistic (by asking if the animal sees the lights as well as the experimenter does—for example, as two different colors or two different shades of gray) and the other behavioristic (by asking if the animal responds on the basis of the difference in intensity between the two stimuli or the difference in wavelengths) (Watson 1913). Such an example shows quite clearly what are for Watson the main features that psychology should possess to be an objective science of behavior (Wozniak 1997):

- *Objectivity*, or the minimization of the influence of both observer and experimental subject on the observational data
- *Quantitativity*, or the use of data collected and analyzed in mathematical and statistical terms
- *Reproducibility*, or the fact that the work of one investigator should be in principle repeatable and testable by other experimenters
- *Flexibility*, or the fact that stimuli and responses could be varied in kind of complexity

These features do not seem so different from those required in today's experimental psychology.[3] What changes is the definition of the terms *stimulus* and *response*, which have been replaced, respectively, by *independent variable* (that is, any variable that is specifically manipulated by the experimenters so its effects upon the dependent variable may be observed) and *dependent variable* (that is, any variable whose values should be the result of the manipulations of the changes in values of one or more independent variables) (Reber and Reber 2001, 784; McBurney and White 2010, 120–22).

These variables, as the stimuli and responses, can be studied building up the experimental conditions that can reduce the influence of the observer or of the subject. For this reason, it is clear that the best place for behavioristic research is the laboratory, where the experimenter can control a great number of variables.[4] In this sense, the behavioristic experimental procedure is not so different from that used in the other natural sciences. I can summarize such a procedure in the following six points:

1. Seek a phenomenon to explain and make one or more testable hypotheses about it.
2. Control and define the experimental conditions, the stimuli (or independent variables) to manipulate, and the responses (or dependent variables) to observe or register via instruments.

3. Manipulate the stimuli (or independent variables) and collect the experimental data through the observation of the responses (or dependent variables).
4. Assess the stimuli (or independent variables) that have caused one or more responses (or dependent variables) and those that have not.
5. Assess the value, strength, and plausibility of the S-R links found through mathematical and logical analysis.
6. Check whether the data collected and analyzed fit with the hypothesis (or hypotheses) assumed at the beginning. In this case, as well as for point 5, the instruments of logic and mathematics are fundamental.

This procedure could be replicated and reevaluated in different laboratories by different researchers.

For Watson, the application of the S-R formula (and of the experimental procedures related to it) to psychological problems allows psychology to be free from the method of introspection and its difficulties.

Varieties of Behaviorism in Watsonian Behaviorism

The philosopher Graham proposes to classify behavioristic psychologies on the basis of their commitment to (at least one of) these three claims (2005):

1. Psychology must be the science of behavior, not the science of the mind.
2. Behavior is describable and explainable without making any reference to mental events of any type. The sources of behavior can be found in the environment, not inside the mind.[5]
3. If in the course of the definition of a psychological theory it is possible to introduce mental terms or concepts for taking account of behavior, then these terms or concepts must be eliminated or translated into a behavioral vocabulary.

These three claims are logically distinguished and, if taken alone, each is the central claim of a certain kind of behaviorism. That is, the acceptance of (1) is typical of *methodological or empirical behaviorism*, that of (2) of *psychological behaviorism*, and that of (3) of *analytical or logical behaviorism*. Although Watsonian behaviorism is generally identified as methodological or empirical behaviorism, in "Psychology as the Behaviourist Views It" (1913) and *Behaviorism* (1925) we can also find traces of both the psychological and the analytical ones. I have described methodological behaviorism in the first paragraph and I have pointed out that its central claim is that scientific psychology cannot be the science of the mind but the science of behavior. In this sense, methodological behaviorism is a normative theory about the scientific conduct of psychology.

As I have already mentioned, the reason for shifting from mind to behavior is mainly the discontent with the mentalistic psychology and its introspective method. Methodological behaviorism points out that human psychology is not different from animal psychology and that scientific psychology must be based on objective and observable facts. As Watson clearly pointed out,

> The psychology which I should attempt to build up would take as a starting point, first, the observable fact that organisms, man and animal like, do adjust themselves to their environment by means of hereditary and habit equipment. These adjustments may be very adequate or they may be inadequate that the organism barely maintains its existence; secondly, that certain stimuli lead the organisms to make response. In a system of psychology completely worked out, given the response the stimuli can be predicted. (1913, 167)

This quotation shows quite clearly that, for describing and explaining behavior, we do not need to refer to mental terms or concepts of any kind: The external physical stimuli, the responses given to them, and the learning history of a certain organism (human and not human) are sufficient for telling all about its psychology. This is the definition of psychological behaviorism, that is, the research program within psychology whose aim is to understand how the environmental events control behavior, to discover and explain the causal regularities underlying the chains of stimuli and responses, and to predict the behavioral modifications caused by environmental changes (Graham 2005). I described it above, in particular through the description of S-R associations. However, I want to say something more about two important points of the psychological behaviorism in Watson's thought: the environmentalism and the notion of *observable fact*.

Watson's environmentalism starts from considering that, in everyday life, an organism is assailed continuously by many different stimuli coming from outside its body. When this happens, the organism must do something to respond to these stimuli (Watson 1925, 13). In this way, (animal and human) behavior is defined in terms of patterns of adjustment to stimulus conditions in the environment and factors of habit and drive in the organism (Wozniak 1997).

Watson is not interested in defining the genetic determinants of these patterns. According to his perspective, whether they are innate or acquired is not a problem of psychology. What psychology has to focus on is how these patterns work in a certain environment. And, for doing it, psychologists must study only observable facts, that is, only chains of stimuli and responses.

Watsonian behaviorism leaves no room for anything else: every kind of mental (conscious or unconscious), neurobiological, or genetic variable that could be put between stimulus and response must be ignored. This means that, for Watson, in a scientific psychology we cannot postulate or infer the existence of factors determining behavior different from the observable stimuli. However, Watson admits that most of these chains are difficult to observe, and we need instruments in order to do it. In this sense, when Watson talks of observable facts, he has in mind many degrees of observation, ranging from the most direct (*naked eye observation*) to the most indirect (*observation through instruments*).

An example of *direct observation* in psychology is the so-called *external responses*, that is, the ordinary doings of human beings such as picking up a ball, writing on a paper with a pencil, driving a car, etcetera. In contrast, an example of *indirect observation* is the so-called *internal responses*, that is, all responses of the muscular and glandular systems inside an organism's body. For Watson, these internal responses are difficult to observe not because they are inherently different from the external ones, but because they require instruments to be detected (Watson 1925, 15; Boring 1929, 585).

As we can see, for Watson psychology's closest scientific counterpart is physiology. However, he points out that physiology and psychology must be autonomous. In fact, the former deals with the functioning of the single parts of the animal (such as the digestive system, the circulatory system, the nervous system, etc.). In contrast, the latter deals with what the animal does in its environment (Watson 1925, 11; Boring 1929, 585). From these definitions it is possible to see that psychology is distinct from physiology only in the domain of objects, not in its methods. In fact, both of these disciplines must be considered as natural sciences.

Watson justifies this point by arguing that in both of them we apply the same experimental procedure and the instruments of logic and mathematics to assess the results (19). That is, for Watson the behaviorist works like any other natural scientist, by gatherings facts, by verifying data and subjecting them to logic and mathematics (7). This is a strong claim about the unity of science similar to that proposed by logical positivism.[6] According to such a view, all science is in principle expressible in the same formal language within which it can be axiomatized. This means that all of the different scientific disciplines (from physics to social sciences) share the same fundamental model of explanation and prediction, the *deductive nomological model* (Hempel 1965, 335–47).

Further, neopositivists assume that each theory of a certain domain of inquiry can be logically reduced to a more basic one and, at last, all the theories of every domain can in principle be reduced to those of the physical domain

(Hooker 1999, 541). For example, a psychological theory can in principle be logically reduced to a biological or physiological theory that in turn can be reduced to a chemical theory that, at last, can be reduced to a physical theory. Such a reduction implies that, in the future, it will be possible to deduce the laws of the *higher-level sciences* (such as biology, chemistry, social sciences, etc.) from those of the *basic-level science* (physics). For logical positivists, the unity of method and the possibility of reduction of the higher-level sciences to the basic-level science are a guarantee of the unity of science. In this view, psychology would be part of the natural sciences only if its statements were translatable or reducible to those of physics.

This view is clearly developed in an article by the philosopher Hempel, "The Logical Analysis of Psychology" (1935). Hempel starts by attacking the idea that "apart from certain aspects clearly related to physiology, psychology is radically different, both as to subject-matter and as to method, from physics in the broad sense of the term" (167). Then, he argues that it is impossible to consider psychology as a science if its subject matter is the content of consciousness accessible only trough introspection (168). According to neopositivism, such contents cannot have any room in a scientific enterprise because they are not objective and empirically testable. However, if its subject matter were the *observable behavior* and not the *consciousness*, psychology could be considered as scientific.

Watsonian and Hempelian (or analytical or logical) behaviorisms share all of these considerations. But it is worth noting that they are two rather different enterprises: The former is an empirical research program in psychology, the latter a philosophical thesis whose central claim is that all of the scientific disciplines are in principle of one and the same nature—they are all branches of the unitary science, physics (Hempel 1935, 178). In this perspective, the analytical behaviorism, though connected in many ways to the claims of the methodological and psychological behaviorism, does not imply that the method of psychological research must be based on the study of the responses of an organism to certain stimuli in the environment (177). Neo-positivism is primarily a verificationist theory of meaning, and it does not prescribe any specific formula for giving an account of the behavior. Its aim is to assess according to which conditions scientific propositions can be considered meaningful. As I said previously, according to the logical positivist view, scientific propositions are considered verifiable and meaningful only if they are translatable or reducible in terms of the basic science, physics. That is, for Hempel, "all psychological statements which are meaningful (that is to say, which are in principle verifiable) are translatable into propositions which involve not psychological concepts but only the concepts of physics. The propositions of psychology are consequently physicalistic propositions.

Psychology is an integral part of physics" (173). All of the propositions that cannot satisfy these requirements must be considered *pseudo or metaphysical propositions*. So, as I have pointed out above, because of their subjective character, mentalistic concepts do not appear to be able to satisfy the conditions of verification (that is, they are untranslatable in physicalistic terms) that, instead, are successfully satisfied by behavioral concepts.

For analytical behaviorism, only under these conditions can psychology be part of the natural sciences. This conclusion could be shared by Watsonian behaviorists, although they focus more on the methods and the definition of empirical psychology than on how it is possible to translate or reduce its vocabulary to physics. According to this point, it can be argued that the attention of logical positivists for psychology can be considered only as an example of application of their program of unification of science to a specific discipline.

TOLMANIAN BEHAVIORISM

The S-R formula seems to provide a good empirical ground for psychology: It allows explaining how an organism responds to certain stimuli and even making predictions about its behavior on the basis of the stimuli considered. Further, such an S-R formula can be applied successfully to the study of learning: An organism learns something (or to do something) according to the number of times (frequency) it deals with a determined stimulus (or set of stimuli) and gives a determined response (or set of responses). Thus, all a psychologist has to do is discover all of the possible combinations of stimuli and responses. An example of application of the formula is provided by an experiment with a four-compartment discrimination box. A rat is put in such a box and has to learn which doors are open to arrive at the *food box*. The opening and closing of the doors is determined by the experimenters in terms of its being lighted or dark, left or right, or other combinations. Thus, the rat has to learn the correct sequence of doors open to reach the food. For example, door 1 is open when lighted but closed when dark (or vice versa), door 2 is open when left and closed when right, and so on. That is, for stimulus 1 (door 1) there is a correct (lighted) and an incorrect response (darkened), for stimulus 2 (door 2) a correct (left) and an incorrect (right) response, and so on. Watsonian behaviorists have no difficulties in explaining the rat's behavior and in predicting which doors it will tend to choose after a certain number of trials.

But let us consider a situation in which the experimenters vary the stimuli randomly in each trial. In this case, the rat could not solve the task: It lacks the regularity of the stimuli's presentation on the basis of which it can learn a sequence of correct responses. In such a case, according to Watsonian behaviorism, the result expected is that the rat will not show any regularity in its choices. However, when this experimental variation is applied, it can be seen that the individual rat goes through a succession of systematic choices—that is, regularity in the rat's choices. It is observed that such a rat begins by choosing all dark doors and so on (Tolman 1948, 255). These *well-above-chance systematic types of choices* cannot be exhaustively accounted for only according to chains of stimuli and responses. Something different seems to be relevant. Something different seems to be relevant here. Tolman postulates that something intervenes between S and R, and he aims at explaining what it is. But before considering these other determinants of behavior, let us look at Tolman's behaviorism and how it differs from Watson's.

Behaviorism beyond Watson

Tolman declares himself as a behaviorist by assuming the two core notions of behaviorism: how an organism behaves is the legitimate and main source of data for psychology (Reber and Reber 2001, 754), and the aim of psychology is the description, prediction, and control of behavior (Lehaey 1980, 334). Thus, he rejects consciousness and its subjective character as the subject matter of psychology: "the definition of psychology as the examination and analysis of private conscious contents has been something of a logical sticker. For how can one build up a science upon elements which by very definition are said to be private and non-communicable?" (Tolman 1922, 1).

Curiously, in this early paper (1922), the real target is not a form of mentalism or introspectionism but rather the Watsonian behaviorism. Tolman defines this kind of behaviorism as the analysis of the S-R relation such that, having a certain S we can predict a certain R and, vice versa, having a certain R we can predict a certain S. However, he argues that in Watson's work these S and R are generally defined in physiological terms: The former, for example, a ray of light of a different wave length; the latter, for example, a muscular contraction or a glandular secretion (1–2). In this sense, Tolman finds the Watsonian proposal unacceptable, because it seems to suggest a reduction of behavior to physiology. Thus, he points out that "the only difference between our point of view and Watson's would be that we should insist that . . . an account in terms of muscle contraction and gland secretion would be not behaviorism at all but mere physiology" (2).

According to this criticism, Tolman defines Watsonian behaviorism as *molecular* and his as *molar*. Molar means that a behavior must not be considered as a mechanistic series of S-R connections or of simple muscular or glandular reflexes but rather as a function of the organism as a whole. What characterizes the notion of behavior interpreted in this meaning is its *purposiveness*.

For Tolman the behavior must be seen in terms of how a certain organism uses the objects in the environment, and so it develops a certain *means-end readiness* with regard to them and their role in relation to its behavior (Marx and Hillix 1963, 283). This means that the behavior in general must be seen as always goal-oriented, and for Tolman such an orientation can be observed intersubjectively and is thus definable in objective terms.

An example of purposive behavior is the following: When a rat runs a maze, it is observed that his running and searching activities persist until food is found. It seems that his persistence is the result of the physiological condition of hunger. We do not know whether the rat in so persisting is conscious, or if he feels the purpose (to use a mentalistic terminology). However, we know that, given (1) the physiological condition of hunger and (2) the objective conditions of the maze, the rat persists until the food is found. For Tolman, "it is purely objective fact of persistence until a certain specific type of goal object is reached that we define as a goal seeking. And as thus defined, a goal seeking is a wholly objective and wholly behavioristic phenomenon. There is nothing mentalistic about it" (1925a, 38–39)—probably nothing mentalistic, but also nothing strictly behavioristic (that is, strictly Watsonian), except the conditions (1) and (2). In fact, the explicit aim of this paper (1925a) is to introduce into experimental psychology new concepts that could be useful for description and explanation. *Purpose* is only one of these new concepts that Tolman considers different from the usual ones in not being restricted to the customary physiological notions of stimulus, neural excitation, synaptic resistance, muscular contractions, or glandular secretions (38).

Another one of these concepts is *cognition* or *cognitive hunch*. We can understand this notion by coming back to the example of the rat in the four-compartment discrimination box. Let us imagine that we have trained two rats in a situation in which stimuli are varied randomly by experimenters. One rat shows an above-chance tendency to choose the left rather than the right doors, the other vice versa. The notion of *cognitive hunch* allows us to explain the two different performances. The animals, in search of food, cannot learn defined sequences of S-R because they are randomly determined. But, despite that, their behavior seems to be guided by a sort of hunch about the regularity of the door-stimulus presented. In Tolman's words,

> the tendency to try all doors (but each one not more than once), the tendency to work in regular fashion from left to right or from right to left, the tendency to try the same door several times, either with or without intervening attempts at other alleys, and finally, the tendency to persist at some small group of doors over and over again are pretty evidently objective descriptions of the . . . animal's exploratory tendencies (cognitive hunches of how to get there). The animal that persists at the same door over and over again has an inferior set of exploratory

> tendencies (cognitive "hunches") to the one that tries other doors in between. (Tolman 1925a, 42)

Or, for using different definitions, we can say that the rats have *construed a cognitive map of the environment* (Where? Maybe in their minds?), so they follow its coordinates for reaching food. Or, still, rats' behavior is guided by a *hypothesis* about the position of the food in the maze. Thus, the differences in the rats' performance can be explained by the differences in *cognitive hunches* (or maps or hypotheses) upon which the rats rely. Purpose, cognition, cognitive hunch, cognitive map, and hypothesis are all terms that can be used instead of the usual ones referring to physiology (47).

In his early papers (1922, 1925a, 1925b) Tolman argues that purpose and the other *mental-flavored concepts* must not be considered as mentalistic at all. For him, using mentalistic terms of every sort would mean introducing an unacceptable mind-body dualism in psychology, especially because it is possible to give an account of purpose in behavioristic terms. He points out that purpose must be considered as an objective aspect of behavior. When an animal is learning to find the exit of a maze or to escape from a puzzle box, or he is simply going about his daily business of sleeping, nest building, looking for food, and so forth, in all such performances certain persistence toward a goal can be clearly observed. For Tolman it is this persistence that psychologists must define as purpose (1925b, 33). He strongly points out that a psychologist's attribution of purpose or persistence to a certain behavior must not be considered at all as the result of an inference from behavioral data made by the experimenter. Such an inference would be fallacious and redundant because, by making it, it would attribute a subjective mental state to a behavior that, instead, is directly observable in the organism's behavior.

In other words, according to Tolman, whereas mentalists merely infer the purpose starting from the observation of certain aspects of behavior, behaviorists identify it with these aspects. When the animal's performance is observed, it is not possible to say anything about the possible *contents in the animal's mind.* Thus, observing purpose in the animal's behavior does not permit inferring *mental contents* of any kind. The only things necessary and sufficient for defining purpose are these three behavioral characteristics (35):

1. The constancy of a goal object instead of the variations in adjustment to intervening obstacles
2. The variations in final direction corresponding to differing positions of the goal object
3. The stop of activity when a given goal object is entirely removed

However, Tolman says that a supporter of a mentalistic position can reply to this description by arguing that these three are not sufficient for giving an account of the behavior. In fact, the mentalist can point out that the addition of a certain mental state or function (for example, memory) to this description can provide a better and richer explanation of the behavior itself. In Tolman's words:

> The organism has to note and remember the changes in the position or character of the goal object, if his behaviour is to be thus affected. If a rat readjusts his behaviour to changes in the position of the food box or to changes in the intervening route, he can do so only by virtue of remembering the old and new position of the food box. Hence mentalists will declare that, even if purpose itself were not an ultimately mentalistic phenomenon, the actual working of it must be based on memory, and memory at any rate is a mentalistic phenomenon. (35)

I think that this point is crucial in the discussion of Tolman's theory. That is, in his early papers, Tolman is aware of the limitations of the Watsonian paradigm and of the fact that behavioral responses can be influenced by determinants other than external stimuli. In this sense, it seems to him that mentalistic concepts could not be as wrong as they appear and thus they can have a place in a scientific psychology.

However, it is worth noting that Tolman explicitly refuses to define them as a result of an inferential process, and thus he proposes to reduce them to the observable aspects of behavior. So, in his early writings, he does not propose a defined alternative to Watson's behaviorism, but only offers criticisms of his concept. In this sense, the core of behaviorism is maintained so that Watsonian and Tolmanian behaviorism look similar in their attempt to provide an account of psychology in empirical and behavioristic terms.

Their proposals differ in two ways: first, in the level of analysis of the behavioral components (molar versus molecular); second, whereas Watson proposes eliminating mentalistic vocabulary, Tolman proposes reducing it to the behavioral vocabulary. This is clear in Tolman's reply to the mentalists that argues for the introduction of *memory* in the explanation of purpose: memory, like purpose or other mentalistic-flavored concepts, can be conceived in terms of *purely empirical aspects of the behavior*. Saying that an animal *remembers something* is merely another way of saying that his present behavior can be shown to be causally dependent upon something (35).

Mind as a Set of Intervening Variables

In a late paper, Tolman argues that his behaviorism share two features with the Watsonian version (Tolman 1935, 365):

1. Every organism (human or not) responds to stimulation coming from its environment and suffers from a certain number of internal physiological changes.

2. Every organism behaves because of this stimulation and these physiological changes.

Further, Tolman says that both kinds of behaviorism assume that behavior is determined by a set of *intervening variables* lying in the organism. However, the two kinds of behaviorism differ in how these variables are interpreted. He says they are not incompatible, but rather they refer to two different and complementary ways of explaining behavior. More precisely, Watsonian or molecular behaviorism focuses on the physiological determinants of behavior and thus it conceives intervening variables in terms of concepts such as chemical or physical action, operations of certain neural pathways, sympathetic reverberations, and so forth. Tolmanian or molar behaviorism conceives the intervening variables in terms of psychological determinants of behavior, and thus it defines them as specific types of *behavior readiness* or as objectively defined behavioral conditions of *intention*, *expectation*, *demand*, and so forth. In other words, in this paper Tolman uses the expression intervening variable as an umbrella-term, clustering all of the mentalistic-flavored concepts such as *purpose*, *cognition*, *attainment*, and *learning*.

For a better understanding of the difference between the two kinds of behaviorism, let us consider the following experimental example: If rats are trained to reach food in a maze and then, when hungry, they are put in a new maze where they have to reach other food, they are observed to learn the new maze more rapidly than previously trained but satiated rats in the control group. As I pointed out above, it is easy to see that the different performances (R) of the *hungry* and *satiated* rats at the same situation (S) cannot be exhaustively accounted for by a simple S-R model as that proposed by molecular behaviorism. But if we introduce the intervening variable *appetite* in our explanation as proposed by molar behaviorism, we can easily provide an account of the different behaviors observed. It is worth noting that appetite is not here conceived as something directly observable. That is to say, for Tolman such a variable is not detectable by observing the physiological differences between the two groups, and thus it is not reducible to any molecular intervening variable. Rather, it is something inferable or interpretable on the basis of the systematic manipulations of one or more independent variables and the observation of the concomitant changes of one or more dependent variables (Reber and Reber 2001, 784). In other words, appetite seems to be nothing but an inferred and unobservable mediating process allowing connecting an independent to a dependent variable.

This is clearly an important difference between Tolmanian and Watsonian behaviorisms because for Tolman the relation between an organism and the external world cannot be conceived as so direct and close as Watson thinks.

Such a relation must take into account other factors internal to the organism definable as "functional processes which interconnect between the initiating causes of behavior, on the one hand and the final resulting behavior itself, on the other" (Tolman 1936, 117). In other words, an intervening variable can be said to be an intraorganismic function or disposition (for example, appetite) postulated to account for a certain kind of behavior (for example, eating) in a particular stimulus situation (for example, presentation of a piece of cheese after one day of food deprivation) (Marx and Hillix 1963, 289). The introduction of this notion in the psychological theorizing has three closely related aims:

1. The legitimization of a mentalistic vocabulary in a behavioristic psychology. It is obvious that this vocabulary has not to be ill conceived by subjectivity as that used in the late nineteenth- and early twentieth-century experimental psychology. For Tolman, psychology must deal only with objectively and behaviorally defined concepts. Only assuming a molar point of view, things such as intention, expectation, and purpose can be defined in this way (Tolman 1935, 363).
2. The discovery of theories and laws for predicting, controlling, and describing behavior. In fact, he argues that psychology must always look for laws explaining the processes governing behavior. For such an aim, it has to discover all of the fundamental (internal and external) factors causing behavior and define them objectively (356).
3. The autonomy of psychological science from other disciplines such as neurology or physiology (in opposition to Watsonian behaviorism). On this point, Tolman argues that

> the psychological facts and laws are to be gathered and established in their own right. A psychology cannot be established by a physiology until one has a psychology to explain. Further, it appears to me that it is the primarily job of us psychologists, or at any rate of the "purer" among us, to gather the psychological facts and laws and to leave it to our less pure, physiologically minded brethren to gather the neurological, glandular, and biochemical data which underlie such psychological facts and laws. (Tolman 1936, 118)

These three points make it appear that Tolman conceives intervening variables as real determinants of behavior. In fact, without their postulation, it would be very difficult to explain how a certain S can be the cause of a certain R. It is worth noting that, contrary to Tolman's declared adherence to the basic tenets of behaviorism, his stress upon these variables in the psychological theorizing seems to be at least a partial abjuration of them. This is because by assuming that these variables cannot be directly observed but they need to be inferred from their behavioral effects, Tolman appears to commit himself to postulating the real existence of a mind (Leahey 1992, 327). However, the question of whether Tolman conceives the intervening variables as mental entities is highly controversial, and I will consider it in the following paragraph.

The Two Interpretations of the Notion of Intervening Variable

In his early papers (1922, 1925a, 1925b), Tolman points out that things such as purpose, cognition, demand, and all of the other mentalistic-flavored concepts (not yet grouped under the umbrella-term intervening variable) have to be interpreted as directly observable aspects of behavior. That is, by assuming a molar point of view and rejecting a molecular one, we can identify such concepts with specific aspects of behavior clearly open to observation (Tolman 1925a, 33). However, it is clear that this definition of mentalistic-flavored concepts appears to be too vague and not so well defined to be useful in theory construction (Marx and Hillix 1963, 282). But we have also seen that, with the introduction of the umbrella term intervening variable in his late papers (1936, 1948), Tolman provides a clearer definition of such concepts: He argues that it is possible to give an account of them only through a careful examination of the experimental setting. In Tolman's words:

> Whence . . . come our notion and definitions concerning the intervening variables? My answer is as follows: in certain carefully chosen controlled and "standard" experimental setups, one tries to hold all but one, or one small group of the independent variables constant and studies the functional connection between the variations of this one independent variable, or this one limited group of independent variables, on the one hand, and the correlated variations in some quantifiable feature of the final behavior. (1936, 122)

Such a quotation shows Tolman's apparent adherence to the principles of *operationalism*. Very briefly, according to this doctrine, the theoretical terms of a certain discipline do not refer to anything but are only convenient ways of summarizing observations and experimental conditions (Leahey 1992, 328). This means that it is legitimate to use these terms in theorizing as long as they refer to concrete operations or experimental conditions used in their measurement (Tolman 1936, 115; Reber and Reber 2001, 486).

In this view, psychological concepts denote something only if certain concrete criteria for their applicability in an experiment are defined, and psychological propositions have empirical meaning only if the criteria for assessing their truth or falsity consist of *concrete operations* that can be performed upon demand (Stevens 1963, 53). In this sense, here the adjective *concrete* means *intersubjectively or publicly observable or replicable in different (experimental) situations* (73). On this point, it is important to note that operationalism shares very much with logical positivism (62). Thus, the same considerations made above about the comparison between Watsonian behaviorism and logical positivism can apply here. That is, operationalism must be distinguished from logical positivism because the former (similarly to Watsonian behaviorism) is a philosophical position pointing out that all concepts of science must be defined in terms of concrete operations used in their measurement and the latter a philosophical position aimed at establishing the logical conditions according to which the propositions of every science can be said to be meaningful or not. On the basis of this operationalistic view, an intervening variable is presented as having these four characteristics (MacCorquodale and Meehl 1948, 103):

1. It is quantitatively defined through the experimental manipulations of the independent variables and the observation of the resulting dependent variables.
2. It does not comprehend any hypothesis about the existence of unobservable entities or unobservable processes involved in causing behavior.
3. It does not contain concepts that are not definable by reduction sentences in terms of the observable independent and dependent variables.
4. The validity of the empirical laws involving only observables establishes the necessary and sufficient conditions for the validity of the laws involving the intervening variables.

This interpretation of Tolman's intervening variables as operationally defined in terms of observables is probably the most widespread among psychologists and philosophers (Amundson 1983, 269; Amundson 1986, 525; Sober 1998, 470, note 1)[7] and allows Tolman to be classified as a behaviorist. However, the plausibility of such an interpretation is a matter of controversy. Some argue that this does not represent Tolman's real notion of intervening variables.[8] According to this alternative interpretation, Tolman conceives the intervening variable as a construct with *surplus meaning* and a relatively low degree of operational specificity (Marx 1963, 42). That is, the notion of intervening variable is something more than the sum of all of the concrete operations defining it in a certain experimental setting (29). This appears to be particularly evident in Tolman's 1948 paper, where the intervening variables seem to be *real* psychological entities not operationally reducible to observable terms (Leahey 1992, 328).

In fact, let us consider the following quotation, where Tolman describes the construction of a cognitive map by a rat: "the incoming impulses are usually worked over and elaborated in the central control room into a tentative, cognitive-like map of the environment. And it is this tentative map, indicating routes and paths and environmental relationships, which finally determines what responses, if any, the animal will finally release" (Tolman 1948, 244–45). In such a map, the "environment is represented, so that, if the starting position of the animal be changed or variations in the specific routes be introduced, this . . . map will allow the animal still behaving relatively correctly and to choose the appropriate new route" (246). Tolman here conceives the cognitive map as *something having a meaning* for the rat: the rat *knows* what the maze is and that in it he can find food and no other stuff (thus it knows also what food is). Thus, the rat makes a *representation* of the maze, because it intends to arrive at the food (Amundson 1983, 277). All of these terms (knowledge, cognitive map, representation, or intention) do not seem here merely metaphorical but seem to possess a *semantic content* that resists every attempt at operational reduction. In other words, Tolman's intervening variables as intended in his 1948 paper do not meet the characteristics mentioned before. That is, according to psychologists MacCorquodale and Meehl, they are not definable as *operational constructs* but rather as *hypothetical constructs* having these three characteristics (1948, 104):

1. They involve a vocabulary that cannot be reduced wholly to an empirical and behavioral vocabulary.
2. They refer to entities or processes not directly observable from the data or from the concrete operations defined in an experiment.
3. The validity of the empirical laws involving only observables is a necessary but not a sufficient condition for the validity of these constructs.

It is important to say that this interpretation of the notion of intervening variable as a hypothetical construct can be found very explicitly formulated in other of Tolman's late papers. For example, consider the following quotation (1949, 49): "to use Meehl and MacCorquodale's distinction, I would now abandon what they call pure intervening variables for what they call hypothetical constructs, and insist that hypothetical constructs be parts of a more general hypothesized model or substrate." However, I don't think that such an admission can be considered as the final argument for saying that the late Tolman takes a position in favor of this interpretation. This is because, if we take a look at another one of his latest writings (1959), he does not seem to have renounced trying to give an operational definition to his constructs.[9] In fact, in this article he provides clear examples of this attempt with terms such as *hungriness* (110), *means-end readiness* (113), *cognitive map* (128), and psychoanalytic *repression* (145–46).

In a very brief summary, we can say that Tolman's notion of intervening variable has two different interpretations: The first is reductionistic (mentalistic terms can be reduced to concrete and observable experimental operations); the second is non-reductionistic (mentalistic terms can be inferred from both the concrete experimental operations and the observable behavior but cannot be reduced to *something more than the sum of them*) (Kukla 2001, 54). It is quite clear that only the latter interpretation can be conceived as genuinely mentalistic, although in a completely different way from late nineteenth- and early twentieth-century psychology. This is because, all through his work, Tolman has emphasized the importance of defining the psychological terms objectively and thus of avoiding such things as subjectivity and introspection. The following quotation seems to support this idea: "the human subject arrives at the correct solution (of a certain task) without, however, himself being able consciously to formulate the nature of his hypothesis" (1935, 377). He points out that, in a series of experiments, it was observed that the subject was able to make the correct choice but "he was not conscious of his hypothesis and yet this hypothesis successfully governed his behavior. We must conclude, therefore, that to be conscious—to be introspectively formable—is not essential to even human hypotheses" (Tolman 1936, 377). This quotation and other similar ones[10] can make Tolman appear as a *cognitivist realist* misusing empiricist technical vocabulary (Amundson 1983, 276) and conceiving the mind as a set of unconscious causal processes similar to those postulated by current cognitive psychology (Amundson 1986, 526–27 and 530). Obviously, such a view would be plausible only if we interpret the intervening variables as hypothetical constructs and not as operationally defined constructs. However, I think that for now none has yet provided convincing arguments that favor one of the two positions.[11]

This situation is probably not due to a defect in creativity and ability to argue on the part of Tolman's critics but to a great lack of definitional precision and formal definition of his proposal (MacCorquodale and Meehl 1954, 189 and 196–97). That is, Tolman does not appear to aim at specifying the axiom set of its system, and for this reason his proposal seems to be programmatic in nature (198). It must be said that Tolman explicitly (and auto-ironically) admits this difficulty in different parts of his work. For example, consider the following quotation (Tolman 1959, 150): "All I can say here is that my system is based on hunches and common-sense knowledge. It is certainly not hypothetico-deductive. I have not the type of mind that can remember which were my axioms and which were my deductions."

CONCLUDING REMARKS

The main issue emerging from the analysis of Watsonian and Tolmanian behaviorism is probably the relation between observation and theory. In other words, the question underlying the foundation of an *objective and scientific psychology* regards what a psychologist can observe and what inferences she is allowed to make from her observations. On this point, it seems that Watson and Tolman start with the shared assumption that the object of psychology must be the observable behavior and not the mind as defined by the late nineteenth- and early twentieth-century mentalists. In other words, both basically seem to assume that psychology could finally join the ranks of legitimate natural science by refusing introspection as a research method and appealing to an objective vocabulary (Hatfield 2002, 213–16). However, they diverge on the level of analysis of behavior that has to be considered and on what is possible to infer from the behavioral data.

In regard to the first point, it is clear that Watsonian behaviorism aims to look at a more restricted and circumscribed *area of observation* than the Tolmanian. Although Tolman is probably right in arguing that the two kinds of behaviorism are complementary, the attempts to find some connection between them seem to be (at least for now) unsuccessful. The second point is linked to the first: Because Tolman's level of analysis is wider than Watson's, it seems clear that the former requires more inferential commitment from observation to theory than the latter. In fact, at a first look, purpose, cognition, and the other mentalistic-flavored terms do not seem to be as *strictly empirical* as the S-R formula is. In other words, Watsonian behaviorism seems to attempt to avoid the use of any kind of inferred theoretical constructs and to build up a psychology based entirely on observable data (Greenwood 1999, 13), contrary to Tolmanian behaviorism that seems to admit their use (Spence 1963, 70).

Unfortunately, we have seen that Tolman appears to be uncertain whether to define operationally or as having a surplus meaning irreducible to observable data. It is important to note that, apart from Tolman and his interpretation of the notion of intervening variable, to accept the surplus of meaning of the mentalistic-flavored terms means to get the behavioristic psychology into trouble. In fact, it means to admit that psychology must be based on something more than the observable behavior and so not accept one of the fundamental tenets of behaviorism.

NOTES

1. For an exhaustive review of the anti-introspectionistic positions before the publication of the Watson's manifesto see Marx and Hillix 1963, 130–36.

2. In confirmation of this point, consider the fact that Watson describes introspection in a very superficial and incomplete manner, by simply saying that it is a sort

of retrospective glance at what has passed through consciousness (Watson 1925, 6; Reber and Reber 2001, 369).

3. See, for example, McBurney and White 2010, 510.

4. Of course, this is true also for the controlled introspection experiments conducted by Wundt.

5. It is important to note that not all behavioristic psychologists deny that the mental processes exist and influence behavior. Rather, they tend to deny that these processes can be analyzed psychologically (Bechtel 1994, 2).

6. For other accounts of the unity of science, see Hooker 1999, 540–49.

7. Marx (1951b), Spence (1951), Hilgard (1958), and Stevens (1963) are examples of the success of this interpretation.

8. For a spirited defense of this interpretation, see Amundson 1983 and 1986.

9. Although he explicitly admits that providing such a definition does not come easily in many cases (Tolman 1959, 131 and 132).

10. As, for example, the one about the *cognitive maps* elaborated in a central control room quoted above (Tolman 1948, 244–45).

11. I think that, in this sense, Tolman behaviorism can be seen as a *curious (epistemological) case* in the history of psychology generating *curious (epistemological) situations*. An example of such a curious situation can be the following one: the fact that, according to whether interpretation of intervening variable is preferred, Tolmanian behaviorism can be always compatible with logical positivism. In fact, if we interpret the intervening variables operationally, this means that they are reducible to behavioral terms, compatibly with the early and more conservative versions of logical positivism that we have met describing the Watsonian behaviorism. But if we interpret the intervening variables as hypothetical (or mentalistic) constructs, this means that they can be considered as part of the theoretical vocabulary of psychology, compatibly with the statements of the late and *more liberal* versions of logical positivism. In fact, these later more liberal versions of the logical positivism point out the great difficulty of translating or reducing exhaustively all of the theoretical terms to observable ones. Thus, they admit the introduction of autonomous theoretical terms, not translatable and not reducible to the observational terms (Castiglioni and Corradini 2011, 32–39).

Chapter Three

New Mentalism

In the previous chapter we saw that Tolman's attempts to justify the use of a mentalistic vocabulary in experimental psychology can be considered unsatisfactory. The main problem with his proposal is its ambiguity: On the one hand, Tolman seems to refuse an operational definition of the intervening variables; and, on the other hand, he does not seem explicitly to accept defining them in purely mentalistic terms. In other words, Tolman's view does not seem to be defined enough to reintroduce the idea of mind in psychology. This lack of definition seems to be due mainly to the fact that, all through his work, Tolman considers the intervening variables as entities mediating between stimuli and responses (behavior). Thus, although his psychology can admit the existence of mental states, it is strongly committed to facts about stimuli and behavioral responses.

In this respect, the Tolmanian proposal does not look so radically different from the Watsonian one and thus does not seem able to go beyond the fundamental tenets of behaviorism. In spite of these problems, Tolman's notion of an intervening variable is very interesting, because it casts doubts on the possibility of founding a scientific psychology only on the analysis of stimuli and responses. Or, at least, his proposal suggests that the success of many behavioristic experiments might depend upon the experimenter's implicit and involuntary control of other variables, which, when made explicit, involve a non-eliminable reference to an organism's mental states (Levin 2013). For example, the rats-in-the-food-box's behavior seems to be determined (at least partially) by *feelings of hunger*, *intentions to reach the food*, and *cognitive maps of the maze.* Tolman's proposal seems to suggest two weak points of behaviorism:

1. The stimuli in the environment cannot be the only relevant cause of behavior. Other (perhaps mental?) factors are likely to play an important role in its determination.
2. The theories explicitly referring to entities such as feeling, desire, or cognition can provide a more complete account of the organism's behavior than S-R theories.

It seems that cognitivists assume and develop these suggestions and, in a certain sense, they take Tolman's intervening variables *more seriously* than Tolman himself does. More precisely, by using MacCorquodale's and Meehl's distinction seen in chapter 2, the passage from behaviorism to cognitive psychology (CP) can be represented plausibly in terms of the replacement of (operationally defined) intervening variables by hypothetical constructs (having a surplus meaning) (Greenwood 1999, 1). Thus, we can argue that cognitivists' hypothetical constructs show three characteristics:

1. They are *representational mediating states*, internal to a cognitive system, that carry information about the environment external to it and used by it in processing (Brandimonte et al. 2006, 21–22).
2. They are *not directly observable* but are conceived as abstract and unobservable entities functionally defined and definable only through theorization.
3. They are *not introspectively accessible* by consciousness and, for this reason, they must be assumed as *unconscious* (Mandler 2007, 7).

Before starting the assessment of CP's mentalism, I believe it is necessary to set forth a premise: Although I am aware of the relevance of connectionism and dynamical systems theory (DST) as approaches to mind that can be found in CP, I have deliberately chosen to not discuss them and to focus only upon the computationalist perspective in this chapter. This is for two reasons. The first is quite trivial but nonetheless sincere: I admit that computationalism is the approach I know better and about which I think I can say something correct. The second (perhaps more substantial) is that, in spite of the relevance of connectionism and DST, computationalism is still *alive and well* and probably can be considered the most developed (perhaps the mainstream) approach in CP today (Fodor 2011, 1–3).

THE NEW INTERVENING VARIABLES AND THE INFORMATION PROCESSING VIEW

The focus of cognitivistic research is on the intermediate states that play a role in determining the response moving from one stimulus (or more stimuli).

Thus, response (behavior) and stimulus lose their central place in experimental psychology: Cognitivists are primarily interested in assessing which mental states can determine the behavior and how they can do it. But how exactly are these mental states defined?

According to the psychologist Bruner (1992, 780), first cognitivists defined them on the basis of a constructivistic view of mind. A good example is the controversy about the idea of perception, probably one of the first matters of debate between cognitivists and behaviorists. For behaviorists, perception is conceived as a neutral registration of what is out there, whereas for first cognitivists it is an activity affected by other concurrent processes of thought, memory, and so on. In other words, cognitivists conceive perception as something more than a direct response to stimulation, that is, an *elaboration* or a *construction* based on a set of mental operations (memory, thought, and so on) (Lachman et al. 1979, 118; Reber and Reber 2001, 150–51). Such operations are supposed to analyze and treat the features of the external stimuli (for example, through assessing the figure-ground structures, contrasts, constancies, and so on) for constructing our perceptual world.

Today the constructivistic approach the first cognitivists proposed is applied not only to perception but also to all the mental phenomena and can be found in the so-called *information processing view*. According to this view, human beings and the other organisms with a mind are conceived as systems taking up information from the environment, treating, transforming, storing, and using it in action and communication (Lachman et al. 1979, 7; Lycan 1994, 319; Mandler 2007, 189). This means that everything an organism thinks or does depends upon some kind of information processing (Leahey 1992, 446). That is, mind is conceived as composed of a certain number of mental operations taking place in stages or steps, such as input, coding, storage, retrieval, decoding, output, and so on (Reber and Reber 2001, 352). In this view, the behavioral responses are never caused directly by the external stimulation but are the product of a work of construction performed by a set of intervening mental processes (Lundin 1996, 291).

On the basis of the information-processing view, cognitivists' psychological theories appear to be like *lists of things* describing how one or more mental states perform in relation to environmental stimuli, other mental states, and behavioral responses. Or they appear to be like *flow charts*: pictorial or graphical representations of sequences of events connecting stimuli in input to responses in output. For example, in order to give an account of how people drive a car, cognitive psychologists argue that the following mental operations have to take place: Perceiving every familiar landmark anew each time, representing the landmark's appearance in memory, matching the current perception to its previously stored representations, and so on (Leahey 1992, 446).

The flow-chart form of psychological theories is the clearest example of how the language of CP is strongly influenced by information and computer science.[1] Such an influence does not represent only a linguistic convention but something deeper. In fact, one trademark of CP is the (at least partial) acceptance of a parallel between the human mind and the computer program, both conceived as instantiations of a general-purpose machine able symbolically to represent and manipulate everything that can be specified in a symbolic form (Lachman et al. 1979, 103). Such a trademark is clearly shown in Neisser's influential book *Cognitive Psychology*: "The task of a psychologist trying to understand human cognition is analogous to that of a man trying to discover how a computer has been programmed. In particular, if the program seems to store and reuse information, he would like to know by what routines or procedure this is done" (1967, 7). According to this quotation, it seems clear that the analogy between computer programs and the human mind offers scientific psychology not only a formalized and rigorous language, but also a new powerful way to approach mental phenomena. Through the *computer metaphor*, psychologists can study mind in an objective way and, contemporarily, avoid the restrictions imposed by the behavioristic research program.[2]

The information-processing view conceives the human mind as a sort of complex device hierarchically structured and able to perform a certain number of operations (Simon 1993, 638). These operations are performed on symbols, which are definable as patterns, made of any substance whatsoever, that are used to denote, or point to some other symbols, or some objects or relations among objects. The thing a symbol points to is its meaning. The economist and psychologist Simon (1993, 640) defines six operations that a complex device (computational or mental) can perform on symbols:

1. To input symbols.
2. To output symbols.
3. To store symbols and the relational structures of symbols in a memory.
4. To construct, modify, and erase such symbol structures.
5. To compare two symbol structures for identity or difference.
6. To follow one course of action or another, depending on the outcome of such a comparison.

Cognitive psychologists assume that, on the basis of these simple operations, it is possible to provide both a definition and an explanation of all mental processes underlying behavior. More precisely, from this limited number of operations, it is possible to construe models of the mental processes mediating between input and output. In this respect, such processes show some similarities with Tolman's intervening variables. In fact, both play a causal role in the determination of behavior.

Further, in a certain sense, Tolmanian intervening variables seem to be compatible with a constructivistic or information-processing approach. In fact, it is evident that Tolman's rats construe some representations of the environment (or cognitive maps) during the task they perform. However, it must be pointed out that Tolman does not propose any theory for describing and explaining the processes underlying the construction of such cognitive maps as cognitivists do. Thus, his intervening variables do not appear as entities processing the information carried by the stimuli. From this point of view, it seems that Tolmanian and cognitivistic mediating states play a different role in the determination of behavior and so in theory construction. Thus, if we accept that Tolman conceives his intervening variables as hypothetical constructs, they are conceived as entities that take stimuli to responses and even can influence subjects' performances in the experimental tasks, but that do not take any part in the analysis of the external stimuli as the *constructivistic operations* postulated by cognitivists do.

Functionalism and the Abstract Character of the Mental

In chapters 1 and 2 we saw that mentalists and behaviorists offer two opposite solutions to the so-called *mind-body problem*. On the one hand, early mentalists are dualists, because they conceive mind as something distinct from the physical, investigable only through introspection and with its own properties and laws. On the other hand, behaviorists are reductionistic materialists and propose to eliminate mind from scientific psychology in favor of observable chains of stimuli and responses. Now, the question is: What is the notion of mind for cognitivists? Some people could answer in the same manner as I have above: Mind is a sort of mechanical device processing the information gotten from the stimuli and then treating this information for constructing responses. But such an answer does not tell very much about the nature of mental states. Thus, the question remains: For cognitivists, what makes something a mental state?

It is worth noting that cognitivists share with behaviorists the aim of developing a naturalized and objective (in a third-person) account of psychology and the refusal of the dualism of the late nineteenth- and early twentieth-century mentalists.[3] Thus, cognitivists look for a philosophical account of mental phenomena that allows them to avoid both the introspectionistic dualism and the behavioristic reductive materialism and that can be compatible with the information-processing view. Functionalism seems to provide a good solution in this sense. In philosophy of mind, functionalism is the doctrine according to which what makes something a mental state of a certain type depends on the way it functions, or on the role it plays, in the system of which it is part (Levin 2013).[4] More precisely, functionalists conceive mental states or processes as causally mediating links between a person's sensory stimuli and his ensuing behavior (Lycan 1994, 317). As pointed out by the philosopher Fodor,

> Functional differentiation is differentiation in respect to causal role. A headache, for example, is identified with the type of mental state that among other things causes a disposition for taking aspirin in people who believe aspirin relieves a headache, causes a desire to rid oneself of the pain one is feeling, often causes someone who speaks English to say such things as *I have a headache*, and is brought on by overwork, eyestrain and tension.[5] (1981, 124)

In this example, it is clear how a certain number of psychological states (such as *pain*, *feeling*, or *belief*) and behaviors or dispositions to behave (such as *taking an aspirin* or *saying to feel a headache*) are linked in a causal relations' network. It is also evident how and why the appeal to the causal character of mind can be an advantage in respect to the most restrictive kinds of behaviorism (such as the Watsonian one). This is because, on the basis of behaviorism, it seems practically impossible to give a reliable account in purely behavioral terms of situations such as an actress wanting to have an experience she does not really have or a total paralytic who cannot manifest any experience she does not have (Lewis 1966, 20).

However, it is also evident how and why this appeal can be advantageous with respect to the (supposed) liberalized kinds of behaviorism (as the Tolmanian one), which generally require a one-to-one function from mental predicates to behavioral or dispositional predicates such that the satisfaction of a certain mental predicate entails the satisfaction of a certain unique behavioral predicate, and vice versa (McGinn 1991, 187). In other words, according to functionalism, the behavior of a person possessing a certain belief does not depend only on such a single belief but also on the relation among such a belief and various others or among different other mental states or processes such as memory, desires, or feelings (Putnam 1960, 22–23). In this sense, functionalism seems to be able easily to account for the many combinations of mental states and processes of different kinds that can be involved in the determination of behavior (Lowe 2000, 46).

It is worth noting that functionalism defines mental states only by virtue of what function or role they play in the causal relations' network without any reference to the nature of their *physical realization* (or, to put it more simply, without any reference to what they are made of) (Putnam 1960, 26). For this reason, it appears to be a quite liberal philosophical position because in principle it is compatible both with a dualistic position of a certain sort and a physicalistic one (Castiglioni and Corradini 2011, 64; Levin 2013).[6] In a certain sense, we can say that, according to the functionalistic doctrine, mind resembles money. This is because defining something as money does not depend on which material it is made of (for example, gold, silver, paper, or wood) and what position it occupies in the space-time, but on the kind of function it plays in the exchange of commodities in a market (Rey 1997, 165). In such a way, mental states as well as money are abstractly defined (Putnam 1960, 25–26): They are not defined in terms of concrete entities occupying a certain spatial volume at a certain time. In fact, it makes little sense to ask how much space or time a functional role occupies at a certain time, even if it is somehow implicated in the space-time (Rosen 2012).

Thus, mind is conceived as a-spatial and a-temporal. For this reason, it cannot be perceived or directly observed in any way and thus it can be known only through abstraction. So defined, the functionalistic mind appears to be separated and distinguished from the physical matter. Thus, the question here is how it can have a causal power in the physical world. In fact, in this world, only concrete entities occupying a certain spatial volume at a certain time can cause physical effects. As the philosopher Fodor clearly pointed out in a well-known passage, "If the mind is non-physical, it has no position in physical space. How, then, can a mental cause give rise to a behavioral effect that has a position in space? To put it another way, how can the non-physical give rise to the physical without violating the laws of the conservation of mass, of energy, and of momentum?" (1981, 114).

Functionalists tend to respond to these questions by appealing to the *multiple realizability theses*. According to such a thesis, because functionally defined entities are abstractions from the physical, they can be realized in an indefinite variety of physical substrates (Rey 1997, 177). This is clearly exposed in the previous example of the money: Its role in the exchange of commodities in a market is something characterized abstractly but instantiated in many different realizers such as gold, silver, paper, and wood. In the same fashion, abstract mental states or processes (for example, pain, headache, or memory) can be realized in many different physical kinds (for examples, neurons or siliceous chips) (Putnam 1960, 25; Bickle 2006): For functionalists, it is not a crucial point to assess which kind of physical entity has the properties to instantiate mental states (Gardner 1985, 78).[7] More precisely, the multiple realizability theses imply that, if two different persons have some mental properties in common, there is no guarantee that both will share the same physical properties. Rather, they may deploy different physical realizations of the same mental properties (Sober 1997, 303).

Although it is not always explicitly formulated, the appeal to multiple realizability thesis is quite widespread in information-processing and cognitivistic literature. For example, let's consider the following quotation about the study of problem solving from a seminal paper in CP:

> Problem solving—at the information-processing level at which we have described it—has nothing specifically *neural* about it, but can be performed by a wide class of mechanisms, including both human brains and digital computers. We do not believe that this functional equivalence between brains and computers implies any structural equivalence at a more minute anatomical level (e.g., equivalence of neurons and circuits). (Newell et al. 1958, 163)

In other words, psychologists must deal only with *software or program description* of the psychological functioning (*at the abstract level*), leaving aside *hardware description* (*at the concrete level*) (Putnam 1975, 215; Putnam 1997, 34).

As I said above, the abstractness of the mental is the central feature of the functionalistic doctrine (Putnam 1960, 25–26). In fact, the abstract character of a certain entity implies that it cannot be perceived directly and thus defined as observable in any way.[8] This means that concreteness is a necessary condition for the observability of a certain entity. We have seen an example of this point considering behaviorism in chapter 2.

Behaviorists aim to define psychology as the science of behavior and not of the mental. In this sense, behaviorists consider psychology quite similar to paleontology, the study of fossils. In fact, behaviors, as fossils, are *directly observable*—this means that every person with normally functioning eyesight can see them (Okasha 2002, 59). Thus, both fossils and behaviors are to be considered observable terms because their meaning is fixed by their being associated with some observable entities or properties (Hempel 1958, 78; Bird 1998, 126). However, it is worth noting that, if it is true that abstractness implies the unobservability, the opposite is not true. In fact, although observable entities are always concrete, concrete entities can be both observable and unobservable. This means that concreteness is not a sufficient condition for the observability of a certain entity. In fact, many concrete entities cannot be observed directly. In physics, for example, atoms, electrons, quarks, leptons, and other particles cannot be observed directly; at best, they can be detected through instruments. For example, physicists can detect an electron through the observation of the tracks it has left in the bubble chamber but not observe the electron itself (Achinstein 1999, 331).

It is controversial whether to consider detection as a form of observation (Bird 1998, 133–35). That is, observation seems always to be a matter of degree. Although some are clear cases of observable and unobservable entities (for example, all of us can see stones with the naked eye but not quarks or electrons), it seems to be difficult sharply to classify in these two categories many entities of science (Kosso 1994, 118). However, it appears quite clear that the less we can observe an entity, the more we have difficulties in fixing its meaning. Thus, the question here is to define the criteria for assessing the meaning of a term that refers to an unobservable entity. The answer to this question is quite intuitive (but nonetheless problematic): To assess the meaning of a term referring to an unobservable entity, we need to *think about it*. More specifically, to describe a certain entity, we will not refer to an *observational vocabulary* but to a *theoretical vocabulary*. The terms of this vocabulary can be said to be *fictions or inventions*, in the sense that they are autonomous from the terms referring to observable entities and thus they cannot be eliminated in favor of them (Hempel 1952, 31; Hempel 1958, 179).

So, physicists use the observational vocabulary for describing the tracks left by an electron and the theoretical vocabulary for describing the electron itself. That is, electron has to be considered as a theoretical term whose meaning is determined only by assessing its systematic role within the theory (Bird 1998, 128). In this sense, the unobservable physical entities and the mental entities are similar. In fact, the only way to assign their meaning is through theorizing.

However, it is clear that physicists and psychologists appeal to theorization in a rather different way. This is because the physical entities can be both concrete[9] (such as quarks or electrons) and abstract[10] (such as masses or forces), whereas psychological entities (such as attention or memories) can be only abstract.[11] In other words, the only things that can be observed more or less directly regarding such mental states are their (supposed) behavioral effects and their (supposed) concrete realizers (Putnam 1960, 26; Fodor 1968a, 84).

On this point two considerations follow. First, functionalism does not seem to dismiss behaviorism completely, at least methodologically. That is, although functionalists assume that it is not possible to find behavioral correlates or operational definitions of the mental states, they do not deny that such states can be inferred only from their (supposed) behavioral effects. In other words, it seems that for functionalists the observation of how people behave is decisive for assessing the presence of a certain mental state or process (Rey 1997, 197; Reber and Reber 2001, 85). Second, a problem surrounds the multiple realizability thesis and the issue of the causal power of the mental. That is, the fact that we cannot observe or detect in any way the abstract entities, but only their (supposed) realizers, means that such entities can *stay in the physical world* only if they are *anchored* to something concrete.

Now, although it seems reasonable to abstract away from the observable and concrete features to describe the functional role of something, it is not clear how such a role concretely can cause something per se, I mean, *autonomously*. In fact, the appeal to the multiple realizability theses seems to beg the question of how the mental can cause physical effects by implicitly arguing that it is the concrete entity realizing the functional role that has the real powers, not the role itself. If such a characterization of the multiple realizability thesis is correct, mental states appear to be epiphenomenal: causally inert or impotent (McLaughlin 1994, 277).[12] Thus, we can say that, although functionalism seems to permit a level of psychological explanation autonomous from the physical level and to avoid the strictness of the behavioristic models, it fails to account for a genuine causal role of the mental.

The Unconscious Mind

In chapter 1, I pointed out that late nineteenth- and early twentieth-century mentalists conceived mind as introspectively accessible to the subject and conscious by its nature. Thus, according to these psychologists, consciousness was the mark of the mental. Now, both the information-processing and functionalistic views seem to be rather silent about the conscious or unconscious character of the mental. In fact, both of these views can apply in principle to everything (not only mental) that can play a causal role in a certain system (for example, a piston in a car's engine) or can process information or manipulate symbols (for example, a computer program). Thus, the question whether for cognitivists mind is conscious seems still to be open. My answer is that, although cognitivists postulate that mind exhibits both consciousness and unconsciousness, most of them consider almost all of the causal-functional mental operations as unconscious.[13]

But, for cognitivists, what does unconscious mean exactly? My thesis is that cognitive psychological research holds three different meanings of unconscious:

1. Outside of attention: Consciousness is identified with *selective attention*, namely the perceptual process involved in situations in which a subject is confronted with many stimuli and must select only one of them and attend to it (Reber and Reber 2001, 658). Thus, unconsciousness is interpreted as the condition in which the stimuli impinge on perceptual receptors but fall outside the focus of selective attention.
2. Lack or failure of introspection: Consciousness is identified with the *ability to make introspection or accurate verbal reports* of the mental operations involved in the determination of behavior. Thus, unconsciousness is interpreted as the condition in which a subject cannot access introspectively its mental operations and verbally report how they have determined behavior (Greenwald 1992, 767).

3. Outside of (conscious) control: Consciousness is identified with *a controlling or supervising function or activity* of certain mental processes, such as planning and triggering action and thought (Baars and McGovern 1996, 82). Thus, unconsciousness is interpreted as the condition in which mental processes take place automatically, that is, independently of conscious control or supervision (Reber and Reber 2001, 70).[14]

These three different meanings of unconscious obviously refer to three different situations that deal with: (1) the unawareness of the perception of a certain stimulus, (2) the impossibility of describing the cognitive operations determining our behavior, and (3) the impossibility of controlling such operations. Of course, all three can be strongly intertwined. In fact, if a stimulus has not passed through the focus of selective attention (1) and it has produced some effects on a subject's behavior, a set of cognitive operations that cannot be either introspected or verbally reported (2) or controlled by the subject (3) has processed them. But it is worth noting that the mental operations postulated in CP can be introspectively inaccessible (2) as well as consciously incontrollable (3) if the stimulus has passed through the focus of selective attention. In this case, subjects are certainly aware of having perceived the stimulus, but they can neither verbally describe the mental operations involved in the stimulus processing nor consciously intervene in it. Thus, we can say that situations occur in which (1) can be distinguished from (2) and (3).

It is worth noting that (2) and (3) regard the definition of the mental operations more directly than (1). In fact, (1) refers only to those situations in which a stimulus is or is not consciously perceived by the subject without implying the postulation of any mental operation. For that reason, we will focus only on (2) and (3) in this discussion. Intuitively, it seems to be uncontroversial that exerting a conscious control over the mental operations is different from giving a verbal description about how they work. In fact, in the cognitivistic literature, we can find various cases in which subjects are able to give an account of their mental operations but they are unable to exert any conscious control over them and, vice versa—cases in which subjects are able to exert a certain control over their mental operations but unable to give a verbal description of them.

An example of the first case is the well-known Stroop effect. It can be described as follows: In an experimental situation, subjects are presented with a list of color names (for example, blue, yellow, red, or pink) printed in non-matching colors. For example, the word yellow is printed in pink ink or the word blue in red ink. Thus, subjects are asked to report the color of a word in the list with disregard of its meaning (according to the previous examples, the correct responses are pink and red). The results suggest that subjects find some difficulties at looking only at the ink color alone in which the word is printed and are prone to read the word (according to the previous examples, they tend to respond yellow and blue) (Reber and Reber 2001, 217). According to one of the interpretations of this phenomenon, this happens because reading is an automatic process, not readily subject to conscious control.

For this reason, subjects find it difficult to refrain from reading and to put attention on identifying the ink's color by disregarding the word printed in that ink's color (Sternberg 1996, 84). In other terms, the Stroop effect occurs because two completely different processes for color responses (one for the color itself and the other for the color name, that is, the written word) are activated simultaneously. Thus, the tendency to read the word interferes, causing difficulties in telling what the ink's color is. In such a case, subjects are aware of their difficulties, and they are able to ascribe them to the interference between the two kinds of processing, but they are not able to exert any conscious control over them (Lundin 1996, 294).

The implicit learning paradigm offers many examples of subjects able consciously to control their mental operations without being able verbally to describe them.[15] Implicit learning is loosely defined as that kind of learning taking place independently of awareness of both the process of acquisition and the content of the knowledge acquired (Reber and Reber 2001, 392; Frensch and Ruenger 2003, 13). In the tasks developed for assessing this kind of learning, subjects have to manage a certain number of variables to reach a certain goal.

The *Sugar Factory Production* is a good example of this kind of task. Subjects are presented with a computer game representing an imaginary manufacturing situation, such as a sugar production plant, and instructed to maneuver a certain number of variables such as wages, labor peace, worker output, and the like to yield a particular overall production. Experimenters do not tell the subjects that the game operates according to a sophisticated and complex rule system that relates factors to each other. Achieving the goal (the required production standard) needs the rules to be *known* in some sense of that word (Reber 1989, 606–7). The results of the studies using this task (and other similar ones) report that subjects are able to make appropriate adjustments in the relevant variables, which means that they have induced the correct rules system that determines their behavior. However, as I said above, it is reported also that subjects have many difficulties in giving a verbal description of the rules they have to follow for solving the task (St. John and Shanks 1997, 165). But this does not mean that subjects are completely unaware of these rules, because they appear to be able intentionally to control their application throughout the task (Dienes and Perner 2002, 78). In a few words, in the implicit learning tasks participants seem to be conscious of how to apply the rules they have learned (and that the game follows a certain number of rules they must learn), but they are not able to give any verbal account of them (Frensch and Ruenger 2003, 14). Thus, they do not appear to be able to look inward to the mental states or processes used to solve the task.

It is worth noting that the distinction between *being able to exert a control on (something)* and *being able to verbally describe (something)* closely resembles the distinction between *knowing how* and *knowing that*. That is, the distinction between an ability to do something (a *procedural* or *rule-based knowledge*) and an ability to say something (a *propositional* or *data-based knowledge*) (Cohen and Squire 1980, 207).

To better understand it, consider the following example: When a person plays with playing cards, on the one hand she (usually consciously) *knows that* a king has a higher value than a queen; on the other; she (usually unconsciously) *knows how* to shuffle the cards (Mandler 2007, 229–30). The problem with such a distinction is that, although it seems to be graspable intuitively, it has not yet received a satisfying formulation. As the philosopher Crane clearly pointed out, "but why suppose that having an ability is never a state of propositional knowledge, or that having some propositional knowledge is never an ability? . . . If ability knowledge is what is expressed when we say someone knows how to do something, then nothing rules this out from being propositional knowledge too" (2001, 94–95). In other words, we can find situations in which someone is able to control her mental operations as well as to report and describe these operations.

It is important to note here that the plausibility of the distinction is not being denied,[16] but it is only considered that knowing how and knowing that can imply each other. Probably because of such an implication, for assessing whether a subject is able to supervise or control her mental processes (3) during a cognitive task, the experimenters tend to evaluate whether she is able to make good introspections or verbal reports (2). For this reason, it can be said that the assertion that we "have no direct access to higher order mental processes such as those involved in evaluation, judgement, problem solving, and the initiation of behavior" (Nisbett and Wilson 1977, 252) generally means that none (not only the layman but also the cognitive psychologist) are able to make introspection or accurate verbal reports of the mental operations involved in the determination of her behavior (Kilhstrom 1987, 781).

For example, the cognitive processes involved in the determination of the visual estimation of depth seem to be closed to subjective awareness and not verbally reportable. This point is well exposed by the philosopher Fodor: "for example: texture gradients, stereopsis, overlap, flow pattern and other cues contribute to causally determining our visual estimates of depth. . . . Of course, no subject . . . can tell you what cues determine his visual estimates of visual depth" (1968b, 631).

It is worth noting that, according to these definitions, the unconsciousness of mental operations can be conceived as a form of unobservability. That is, the mind is not only unobservable for psychologists, who can only postulate it through theorizing and inferring from its behavioral effects, but also for anyone who tries to introspect them. In principle, no one can access privately her mental processes; thus, she cannot observe how they work in any way. However, this point could sound quite astonishing to many people. It is a legitimate question to ask why, after all, we are conscious of what we are doing and of what happens in our mind. Cognitivists tend to answer this question this way: It is true that we are conscious of what we perceive, feel, believe, talk, and so on. But everything we are conscious about must be considered as the final product (output) of a certain set of computational mental operations introspectively inaccessible. This point is clearly exposed by the economist Simon when he describes the cognitive process of recognition:

> We do not have conscious access to the processes that allow us to recognize a familiar object or person. We recognize our friend, but we do not know what traits and features enable that recognition to occur. Nor can we describe these traits or features to other people accurately enough to enable them to recognize the same person. We are aware of the *fact* of recognition, which gives us access to our knowledge about our friend; we are not aware of the *processes* that accomplish the recognition. (1998, 13)

In other words, the *content* (or the *representational aspects* or *the facts of our knowledge*) of our conscious experience is causally determined unconsciously. Let's take again the example of the visual estimation of depth: This estimation is nothing more than a judgment or belief about what we perceive. We are aware of this belief and thus of our perception, but we cannot access the complex psychological mechanisms that have led from retinical information to such a belief (Stich 1978, 503). In other words, "in general, the world in our conscious mind is a set of representations that result from a set of processes, and the world in our unconscious mind is a set of processes themselves. . . . All mental processes are unconscious. We are aware at best of some of their results" (Johnson-Laird 2006, 57).

THE PUZZLE OF VERBAL REPORTS

As discussed above, cognitivists argue that people's inability verbally to report the mental processes involved in the production of a behavioral output can be considered the empirical criterion for assessing the unconscious character of these processes. Examples of the application of such a criterion may be found outside experimental psychology's laboratories. For example, when someone is asked, *What is your mother's maiden name?*, the answer appears swiftly in consciousness. But if she is asked, *How did you come up with that?,* she is not able to describe the memory processes that brought the answer (Nisbett and Wilson 1977, 232). Or, when someone is driving a car or riding a bicycle, she does not seem able verbally to express the mental operations determining her performances. Thus, such operations are considered to be *unconscious*.

As we can see, at a first glance verbalization appears to be rather different for cognitivists and behaviorists. In fact, although verbal responses provide the commonest data in behavioristic research, they are considered to be a kind of objective behavioral data. For example, in visual perception experiments subjects are asked to say *Yes* or *No* when a certain stimulus is perceived (or not) by them. However, to say *Yes* or *No* is the same as to press *Y* or *N* or *A* and *B* on a keyboard (or, for example, a red or a green button), except that the former is made with the mouth instead of the finger (Ericsson and Simon 1980, 216). In this sense, behaviorists conceive verbal data as behaviors directly observable by external observers and thus define them as third-person data. Instead, for cognitivists, verbal data seem to concern the subjective experiences directly observable only by the subjects having those experiences and thus they are defined as first-person data (Chalmers 2004; Gaillard et al. 2006, 717–18). In such a view, cognitivists appear to assume that the mental states and processes not verbally reportable by subjects are to be considered unconscious.

However, at the methodological level, how are verbal reports conceived in CP? According to the psychologist Ericsson and the economist Simon (1980, 216), two different types of verbal reports are a function of time of verbalization. The first is called *concurrent verbalization*: it is when the subject is asked to describe her mental operations at the time she is attending to a cognitive task. The second is called *retrospective verbalization*: it is when the subject is asked to describe her mental operations after she has attended to a cognitive task.[17]

Such kinds of verbalization show some similarities with the late nineteenth- and early twentieth-century introspection. In fact, in very general terms, both introspectionists and cognitivists ask subjects for a (concurrent or retrospective) report of the covert mental events that are taking or have taken place during or briefly after a certain task (Reber and Reber 2001, 369). In other words, both seem to rely on a subjective or first-person perspective in data recollection.

However, an important theoretical difference separates the introspectionistic and the cognitivistic verbal reports. In introspectionistic research, subjects are assumed always to have direct access to what has happened or is happening in their mind. But in cognitivistic research, subjects are not assumed to have direct access to what has happened or is happening in their minds. In other words, cognitivists do not consider verbal reporting as a form of direct observation of mental events (Newell et al. 1958, 156, note 8; Ericsson and Simon 1980, 217): On the contrary, they argue that these reports represent a kind of indirect evidence of mental events. The reason for it is that subjects are not asked to describe directly their mental operations. Rather, they are asked to describe how the cognitive tasks they have performed or are performing are structured and what they have done or thought (or are doing or are thinking) to solve them. Thus, from the accuracy and completeness of the cognitive tasks' descriptions, cognitive psychologists can infer whether subjects are aware of what has happened or is happening in their minds during their performance (G. A. Miller 1981, 219). This seems quite reasonable to me: What prevents us from saying that someone is conscious of her mental operations if she is able to give a full and veridical account of how she has solved or is solving a cognitive task?

In brief, we can say that the introduction of verbal data in CP does not indicate a return to the introspection of the late nineteenth- and early twentieth-century mentalism (Greenwood 1999, 11). Specifically, cognitivistic methodology for verbal reports seems to differ from introspectionistic methodology in three features:

1. Cognitivistic methodology does not require the long and difficult training necessary in the introspectionistic one, because a cognitive task is the same for all of the experimental subjects.
2. Because experimental subjects do not require any special training, it is possible to collect and evaluate many verbal reports, not just a few as in introspectionistic research. In other words, in this situation, a statistically significant sample can be assessed easily in the same experimental conditions.
3. Assessing the correctness of a verbal report of a task is quite easy, although subjects may arrive at describing the procedures they have used or are using to solve the task in different ways (Ericsson and Simon 1980, 221).

As we can see, the cognitive task can provide an anchor point that allows the verbal reporting of the experimental subjects and the control of the researcher over the experiment. Through this anchor point, researchers from different laboratories can compare the verbal reports obtained intersubjectively and, *via* such a comparison, can gather a certain number of third-person data. More precisely, we can individuate the common and across-subjects features of all of the reports collected[18] and thus to have at our disposal third-person and objective data.[19] In this sense, it seems that cognitivists' assessment of verbal reports as evidence for their inferences to the mind and the behaviorists' assessment of these reports as mere behavior tend to converge. In fact, both assessments appear to include only the across-subjects features of verbal reports, that is, those aspects of reports publicly observable and assessable from an intersubjective/third-person perspective. In other words, the search for the common features of verbal reports could aim to limit as much as possible the subjective/first-person character of this kind of data.

Thus, it seems that cognitivists consider the subjective/first-person character of verbal reports as difficult to treat in a scientific way and thus problematic. Probably because of this difficulty, the treatment of verbal reports as sketched above seems to be something more programmatic than applied in cognitive psychology's research. That is, if we take a look at the empirical literature in cognitive psychology, in most studies verbal reports appear to occupy a marginal or secondary place in comparison to other kinds of data (such as those coming from observable behavior or from physiological measures, for example).

Further, I think that cognitivists have not yet developed a received methodology or at least a certain number of common criteria for dealing with these reports and have preferred to focus on the development of methods for gathering and assessing only the third-person data. In this sense, although cognitivists seem to consider in principle the verbal reports as reliable methods for dealing with the first-person data (of course, as long as it is possible to turn them into third-person data), these methods appear to be still rather *primitive* if compared with those for gathering third-person data. That is, the latter have been defined by years of scientific practice, but the former do not seem to have received nearly as much attention. According to the philosopher Chalmers (2004), the reason for such a primitivism seems to be due to the intrinsic difficulty in dealing with these data and with consciousness in general. In a recent paper, the psychologists Newell and Shanks discuss such a difficulty in a critical review of the role of the unconscious mind on decision making. The main focus of their paper is on the methods used to test whether experimental subjects are conscious of the mental processes involved in the determination of behavior during decision-making tasks (Newell and Shanks 2014, 1–2).

They point out that, in decision-making tasks, a comparison is generally made between a behavioral performance (for example, the number of choices from a set of various alternatives) and a conscious assessment based on subjects' verbal reports (3): Researchers infer that a certain mental state is occurring or has occurred unconsciously if subjects' behavioral performance at the task in question is clearly guided by this mental state and no others, but their verbal reports do not reflect it in any way. According to their proposal, in order to assess the presence or the absence of consciousness reliably, a test must meet four criteria (3–4, table 1):

1. *Reliability*: The assessment test must be unaffected by those factors that do not influence the behavioral performance (for example, experimental demands or social desiderability).[20]
2. *Relevance/Information*: The assessment test must consider only the amount of information relevant to the behavioral performance or the decision in question.
3. *Immediacy*: The assessment test must occur concurrently (so long as it does not influence the behavioral performance) or as soon after the behavioral performance as possible to avoid possible lapses or distortions.
4. *Sensitivity*: The assessment test should occur under optimal retrieval conditions (for example, the same cues or stimuli must be provided both for evaluating consciousness and for eliciting the behavioral performance).

It is important to note that, although Newell and Shanks's article is very recent, the idea behind their criteria for assessing consciousness dates back to two papers written by Shanks and the psychologist St. John in 1994 and 1997. In these papers, Shanks and St. John focus on the implicit learning paradigm and provide an articulated criticism of what they call the *Thesis of Implicit Knowledge and Learning*. According to this thesis, most of people's knowledge is the primary cause of their behavior, but it cannot be represented into consciousness as well as the learning of this knowledge (both at the time of learning and at the time of retrieval) (St. John and Shanks 1997, 164).

According to their criticism, most studies in favor of the Thesis of Implicit Knowledge and Learning use invalid tests of consciousness, that is, tests clearly violating criteria (b) and (d) of the previous list (Shanks and St. John 1994, 73–75 and 377; St. John and Shanks 1997, 167). For this reason, they conclude that the empirical evidence in favor of the Thesis of Implicit Knowledge and Learning is not as grounded and well established as it can appear at a first look (Shanks and St. John 1994, 367 and 394; St. John and Shanks 1997, 162–63). In this sense, the Newell and Shanks 2014 paper can be seen as an application of the Shanks and St. John of 1994 and 1997 to the area of decision making (where the Thesis of Implicit Knowledge and Learning seems to be prevalent).

Beyond the discussion on the validity of Shanks' and colleagues' conclusions, I believe that, on the one hand, the four criteria Shanks and colleagues proposed appear to be balanced and very useful in guiding the construction of adequate tests of consciousness able to support the experimental subjects in their verbal reporting during a cognitive task. On the other, they appear to require a lot of work and attention to be met, although they do not set too high a standard for researchers (Newell and Shanks 2014, 4).

However, I believe that, more than an intrinsic difficulty in dealing with first-person data, the reason for this situation is the one I pointed to above: Consciousness and the first-person data have a *bad reputation* among cognitive psychologists because they do not fit with a certain scientific image of the world (more precisely, a physicalistic one). Because of that, these data are often considered a sort of *second-rate data*, not reliable and not veridical. The psychologist Johnson-Laird explicitly argues this point in a 2006 book: "It is impossible to establish the veridicality of subjective reports. At worst, they may be fraudulent . . . ; at best, they may be misleading, because none of us has access to the wellsprings of thought" (27).

Although less explicitly than Johnson-Laird, the psychologist Sternberg dismisses verbal reports as a reliable source of data when he argues that "whereas experimental research is most useful for testing hypotheses, research based on self-reports . . . is often particularly useful for the formulation of hypotheses." Sternberg asserts this position by saying that these reports are limited "because many cognitive processes may be altered by the act of giving the report and many cognitive processes may occur outside consciousness" (1996, 20). It is worth noting that in a more or less explicit way Johnson-Laird and Sternberg appear to endorse the position proposed by the psychologists Nisbett and Wilson in a 1977 seminal article.[21]

According to such a position, the subjective verbal reports have to be considered unreliable not only when they are incorrect or incomplete, but also when they are correct and complete. This is because when subjects verbally report on their mental operations, they do not do it on the basis of any true introspection, but on their theories or judgments about how such processes work. Thus, because they are not based on true introspections, the verbal reports that look rich and accurate cannot be reliable (Nisbett and Wilson 1977, 249). Very briefly, the crucial argument of the Nisbett and Wilson article can be summarized in briefly two points (Wilson 2002, 106):

1. Many (maybe all?) emotions, judgments, thoughts, feelings, and behaviors are caused by an unconscious mind.
2. Because people cannot have any conscious and first-person access to the unconscious mind, the conscious mind confabulates reasons for explaining emotions, judgments, and so forth.

Nisbett and Wilson's position against verbal reporting is very influential and can be considered a paradigmatic example of CP's anti-introspectionism. In fact, Nisbett and Wilson's review is often quoted as decisive in demonstrating the assumption that (almost) all of our mental life is unconscious.[22] However, it must be pointed out that their argument is evidently formulated in a non-falsifiable fashion because both correct and incorrect reports are used to support it (Smith and Miller 1978, 355–56). That is, there is no way to falsify it, even by demonstrating that in some situations people are correct in reporting their mental operations verbally. So conceived, Nisbett and Wilson's argument seems to be an ad hoc argument made for supporting the assumption that mental states are (almost) all unconscious. We have seen above a consequence of this assumption is that people can be conscious only of the products (or contents) of a series of mental processes that are inaccessible to introspection (Nisbett and Wilson 1977, 255–65). In this view, verbal reports about how people solve problems or cognitive tasks cannot be used as data for testing the accessibility to mental processes (G. A. Miller 1981, 281).

However, through the years many authors had criticized the distinction between unconscious mental processes and conscious mental contents that Nisbett and Wilson assume.[23] The general point underlying all of the criticisms seems to be that such a distinction has never been clearly drawn and thus it is more confusing than it appears at a first look (G. A. Miller 1981, 218–19; Ericsson and Simon 1985, 26). In fact, the cognitivistic literature includes many examples of processes that are clearly conscious and of contents clearly unconscious.

An example of conscious process can be the construct of working memory, defined as a limited capacity (that is, it cannot take into account vast amounts of information) mnemonic process allowing holding things in mind in the moment we work on them. This process is considered to be at the basis of conscious reasoning, and people are always aware of it (for example, when they are mentally making a division or a multiplication) (Johnson-Laird 2006, 72 and 430). An example of unconscious contents influencing the behavior involves the blind patients. Although they declare to be blind, these patients display a great ability to respond to the visual stimulations that they are not able to see (Reber and Reber 2001, 96). For example, if they are asked to guess in which part of a screen placed before them a certain stimulus has appeared, they tend to give accurate responses. This means that they possess an unconscious representation of the stimuli presented in the blind field, although they are not able to make spontaneous intentional actions with regard to these stimuli (Marcel 2003, 174).

It is worth noting that, in addition to the fact that the distinction between unconscious processes and conscious contents (products) has encountered different empirical disconfirmations, it seems to be ill conceived in its theoretical formulation. As the psychologist Greenwald (1992, 778) has pointed out, the distinction is flawed because it serves simultaneously to give account of two different distinctions, that between process and content and that between unconsciousness and consciousness. In this way, the process = unconscious and content = conscious conception seems to work as a set of circular definitions with a loose explanatory value. Thus, as interpreted in these senses, *conscious mental process* and *unconscious mental content* are no more than oxymoronic notions.

In summary, we can see that the status of verbal reports as empirical evidence for CP's theories appears to be highly controversial. In fact, it seems that cognitivists consider these reports relevant only insofar as their subjective character can be strongly reduced or eliminated. And because of the difficulty of this reduction or elimination and the possibility of having other kinds of evidence at their disposal, they tend to dismiss verbal reports as unreliable and not veridical. However, it seems to me that the dismissal of verbal reports as a valid source of data for psychology implies the dismissal of a part of the mental as an object of inquiry. This part is the consciousness, of course.

ARE COMPUTER SIMULATIONS EMPIRICAL OR THEORETICAL TOOLS FOR PSYCHOLOGICAL RESEARCH?

As I said above, computer programs have a crucial role in CP theorization. In fact, to provide an explanation of the behavior of an organism (or a machine), cognitive psychologists tend to work through building up a computer program composed of a certain number of information processes generating the behavior in question (Newell et al. 1958, 151). In other words, the program aims to describe the internal and not directly observable set of activities taking place between an input and an output under certain conditions (Lachman et al. 1979, 89–90). That is, it aims to describe the (unconscious) mind from an objective and in a third-person point of view.

As we can see, a computer program is literally a system of difference equations that can be used to explain behavior of every sort of organism or machine (Simon 1992, 6). In this sense, the theoretical work of cognitive psychologists does not differ from that of other scientists whose discipline requires an inference of unobservable theoretical entities (expressible in terms of difference equations, but not only) from gross observable behavior (Simon 1992, 22; Lachman et al. 1979, 90 and 123–24). It is important to note that for cognitivists, using computer programs for simulating mental states is not to be considered only a way for theorizing about the mind, but also a new manner for testing psychological theories empirically. This is a central point throughout the pioneering work of the economist Simon and the computer scientist Newell:

> Computer science is an empirical discipline. . . . Each new machine that is built is an experiment. Actually constructing the machine poses a question to nature; and we listen for the answer by observing the machine and analysing it by all analytical and measurement means available. Each new programme that is built is an experiment. It poses a question to nature, and its behaviour offers clues to a new answer. Neither machines nor programmes are black boxes; they are artefacts that have been designed, both hardware and software, and we can open them up and look inside. (Simon and Newell 1976, 81–82)

In this long but very crucial quotation, Simon and Newell defend the view that programming computer simulations of the cognitive tasks is a form of empirical inquiry, along with observation and controlled experimentation (Nickerson 2003, 549). Certainly, the validity of a computer simulation must be assessed on standards different from those used in observational and experimental inquiries. For example, simulation does not require a statistically significant number of observations of a phenomenon to confirm or disconfirm a theory. Rather, a single experiment (that is, a single simulation) could be sufficient to assess it (Simon and Newell 1976, 82): Once the program is built, it is sufficient to see if it runs in the machine (computer). But, as clearly stated by the philosopher Kukla, this does not seem sufficient for considering computer simulation as an empirical tool and thus computer science as an empirical discipline.

We can set the adequacy of a computer program theoretically, as in mathematics. In this sense, simulation is nothing more than constructing programs that perform in a defined manner, which is a deductive and aprioristic task. In fact, computer scientists have only to assess the adequacy of the structure of a program with the sequence of steps they instruct the computer to take, and this has nothing to do with the experimental way of inquiring (Kukla 1989, 56). Thus, in principle, computer simulations cannot be tools for empirical enquiry but, rather, they are tools for theoretical enquiry.

A possible reply to this criticism is that, although it can be correct in principle, it does not work in practice. In fact, computer programs are too complex to assess their validity only on a theoretical ground (Simon 1993, 638). That is, to evaluate this validity we must execute the program implemented in the computer and observe whether it works adequately. Because of this appeal to observation, Simon and other computer scientists point out that testing a computer program is the same as testing a hypothesis in natural sciences (Colburn 2000, 8). In fact, they argue that, similarly to what happens in controlled experimentation, after having implemented the theory/program according to a set of specific conditions sufficient to produce a certain output behavior, the fact that this behavior takes place (or not) counts as empirical evidence for confirming (or disconfirming) the theory/program (Newell et al. 1958, 155–56).

It is worth noting that, according to this argument, the attempts to demonstrate a theorem made by a mathematician also should be considered empirical. In fact, a mathematician does not know a priori whether her attempts at demonstration will be successful, and thus she has to observe (in a certain sense) where they will lead. Thus, there does not seem to be a difference in principle between relying on computers and relying on paper and pencil (or on thinking!) (Kukla 2001, 108): Defining a step-by-step procedure, implementing it in the computer, and observing how it runs is an a priori and deductive job similar, for example, to theorem demonstration. It is clear that such a job does not permit us to concretely and directly observe how a certain phenomenon occurs.

I think that Kukla is right in considering the construction of a computational model for simulating a certain cognitive system as a kind of theoretical job and not of empirical inquiry. The crucial point here is the meaning given to the term *observation*. Observing how an experiment is going on is not the same as observing how a computer simulation (or a theorem demonstration) is going on. In fact, as I pointed out above, the concrete entities can in principle be directly or indirectly observed but not the abstract ones. Thus, if we define the cognitive processes abstractly (similarly to the mathematical objects), computer programs built to reproduce them are artifacts simulating objects knowable only through theorization and not through observation. In this view, cognitive psychologists consider computers and programs not as tools for observing mental operations but rather as tools for formalizing theories and models of the human mind. So conceived, computer programming is very useful for psychologists because it allows them to write down with clarity and precision the sequence of inner and unconscious mental processes that are postulated to mediate between input and output (Longuet-Higgins 1981, 200; Colburn 2000, 71).

However, it is worth noting that Kukla's criticism does not seem to apply when we compare the computer simulation of a certain cognitive task with the behavior of a human subject performing the same task in the laboratory (Simon 1992, 3). That is, "since the theory takes the form of a computer program, the theory must be wrong if a computer, operating under that program and given the same tasks as a human subject in the laboratory, does not emit the same behavioral responses" (Newell and Simon 1965, 111). In this view, it seems reasonable to consider computer simulations as empirical tools of enquiry. This is because comparing the performances of a computer program with those of a human subject in the same cognitive task for assessing the validity of a certain theory is not an aprioristic and deductive work as the theory-construction through computer language. Rather, such a comparison can be regarded as a way of inductively certifying that the behavior of a machine and that of a human subject, once assessed to be identical in the relevant respects, depend upon some internal events or processes postulated as causally determinant for the behavior itself.

This is possible on the basis of an inductive principle that permits us to infer the unobservable (unconscious) mental processes determining the behavior by the comparison between the performance of a computer program and that of a human subject at the same cognitive task. Such a principle is clearly stated by the philosopher Fodor: "If D is a true description of the etiology of an event e, and if e' is an event numerically distinct from e but of the same kind as e, then it is reasonable to infer, ceteris paribus, that D is a true description of the etiology of e'" (1968b, 639). Thus, according to this inductive principle, the comparison between computer simulation and human behavior seems to be a legitimate empirical procedure for assessing the validity of the postulation of internal operations or processes in psychological explanations.

In conclusion, it seems to me that the introduction of computer programming in psychology primarily has had a crucial role in theorization. In fact, as I said at the beginning of the chapter, most CP theories look like computer programs or, very roughly, lists of processes or states describing what mind does for producing an observable behavior. I think that, in this sense, this change in the way of theorizing can be seen as a revolutionary aspect of cognitivism with respect to behaviorism. However, I believe it is quite controversial whether computer programs and simulations can be said to be tools for empirical enquiry. Personally I do not see strong arguments for conceiving them in this way. This is because they can have an empirical role only when we compare their behavior (or output performance) with that of human problem solvers (Newell et al. 1958, 152) but not if considered alone. In fact, in such a case, computer programs and simulations can work only at an abstract level, that is, at the level of the construction of a theory or of a theoretical model. In other words, computer programs and simulations appear to be tools for defining and describing the unconscious mind.

CONCLUDING REMARKS

In an article about the history of the so-called *cognitive revolution* in psychology, the psychologist Miller describes behaviorism as based on two tenets: the assumption that mental events are not publicly observable and that the only objective evidence available for a scientific psychology is behavioral (G. A. Miller 2003, 141). Curiously, such a definition seems to apply quite well also to CP. In fact, as I said above, for cognitivists the abstractness and the unconsciousness are what characterize the mental. Now, although these features refer to different domains of inquiry dealing with different problems, both assume that the mind is an unobservable entity requiring theorization to be understood (Mandler 2007, 9 and 44).[24]

Further, it is a matter of fact that the study of behavior is at the core of CP and that, like behaviorists, cognitivists assume a strong anti-introspectionistic and anti-subjectivistic position. We have seen above that such a position is defended through the appeal to two different but related strategies: on the one hand, the maintenance of the distinction between unconscious processes and conscious contents; and, on the other hand, the dismissal of verbal reports as reliable tools of inquiry. In other words, at least in the experimental practice, most cognitive psychologists seem to get along very well dismissing consciousness and its subjectivity as mere *folk psychology* and thus preferring to rely on publicly observable behavior to test their theories (Kihlstrom 1999, 173; Marcel 2003, 178).

Thus, according to Miller's definition of behaviorism, cognitivists do not appear to be anti-behavioristic at all. In fact, by following the behavioristic tradition, they tend to make most observations and experiments under strictly controlled situations (in a laboratory) (Lachman et al. 1979, 39 and 115, table 4.2; Simon 1992, 23). However, it is undeniable that, in opposition to the behavioristic tradition, cognitivists assume that it is legitimate to appeal to the operations of the *black box* as the causes of the behavior. We have seen above that, because of the abstract character of the mental emphasized by functionalism and the information-processing view, to justify such an appeal in psychological theorizing, theoretical and deductive work is required. An important tool for doing this job is the computer. In fact, computer programming allows drawing abstract models of the unobservable mental events postulated to be the causal determinants of the behavior.

However, CP is not only a theoretical enterprise hypothesizing internal mental operation. In fact, its practitioners offer empirical evidence for confirming or disconfirming the plausibility of their hypotheses (Bechtel 2005, 320). As for every empirical science, the point for CP here is that of the connections between the theoretical and the observational terms. In fact, these connections can exist only if the theoretical terms have an empirical content (Hempel 1952, 23). Thus, the question here is what guarantees the empirical content in CP and, as a consequence, its status as an empirical discipline. Because of the dismissal of the first-person data, such a status appears to be guaranteed by behavioral data.

In fact, I said above, computer programs can be used as empirical tools for providing an empirical justification of the psychological theories postulating unobservable mental events. But this justification is possible only through the comparison of the computer simulations of the theoretical models proposed with the behavioral performances assessed by observation and controlled experimentation. Thus, in this view, stimuli and responses (that is, the behavior) are to be considered crucial for CP as an empirical enterprise. In this sense, we can agree with the psychologist Leahey when he points out that "the coming of CP is best regarded not as the revolutionary creation of a new paradigm slaying the older one of behaviorism, but as the appearance of a new form of behavioralism based on a new technology, the computer" (1992, 316). In such a view, cognitive psychologists seem to conceive behavioristic psychology as an incomplete but not wrong approach that fails to give account of the unobservable mental phenomena (such as learning, thinking, problem solving) determining the behavior (Neisser 1967, 5; Reber and Reber 2001, 129).

Thus, consciousness (and subjectivity and introspection) appears to have little or no room in CP. As clearly stated by two prominent cognitivists: "one of the dirty secrets of CP is that many of those who practice it can get along perfectly well without displaying any interest in consciousness at all" (Kihlstrom 1999, 173). "Supported by many philosophers, many psychologists considered consciousness an epiphenomenal occurrence that hid the more[25] interesting unconscious effects" (Mandler 2007, 230).

NOTES

1. For an exhaustive account on this point, see Lachman et al. 1979, chap. 4, 87–129.

2. It is worth noting that pioneers in CP assumed the analogy mind = computer program only as metaphor (and nothing more). In fact, they had clearly in mind that the concept of a computer program as a set of cognitive processes has nothing to do with real computers and real minds (Newell et al. 1958, 152–53; Greenwood 1999, 17).

3. As clearly pointed out by the philosopher Greenwood (1999, 3), almost nobody in the CP community has argued for the general inadequacy of the conditioning theories of behaviorism. Rather, cognitivists have argued for a delimitation of the scope of explanations in terms of conditioning and an extension of cognitive explanations in those areas where the conditioning theories had resulted to be inadequate.

4. In this work I will refer to the general features of functionalism without distinguishing among the many varieties of it. For good descriptions of these varieties, see Rey 1997, 165–207, and Levin 2013.

5. It is worth noting that the mental states used in this example do not need any appeal to introspection to be explained and described. In fact, when the person of the

example says *I have a headache*, she does not need to reflect upon it and then consciously describe it to know that she has such a pain (Putnam 1960, 23).

6. A physicalistic version of the functionalistic position can be found in the 1958 seminal paper of Newell, Shaw, and Simon. Here (151) the authors describe two basic elements of their theory of human problem solving, memories, and the primitive information processes. They argue that, although it is clearly obvious that defined physical mechanisms for implementing these elements exist, their theory is not concerned at all with them. This is because it deals with the level of information processing (that is, with "the ability of a computer [or a different kind of machine] to do certain things"), not with the level of its physical implementation.

7. Of course, not all members of the CP community accept this position. For example, the prominent cognitivist Mandler (2007, 3 and 15) declares himself to be a functionalist accepting that the mind is what the brain does and thus adopting a basic materialistic stance.

8. In this sense it can be interpreted as the following affirmation by the cognitive psychologist (and self-declared functionalist) Mandler (2007, 1): "Mind—at least in one of its versions—is one of those things in the world that everybody is willing to talk about but nobody has ever seen or touched."

9. Thus, they are assumed to be unobservable only because physicists have not yet developed sensible instruments to observe or detect them directly.

10. Thus, they are assumed to be unobservable because the possibility of observing or detecting them does not (and cannot) depend in any way upon the sensibility of an observational instrument.

11. It is important to note that such a situation is not peculiar to psychology but also applies to other sciences—or example, economics. In fact, galloping inflation or marginal utility requires a certain degree of abstraction from its observable effects to be described adequately. Such a parallel between psychology and economics is clearly described by the psychologist Neisser:

> The same point can be illustrated with a quite different analogy, that between psychology and economics. The economist wishes to understand, say, the flow of capital. The object of his study must have some tangible representation, in the form of checks, gold, paper money, and so on, but these objects are not what he really cares about. The physical properties of money, its location in banks, its movement in armoured cars, are of little interest to him. To be sure, the remarkable permanence of gold has some economic importance. The flow of capital would be markedly different if every medium of exchange were subject to rapid corrosion. Nevertheless, such matters are not the main concern of the economist, and knowledge of them does not much simplify economic theory. Psychology, like economics, is a science concerned with the interdependence among certain events rather than with their physical nature. (Neisser 1967, 6–7)

12. For a proposed attempt to maintain both the distinction between *abstract* and *concrete* and the causal efficacy of the mental, see Lachman et al. 1979, 96 and 97.

13. On this point see, for example, Lachman et al. 1979, 7–8; Von Eckardt 2003, 553 and 555; Johnson-Laird 2006, 21–59; Mandler 2007, 226 and 228.

14. A consequence of the distinction between controlled and automatic processes is that the former are conceived as slow and not routinary and the latter as fast and routinary (Baars and McGovern 1996, 71).

15. However, the empirical validity of these examples is rather controversial. See Shanks and St. John 1994 and St. John and Shanks 1997 for an exhaustive assessment of this issue.

16. In a famous article (1980, 209) the neuroscientist Cohen and the psychologist Squire report compelling evidence of the plausibility of this distinction. In this study they found that amnesiac patients appear to be able to learn the encoding procedures and rules for acquiring a certain skill but not to remember (to report verbally) the information that results from applying them.

17. For an interesting application of these techniques in the field of decision-making studies, see Gigerenzer et al. 1999, 141–67.

18. Of course, each one represents the first-person or subjective point of view of the experimental subject.

19. Here I mean objective data as synonymous for data upon which a certain degree of intersubjective agreement among researchers is reached. On this point, see Kelly 2014.

20. Very briefly, a bias or a set of biases that can lead a person to respond to self-evaluative questions in a socially approved manner so as to appear more socially desirable either to oneself or to others (Reber and Reber 2001, 688).

21. For two convincing critical analyses of this article, see Ericsson and Simon 1985, 25–30, and Newell and Shanks 2014, 4–5.

22. On this point see, for example, Dijksterhuis et al. 2005, 81; Gaillard et al. 2006, 713; Johnson-Laird 2006, 61.

23. On this point see, for example, Smith and F. D. Miller 1978; White 1980; Ericsson and Simon 1980; G. A. Miller 1981; Greenwald 1992; Ericsson and Simon 1985; Lehaey 1992; Newell and Shanks 2014).

24. In this sense I agree with the psychologist Mandler, who defines the so-called cognitive revolution as “the rebirth of a theory-rich psychology” after behaviorism (Mandler 2007, 178).

Chapter Four

New Antimentalism

In chapter 3 I described CP as a kind of behavioral psychology that admits the appeal to mentalistic terms in its theories. I also argued that these terms refer to abstract entities that can be known only through theorizing and implemented in different physical supports. Such a characterization implies that we cannot obtain any information about the mental from the physical features of the support implementing it. Thus, the level of explanation of the physical support has nothing to do with that of the mental states or processes (Simon 1992, 7–8). In this sense, even if we can agree that the mind is placed inside the brain, psychology can be considered autonomous from neuroscience. As clearly stated by the psychologist Johnson-Laird, "Psychology can be pursued independently from neurophysiology. The physiological substrate must provide a physical basis for the processes of mind, but granted that the substrate offers the computational power of recursive functions, its physical nature places no constraints on the pattern of thought" (1980, 9).

In other words, according to such a position, neurophysiology (and, in general, neuroscience) and psychology pertain to different domains of inquiry and they use distinct vocabularies in their theories. The former uses a biological vocabulary (with terms such as neuron, neurotransmitter, axon, and synapse) and the latter a psychological vocabulary (with terms such as cognition, memory, perception, and thought). Thus, neuroscience cannot be informative for CP and vice versa. It is even assumed that some conceptual difficulties may arise in confounding the two vocabularies (Fodor 1968a, 112–13). However, it is worth noting that many (most?) experimental psychologists may not agree with such a position. A clue in this sense comes, for example, by looking at the voice *neurocognition* of the 2001 edition of the *Penguin Dictionary of Psychology* (464). Here the psychologists Arthur and Emily Reber note that, in comparison to the 1995 edition, their dictionary contains an astonishing number of terms from neuroscience. This means that the recent growth of such a discipline (in terms of comprehension of how the brain works and of advancement of the technologies that permit observing or detecting the nervous system's activities) have oriented experimental psychologists to explore the connections between neurobiological structures and functions and mental processes.

In this chapter I will use the term Cognitive Neuroscience (CN) as a general term to refer to every discipline that tries to clarify these connections. Thus, I will provide a critical examination of the methodology used in CN and of the idea of mind at its basis.

THE METHODOLOGICAL ASSUMPTIONS OF COGNITIVE NEUROSCIENCE (CN)

As I said above, CN can be defined as a *bridging discipline* between CP and neurobiology. Its aim is to provide a means to test the accuracy of the CP's constructs by determining how the cognitive operations described by such constructs are performed in the brain (Ward 2006, 6). In this sense, a fundamental job of CN is to define and explore the relationships between specific neuroanatomical structures of the nervous system and specific cognitive processes (Tranel and Damasio 2000, 119; Reber and Reber 2001, 464).

For this reason, cognitive neuroscientists have focused their research primarily on cerebral lesion studies.[1] In fact, these studies offer the clearest example of how the damage (or malfunctioning) of a certain brain area is followed by the loss (or malfunctioning) of a certain mental function. Thus, they show how CP and neurobiology can interact, the former by examining the behavioral performances of the brain-damaged patients at some tasks and thus inferring the cognitive functions impaired and the latter by assessing the cerebral locus of the damage.

From such a description it follows that a fundamental principle of CN is the *localization of (mental) functions*. That is, cognitive neuroscientists assume that specific mental functions have relatively precise and circumscribed cerebral locations (Reber and Reber 2001, 401). This principle is at the basis of the most important method of CN, the *dissociation method.* According to this method, we can observe or detect a *dissociation* when a brain-damaged patient (or a group of patients) that has to perform the tests A and B, which examine, respectively, the functions F1 and F2, has a poor performance at test A and a good performance at test B (Mondini et al. 2003, 4). However, such a method does not guarantee a reliable conclusion because the performances of the patient (or the group of patients) could depend upon the different degrees of difficulty of tests A and B and not upon the real difference between the cognitive functions under examination (Shallice 1988, 35–36).

For this reason, it is preferable to find a *double dissociation*. We can observe or detect a double dissociation when two patients (or two groups of patients) perform the tests A and B, which examine, respectively, the functions F1 and F2, where one shows a bad performance at test A and a good performance at test B; the other, a good performance at test A and a bad performance at test B (Mondini et al. 2003, 4).

An example of double dissociation is the following: a brain-damaged patient who has lost her ability to use syntax (thus, she is able to understand the meaning of words but unable to string words together to produce sentences) and another who has lost the conceptual knowledge (thus, she is able to string words together but unable to understand the meaning of words) (van Orden et al. 2001, 111). It is worth noting that, although in CN the principle of localization of (mental) functions is at the basis of the dissociation method, the latter can be considered autonomous from the former. In fact, in the experimental practice dissociation is used as a general term for referring to any procedure that allows the researchers to distinguish between two functions (Reber and Reber 2001, 216). In this sense, dissociation between two functions is no more than dissociation in the dependent variable due to researchers' manipulation of a certain independent variable (or variables). In the previous example the test measuring the use of syntax and that measuring the conceptual knowledge are the independent variables and the patients' behavioral performance is the dependent variable (Phelps 1999, 297).

Thus, if from the previous example we omit the fact that the two patients have brain damage (or if we hypothesize that they have the same brain damage or that they have no brain damage), we can find a double dissociation of functions only on the basis of their behavioral performances, but we cannot make any inference about their localization in the nervous system. On the contrary, if we consider that the first patient has damage in Broca's area, in the left-frontal cortex, and the second damage in Wernicke's area, in the temporal-occipital cortex, we are allowed to infer that syntax and conceptual knowledge are distinct not only as cognitive functions but also as brain areas (van Orden et al. 2001, 112).

It is important to note that cognitive neuroscientists do not focus their research only on lesion studies. In fact, many of these studies are based on experiments or observations on single or few subjects because cerebral lesions depend upon accidents of nature occurring (Phelps 1999, 301); thus, it is very difficult to collect a sample of patients with a lesion in the same cerebral area. Thus, such data do not seem to be representative of all of the population of subjects with such a cerebral damage. In this sense, the lesion studies seem to suffer from a lack of *population validity*, that is, the degree to which the results of the experimental sample can be generalized to the population from which it is drawn (Pedon and Gnisi 2004, 136).

Further, although the correlation between a cognitive and behavioral deficit and brain region damage shows that this region is necessary for the normal cognitive performance, it does not reveal how this region contributes to the normal performance (Bechtel and Mundale 1999, 185). Because of these problems, it is puzzling to assess to what extent the data from the lesion studies can be informative for understanding cognition. For this reason, cognitive neuroscientists are convinced that observing the changes in the activity of intact-brain (or nervous system) subjects provides a more reliable basis for such an understanding (Sarter et al. 1996, 3). Thus, for studying samples of intact-brain participants, two categories of techniques are generally used: neuroimaging and physiological.

The neuroimaging techniques[2] measure indices of blood flow in the brain, assuming that such a flow is related to neuronal activity (Phelps 1999, 309). The main idea at the basis of these techniques is that one can isolate the cerebral area active during a specific cognitive process (311). In the studies using these techniques the experimental subjects have to perform two different tasks, chosen so that the one is assumed to require the same cognitive operations as the other plus an additional process (or more additional processes).[3] The average activation of each cerebral location measured during the first task (the easier one) is then subtracted from that measured during the second task (the more difficult one). The result is a *difference image* showing the added (or reduced) cerebral activation elicited by the more difficult task. Thus, this area of *additional cerebral activation* is considered to be the locus of the *additional cognitive process* (Bechtel 2008, 47).

As we can see, the assumption of localization of (mental) functions and the dissociation method seem to apply very well to the studies using neuroimaging techniques. In fact, in these studies cognitive neuroscientists manipulate certain independent variables (in this case, two cognitive tasks) and observe the dissociation in the dependent variable (in this case, the blood flow in different cerebral areas) (Phelps 1999, 312).

Here we use the expression *physiological techniques* as an umbrella term including a wide range of measures—for example, electrical responses, cardiovascular responses, glandular responses, and so forth.[4] The dissociation method seems to apply very well to these techniques. For example, in the studies using the event-related potentials (ERPs)[5] the experimenters manipulate two stimuli as independent variables and observe the dissociation in the dependent variable (in this case, the possible differences in the electric potential evoked by the two different stimuli).

The principle of localization of (mental) functions does not seem to apply as well. In fact, at present, no physiological measure seems to be able to provide a clear indication of the brain areas specific for certain mental functions. Rather, they can inform about how and which physiological activities are related to certain mental functions (Phelps 1999, 308). The point here is how to interpret the principle. If we interpret it in a narrow sense, according to which localization of (mental) functions means only the individuation of specific cerebral areas where specific mental processes take place, the principle cannot be applied to the physiological measures. However, if we interpret it in a broad sense, according to which localization of (mental) functions means also the individuation of certain nervous system's activities related to certain mental functions, the principle can count also for the physiological measures.

I think that this second interpretation is the most widespread among today's cognitive neuroscientists. In fact, they tend to argue that physiological techniques can provide a tool for analyzing the neuronal components underlying cognition and thus they apply them widely in their studies (Mehler et al. 1984, 83–85; Uttal 1998, 5; Phelps 1999, 303–8). In other words, although these measures do not permit us to explore the connections between nervous system and the mental as directly as lesion studies and neuroimaging techniques do, they nonetheless permit us to make such an exploration at least at a certain degree of detail.

In conclusion, it seems that the principle of localization of (mental) functions interpreted broadly is what characterizes the cognitive neuroscientific research. In fact, such a principle is what distinguishes CP from CN, because the former does not recognize the individuation of the neural basis of cognition among its tasks as the latter does. At this point, the question is on which theoretical assumptions the principle is founded and which idea of mind is implied in it.

IS THE MENTAL IDENTICAL WITH THE CEREBRAL?

In chapter 3 I pointed out that the definition of the CP's vocabulary is possible only through a work of abstraction and theorization from the observable behavior. This seems to suggest that a detailed understanding of the *gory details of the nervous system* cannot provide any useful information about the mental to experimental psychologists (Bickle et al. 2006). In this and the previous chapter we have seen that cognitivists constantly stress this concept.[6] However, it is a fact that, at least in the past two decades, cognitivists have started to focus very much on such details in their experimental studies and stress the inevitability of putting together neuroscience and CP in their theorizing.[7] So, the question here is what reasons induce them to do this.

I think the answer relies mainly on the dissatisfaction with the abstract and theoretical nature of psychological constructs. That is, psychologists often consider this abstractness as an Achilles' heel of their discipline and what prevents them from giving an adequate definition to their object of inquiry. In this sense, neuroscience seems to offer a way to give a strong and physical (perhaps concrete?) foundation to psychology. As the psychologist Solso has clearly pointed out, neuroscience can respond to

> [t]he need to find physical evidence for theoretical structures of the mind. The search for the properties of the human mind . . . has been constantly frustrated because of the tenuous nature of the supporting evidence. The development of sophisticated equipment has made it possible to materially prove the existence of certain hypothetical structures and thus validate some theories of language, perception, form identification, motor function, and memory. (1991, 37–38)

In other words, through neuroscience, constructs such as memory, problem solving, and cognition can lose their abstract character, becoming physical and thus open to some form of observation (or, at least, detection). It is important to note that this does not mean an elimination of the mentalistic vocabulary of CP, because its terms are assumed to play an essential role in CN (Ward 2006, 14). Rather, the point here concerns the definition of the nature (or of the *ontological status*) of the entities to which the psychological terms refer. According to this view, the mental properties are conceived as physical properties, more precisely as cerebral or physiological properties observable or detectable through instruments (J. Kim 1998, 53–54). Philosophers call such an assumption *identity theory* (IT), which holds that states and operations of the mind are identical to states and operations of the brain (Place 1956, 45; Smart 1959, 144–45; Smart 2007).

But what does it mean to be identical in such a case? Consider the following example (Putnam 1960, 29): Why is light assumed to be identical to electromagnetic radiation (of certain wavelengths)? In the history of physics, before this identification was recognized, two distinct theories were at stake: the optical theory and the electromagnetic one. Very briefly, physicists decided to define light as electromagnetic radiation when:

- It was possible to derive the laws of optics from the *basic* laws of physics.
- It was possible to derive new predictions in optics (considered now as the reduced discipline).

Thus, like light and electric radiation, mind and brain (or nervous systems in general) refer to the same phenomenon (J. Kim 1998, 199). This is because it is plausible that what happened to optical theory in the past will happen to psychology in the near future. That is, in the near or distant future, cognitive neuroscientists will discover how to derive the laws of psychology from the more basic laws of neurobiology and will make new predictions in the reduced discipline (psychology, of course). More simplistically, the advancements in the empirical and theoretical research in neurobiology and psychology will show us that specific mental states will be identical to specific neural or physiological processes (Smart 1959, 142).

As we can see, in this case *being identical with* means simply *being reducible to.* Thus, IT is a reductionistic claim[8] that can be interpreted ontologically (in virtue of the identity claim, the *abstract mental properties* are reduced *to physical cerebral or physiological ones*) and/or explanatorily (in virtue of identity, the psychological level of explanation is reduced to a neuroscientific one). An example of a reductionistic proposition in both senses is the following: Face recognition is the same as the responses in the nervous system and can be explained in terms of neuronal or physiological responses (Uttal 1998, 12). However, it is quite easy to conceive either an ontological reduction without an explanatory one or an explanatory reduction without an ontological one (Crane 2001, 55).

For instance, if we consider the previous example, we have an ontological reduction without an explanatory one if we accept that face recognition is the same as a certain number of cerebral or physiological entities but we refuse to explain it through neurological or physiological theories. On the contrary, we have an explanatory reduction without an ontological reduction if we accept that face recognition can be explained through neurological or physiological theories but not that it is the same as a certain number of cerebral or physiological entities.

It is important to note two further important features of the IT: First, it does not assume that the mental is caused by the cerebral or the physiological but that the mental is just the cerebral or the physiological (Smart 1959, 147). Second, it does not say that nonphysical entities are really physical, because this view does not conceive that there are not nonphysical things (Guttenplan 1994, 91). Thus, according to this view, the mental processes cognitive psychologists postulate in their theories cannot be considered as abstractions in any way: they are just physical (brain or nervous system) properties. It is clear why IT easily avoids the *epiphenomenalistic risk* implicit in the functionalistic position described in chapter 3. In fact, the mind does not need any physical realization to exercise its causal power in the physical world because *it is the realizer itself.*

In philosophical literature IT can be found formulated either in terms of *types* or in terms of *token*. The *type/token distinction* can be understood as a distinction between instances and sorts of things (Guttenplan 1994, 597). Tokens of things are individual things— for example, each single copy of a book that possesses a specific location in space and time— whereas types of things are classes of all tokens that are similar in some respect (Rey 1997, 548). By paraphrasing a brilliant example of the philosopher Rey, we have only one type of Charles Bukowski's masterpiece *Post Office* (because every copy of this book consists of the same words in the same order) but many tokens of it (because there are many different copies of it in many different formats).

Applied to a mental state like a certain belief, we can think of it as a type when we say that we have always (or many times) had a certain belief about something; or as a token when we speak of a certain belief we are currently having. In this sense, according to the type IT, every instance of a certain mental state must always (or many times) be considered as an instance of the same physical state. Instead, according to the token IT, an individual instance of a particular mental state occurring in a particular subject at a particular time is identical to a particular physical state of that subject at that time. It is clear that the token version of IT is much weaker than the type version and is not able to give a real account of the relation between mind and body. In fact, by adapting an example of the philosopher Crane (1994, 483), it is as if we would explain why all Italian prime ministers have been white males by simply asserting that each particular Italian prime minister is identical with some particular white male.

Because of this weakness, token IT is commonly said to be in principle compatible with functionalism (see Lycan 1994, 318; Smart 2007). In this chapter I will focus only on a specific version of the type IT.[9] The reason for this choice is twofold: On the one hand, because we can see a current revival of this position;[10] and on the other hand, because I think that the aim of CN is to identify the types of mental states or processes in the nervous system, not their simple tokens.

In general, it must be said that the early versions of the modern type IT[11] are widely rejected today because of their empirical and logical implausibility. In specific, they aimed to provide a plausible account for identifying conscious phenomena (such as sensations) with cerebral or neurophysiological processes, but they seem to have failed because of certain difficulties. In fact, as the philosopher Rosenthal (1994, 354) has pointed out, in order for a mental state to be classified as conscious, someone or something must be in that state. So, to understand such a state, we must adopt the point of view of the creature that is in this state.

Now, an account of something can be objective only if it does not depend on any particular point of view (in other words, only if it is considered in a third-person perspective). But consciousness is inextricably related to a specific point of view (in other words, consciousness can be considered only in a first-person perspective), so no objective or third-person account of it seems to be possible. Thus, it follows that a certain conscious (subjective/in a first-person) state cannot be identical with a certain cerebral (objective/in a third-person) state in any way. However, as discussed in chapter 3, the subjectivity does not concern the unconscious mental states or operations cognitive psychologists postulate in their theories. Thus, in principle, these unconscious processes appear to be better candidates than the conscious states for the (ontological and/or explanatory) reduction to the cerebral and physiological functions.

This point seems to be quite widespread in psychological and neuroscientific literature. For example, the psychologist Gray explicitly argues that describing the brain processes is the same as describing the unconscious mechanisms responsible for the construction of the representation of the external world (2004, 107).[12] The psychologist Johnson-Laird makes similar considerations when, discussing the mental imagery's debate in CP, he says that "all mental representations reduce to nerve impulses in the brain cells, just as the execution of any computer program reduces to the shifting of electrical bits from one memory register to another" (2006, 31). What Gray and Johnson-Laird seem to assume here (more implicitly than explicitly) looks like an IT[13] that maintains an ontological reduction (they argue that the mental is the same as the cerebral or the physiological) but rebuts an explanatory reduction (they maintain that the psychological theories cannot be reduced to the neuroscientific ones).

In agreement with Gray and Johnson-Laird and in contrast with the early versions of the modern IT, the philosopher Bechtel has developed a version of type IT called *Heuristic Identity Theory* (HIT) that focuses on the unconscious mental operations or processes and not on conscious mental states or sensations: This allows him to avoid those tricky issues about subjectivity and introspection that have put the previous ITs in trouble. Bechtel's proposal starts by pointing out that the multiple realizability thesis at the basis of the functionalistic doctrine is what makes considering the information about the brain or the nervous system of little or no relevance for understanding the cognitive processes (Bechtel and Mundale 1999, 176). In fact, to assume that the same abstract mental process or state can be realized by many different physical supports implies not accepting in principle that the nervous system put some constraints on the cognitive system and thus precludes any possibility of localizing the mental functions somewhere in the brain.

Against the multiple realizability theses, Bechtel argues that cognitive neuroscientists implicitly reject it in their experimental practice (184). This is because the core of such a practice is the identification of neurobiological or neurophysiological types with psychological types. That is, in their experiments researchers attempt to make a *one-to-one mapping* between psychological states (identified by CP) and brain states (identified by neuroscience) (Bechtel and Mundale 1999, 202–3; Bechtel and McCauley 1999, 68–69). It is clear that with the expression one-to-one mapping Bechtel refers to the principle of localization of (mental) functions previously described and rightly shows how it is strictly connected to type IT: "Underlying attempts to localize cognitive operations in brain structures is the assumption that there is an identity relation between particular mechanisms and neural mechanisms. Asserting that it is the same thing that is described in mental and neural or physical terms is the characteristic claim of one of the traditional stances, the Mind-Brain Identity Theory" (Bechtel 2008, 69–70).

It is important to stress that Bechtel's argument in favor of his HIT is based on the fact that, historically, neuroscientists were (and currently are) involved in identifying nervous system areas and processes "across [a] broad range of species as belonging to the same type" (Bechtel and McCauley 1999, 68). In my opinion, the fact that all through its history, CN practice has (implicitly or explicitly) endorsed the identity claim is not per se a good reason for considering it plausible.[14] In fact, the principle of localization of (mental) functions is a methodological assumption of CN that can be empirically confirmed or disconfirmed. In such a view, it appears that Putnam's old argument against the empirical plausibility of the IT still works.

Very briefly, such an argument is based on the empirical likelihood that two creatures (belonging either to the same species or to different ones) that are not in the same identical cerebral or physiological state can nevertheless be in the identical psychological state (Block and Fodor 1972, 160; Bechtel 2010, 360). The strength of this argument relies on the fact that it is sufficient to show only one case in which two creatures (belonging either to the same species or to two different species) share the same mental state but not the same cerebral or physiological state to falsify the IT (Crane 2001, 55–56). Bechtel responds to this criticism by emphasizing the heuristic character of his version of the IT. His HIT maintains the distinction between the psychological and the neuroscientific level of explanation (he calls it *explanatory pluralism*) and the assumption of an ontological type-identity relation between mental and cerebral or physiological processes (McCauley and Bechtel 2001, 738).

But, differently from the early versions of the type IT assuming an ontological reduction without an explanatory reduction (Smart 1959, 144–45), Bechtel proposes to interpret it as a *heuristic of discovery* that allows developing and elaborating hypotheses and theories about the connections between the two levels of explanation (McCaueley and Bechtel 2001, 737). In this view, the localization of (mental) functions appears to be something more than a methodological principle whose plausibility can be empirically disconfirmed by a single falsification (as suggested by Putnam's argument): It is rather a methodological leading principle at the core of CN whose function is to drive cognitive neuroscientists in making hypotheses about the identification of information-processing activities with cerebral or physiological processes (745) and whose validity is not empirically challenged directly in the experimental practice.

According to the HIT, only the single *identification hypotheses* proposed by researchers must be rejected or accepted on the basis of the empirical evidence, not the *heuristic identity principle per se* (751). For Bechtel, the appeal to his HIT is justified by the results gained by the CN in the last years. In Bechtel and Mundale (1999, 190–201) and in McCauley and Bechtel (2001, 745–52), we can find a wide and exhaustive review of visual perception experiments that aim to show how the information about the nervous system has been successful as a guide for functionally decomposing the cognitive system and how such a strategy has provided an improvement at both the functional (psychological) and neuroscientific level of explanation.

As I pointed out above, the HIT is based on an analysis of the experimental practice.[15] I think Bechtel is right when he argues that, if cognitive neuroscientists assume the principle of localization of (mental) functions as correct, they must dismiss functionalism and accept (a version of) the IT. In fact, if we follow the multiple realizability thesis, the taxonomies of brain states and psychological states should be considered independent of each other; thus, brain decomposition should be a poor guide for psychological decomposition (Bechtel and Mundale 1999, 190–91).

However, it must be pointed out that the visual perception experiments Bechtel reported appear to be too controversial to be defined as successful and thus to justify the appeal to HIT. For example, in Bechtel and Mundale (1999, 748–51), McCauley and Bechtel (2001, 195–99), and Bechtel (2008, 89–128), we find reported the debate about the so-called Two Visual System Hypothesis (TVSH). Very briefly, such a hypothesis says that, in the brain, two distinct pathways or streams responsible for different functions of the visual processing can be individuated: the ventral stream of projections that reaches the infero-temporal cortex and the dorsal stream of projections that reaches the posterior-parietal cortex (Goodale and Milner 1992, 396). Although the researchers tend to agree about the anatomical distinction between these two streams, they disagree a great deal about the functional characterization of them. That is, in experimental literature, we can find plenty of proposals for identifying these two pathways functionally, often clearly irreconcilable among them (Previc 1996, 543–45).[16] This means that it is very difficult to make a one-to-one mapping between a certain mental function and one of these two anatomically well-defined pathways.

Bechtel recognizes this problem and thus implicitly admits that the anatomical distinction (the neurological datum) does not seem to help in giving information about the mental functions. Nonetheless, he uses the TVSH debate as an example of fruitful interaction between neuroscience and psychology (McCauley and Bechtel 2001, 748). This seems to reveal an ambiguity in Bechtel's proposal: On the one hand, he argues that only the successful experimental results of CN can justify the plausibility of the HIT. But, on the other hand, he seems to argue that it is sufficient to show the *heuristic fruitfulness* of his proposal to justify it (as the example of the TVSH debate seems to suggest).

In my opinion, to assess the plausibility of the HIT in CN it is not sufficient to emphasize the role it plays as a heuristic of discovery and the fact that it is accepted implicitly by most researchers. Rather, its plausibility should be assessed mainly on the empirical ground: On the basis of the supporting evidence that the neurological or physiological data give for confirming or disconfirming the hypothetical identities' the researchers propose. This means that the data coming from the observation (or detection) of different cerebral or physiological activities must make it possible to distinguish between different mental processes as well as the behavioral data in CP's experiments do.

THE PRINCIPLE OF LOCALIZATION OF (MENTAL) FUNCTIONS UNDER SCRUTINY

It is a fact that many experimental psychologists have welcomed the introduction of neuroimaging techniques in their studies enthusiastically. As clearly emphasized by the psychologist Smith, "It is not just a matter of cognitive neuroscience providing constraints, or more data, about cognition. Neuroimaging techniques may eventually provide more informative and more directly interpretable information than that obtained in strictly cognitive experiments. Furthermore, as we learn more about the functions of different anatomical regions, the power of neuroimaging data will increase greatly" (1997, 72). In this quotation we find the two main themes of the present discussion about the relationship between neuroscience and psychology:

1. The question of the reliability of the cerebral or physiological data in comparison to the behavioral ones.
2. The problem of the validity of the principle of localization of (mental) functions in the nervous system.

In 2006 these issues were discussed in a series of contributions from different authors in volume 42, issue 3, of the journal *Cortex*. This *Cortex* debate is about an article titled "What Can Functional Neuroimaging Tell to the Experimental Psychologist?" written by the psychologist Henson and published in *The Quarterly Journal of Experimental Psychology* in 2005.

Henson's main argument can be briefly summarized in this way: The data from neuroimaging and physiological techniques must be considered as another dependent variable, along with behavioral data, that can be used to test competing theories at the psychological level of explanation (Henson 2005, 193–94).[17] More precisely, Henson argues that the behavioral data should not be considered as having a privileged status in experimental psychology. This is because neuroimaging data can constrain psychological theories in ways that cannot be addressed by behavioral data (195). That is, information about the activity in the nervous system's anatomical structures of the nervous system can provide more direct access to the mental activity and so can allow us to learn more about cognition than behavioral outputs can (Coltheart 2006, 323). In fact, from such information, it is possible to make two different types of inference (Henson 2005, 197–99). Before presenting them, it is important to stress that Henson conceives both these inferences as based upon the hypothetico-deductive reasoning that most experimental psychologists employ.

By following this reasoning, psychologists have two theories, T_0 and T_1, in competition. According to T_1, the experimental conditions C_1 and C_2 will differ only in the engagement of the hypothetical function F. Instead, according to T_0, the two conditions C_1 and C_2 will not differ. If function F will affect the dependent variable Y, then a significant difference in Y under conditions C_1 and C_2 will favor T_1 over T_0 and, in turn, will support the existence of F. Given this premise, let us show the two inferences from the nervous system's activity Henson proposes:

(a) Function-to-structure deduction. If the experimental conditions C_1 and C_2 will produce different patterns of activity in the brain, then the conditions C_1 and C_2 will differ in at least one (mental) function, F.
(b) Structure-to-function induction. If the experimental condition C_2 (referring to the psychological theory T_2) will elicit activity in the brain area R_1 relative to a certain baseline condition C_0 and area R_1 has been previously associated with a certain (mental) function F in a different context (for example, in a previous experiment involving the experimental condition C_1 referring to the psychological theory T_1), then the function F will be also implicated in condition C_2.

It is worth noting that (a) (sometimes called *forward inference*) and (b) (sometimes called *reverse inference*) serve different kinds of jobs in CN (Marshall 2009, 116), and they have different requirements for being used. (a) is a kind of inference from a single experiment having two (or more) conditions that does not require a strong localizationistic assumption (in fact, it does not matter here *where exactly* in the nervous system the differences in activity arise, but only that these differences are observed or detected). Instead, (b) is a kind of inference from two (or more) conditions pertaining to two (or more) experiments that do require a strong localizationistic assumption (in fact, it does matter here *where exactly* in the nervous system the same activity arises) (Henson 2005, 197–98). It is quite easy to see how both of these kinds of inference follow the logic underlying the dissociation method described above. In fact, for both (a) and (b), there are some psychological theories, T_1 and T_2 (both giving account for F) and T_0 (giving account for non-F); and there are neuroimaging data, N, assumed to be decisive for distinguishing among these theories (Coltheart 2006, 324–25). Thus, by following (a), a dissociation detected in N should allow us to choose between T_1 and T_0, whereas, by following (b), a dissociation should allow us to infer that T_1 and T_2 have nothing in common (on the contrary, if the same N would be observed or detected in both of the experiments referring, respectively, to T_1 and T_2, it should allow us to find connections between the two theories).

I previously pointed out that the dissociation method can apply to many different types of dependent variable. That is, many sorts of data (behavioral, neuroimaging, physiological, etc.) are used in experimental psychology to find dissociations among cognitive functions and, consequently, to distinguish among competing psychological theories explaining these functions. CP uses behavioral data for doing such a job. For example, consider two theories about the contribution of semantics to the ability to read aloud (Coltheart 2006, 324):

1. T_1: irregular words require the assistance of access to semantics to be read aloud correctly.
2. T_2: irregular words do not require such assistance to be read aloud correctly.

For determining whether T_1 or T_2 is accurate, the behavior of the patients with impairments in the semantic system (or to the access to it from print) seems to be decisive. In fact, T_1 predicts that most of these patients will not be able to read aloud irregular printed words, whereas T_2 predicts that most of them will not be able to do this. In this case, the behavior appears to be a reliable empirical ground for testing the two psychological theories.

Although cognitive neuroscientists recognize the importance of the behavioral data in research and argue that they should be used together with the cerebral or physiological ones (see Phelps 1999, 316–19; Henson 2005, 212–15), they assume that the dissociation method is more applicable to the latter than to the former. Henson explicitly states the reason for it: "different parts of the normal, healthy brain sub-serve different functions. I expect that few people would dispute this statement—for example, that different parts of the brain are involved in the initial processing of visual auditory input (in the occipital and superior temporal lobes, respectively). Within the occipital lobes, there is also good evidence that different parts are specialized for processing color (V4) and motion (V5)" (2006, 215). Henson calls this statement *the systematic function-structure mapping assumption*. According to this assumption, mental functions and nervous system activities systematically map between them, which allows cognitive neuroscientists to use the dissociation method at its best.

It is clear that Henson's statement is localizationistic in principle[18] and reflects the acceptance of HIT or, at least, another version of type IT.[19] That is, because the localization of (mental) functions in the nervous system is the leading principle at the basis of the dissociation method as used in CN, Henson's position can be considered compatible with Bechtel's.[20] Thus, Henson's examples reported at pages 199–207 aimed at showing how neuroimaging data permit us to choose between two psychological theories can be considered as empirical evidence in support of the veridicality of HIT. However, at pages 325–29 of his editorial article opening the *Cortex* debate previously mentioned, the psychologist Coltheart makes a detailed examination of Henson's examples and concludes that they are more controversial than they first appear.

For example, he notes that Henson reports both cases of competing CP theories receiving equal support (or, better, equal lack of support) from the neuroscientific studies (as in the example 2 about the subsequent-memory paradigm considered at page 326) and cases in which clear evidence is not offered of different activations for different cognitive tasks (as in the example 1 about the remember/know paradigm considered at pages 325–26).Coltheart's analysis suggests that the support adduced by cerebral or physiological data is much more controversial than that adduced by behavioral data, and thus the empirical evidence in favor of the one-to-one mapping between cognitive mental functions and cerebral functions is not so strong (330).

These difficulties with the cerebral and physiological data have brought some authors to question the validity of the principle of localization of (mental) functions in the nervous system. Inside the *Cortex* debate, the psychologist Page attacks Henson's position by arguing that, if we accept a localizationistic position, it is a logical necessity that any two stimuli giving rise to two different patterns of behavior (or perception) must also give rise to two different patterns of cerebral or physiological activity (2006, 430). Thus, it follows that the observation or detection of two different kinds of activity in the nervous system necessarily implies the observation or detection of two different kinds of mental function. But how to consider the cases in which two stimuli give rise to two different patterns of cerebral activity that are not accompanied by any change in behavior (or perception) (431)? This is a tricky question. In fact, in such a case, to accept the observation or detection of two different mental functions through cerebral data, we must accept both that the principle of localization of (mental) functions is undoubtedly correct and that the behavioral data have no particular value. But, because the validity of such a principle is controversial, dismissing the behavioral data in favor of the cerebral data seems to be too risky for experimental psychologists.

Outside the *Cortex* debate, some authors have pointed out that assuming a priori the validity of the localization of (mental) functions in the nervous system can lead to mistaken inferences about psychological theories. That is, assuming that there are isolatable and distinct areas mapping into mental processes leads inexorably to conclude that these processes are localized in those regions in which differential activity is observed or detected (Gray Hardcastle and Stewart 2005, 35–37). Thus, every observation or detection of differential activity in cerebral regions must be interpreted as an index of localization of a certain mental function, even in those cases in which this is clearly implausible (for example, when the activity observed or detected represents only a small part of a bigger activity involving many other areas) (Uttal 1998, 74–75).

That is, the principle of localization of (mental) functions does not seem to admit that a certain mental function can be supported by many different parts of the nervous system. Rather, it says that the nervous system (and thus the mental, on the basis of the IT) is partitioned in *causal micro-components* or *single causes* whose effects are single behaviors (van Orden et al. 2001, 113). So conceived, the principle sounds like an axiomatic belief empirically implausible (136).

As we can see, it seems that to accept the cerebral or physiological data as informative for the psychological theories we must accept that the nervous system puts some constraints on cognition. But, as the identity-theorists clearly point out, such constraints must be really strong to be useful in some fashion; otherwise the connections between the mind's functions and the nervous system's structures risk appearing too loose to be reliable. For this reason, cognitive neuroscientists must embrace the principle of localization of (mental) functions in their research. However, doubts about the validity of such a principle are many because the nervous system appears to resist being partitioned into little components. Thus, because localizing cognitive functions in the brain or in the nervous system seems to be the main work of CN, the situation seems to be quite critical for such a discipline.

CONCLUDING REMARKS

At the beginning of this chapter I defined the CN as a bridging discipline that attempts to unify the results of CP with those of neuroscience. In other words, by assuming the strict relation between the mind and the nervous system, CN aims to find connections and possible reductions between two distinct disciplines that appear to be methodologically and theoretically autonomous. In principle, looking for connections and possible reductions among theories pertaining to different domains of inquiry cannot be seen as something bad.

As the philosopher Crane clearly emphasized about the search for explanatory reductions in the history of science, "genuine explanations are advances in our knowledge, and faced with a possibility of advancing our knowledge it would be irrational to rejects it merely on the grounds that it is reductive. (Or, rather, it makes little to do so, since reduction is just a name for this sort of advancement of our knowledge)" (2001, 55). That is, paraphrasing Humphrey Bogart in the 1952 Richard Brooks masterpiece *Deadline U.S.A.*, "that's the science, baby, and the science. And there's nothing you can do about it. Nothing."

But, in the case of psychology and neuroscience, are there good theoretical and empirical reasons for reducing (or, at least, connecting) the former to the latter? On the basis of the previous examination, I say that there are not. Although cognitive neuroscientists have found, and find, many correlations between psychological and cerebral or physiological data in their studies, it is a fact that a *correlation* is not the same as an *identity-relation* (Smart 1959, 142). More precisely, the former indicates only that there could be a correspondence between a certain cerebral or physiological activity and a certain mental operation (measured through a cognitive task). The latter indicates that a certain cerebral or physiological activity is both necessary and sufficient for a certain mental operation (measured through a cognitive task) (Putnam 1960, 29; Uttal 1998, 71). It is clear that the identity-relation needs more demanding requirements than correlation; and, in the analysis presented throughout this chapter, I believe I have pointed out that they are neither well-justified nor theoretically well-founded. In fact, no experiment in CN has yet provided uncontroversial evidence for this type of relation, and no theoretical examination has provided good reasons for accepting the principle of localization of (mental) functions as reliable. Thus, I think no good reasons exist for considering the cerebral and physiological data as informative as the behavioral ones in experimental psychology.

NOTES

1. On this point, see Shallice 1988.

2. Such as the functional magnetic resonance imaging (fMRI) and the positron-emission tomography (PET).

3. Let's consider two tasks, one where experimental subjects are presented a word and are asked to repeat it (for example, chair-chair) (*repetition task*) and one where subjects are presented a word and are asked to generate another word representing n use of the presented word (for example, chair-sit) (*generation task*) (Petersen et al. 1988, 586–87). It is clear that repeating a word requires seeing, reading, and speaking a word. Generating a word requires all of these components and additional ones, such as forming semantic associations (Phelps 1999, 311). Thus, performing the generation task requires the same cognitive operations for performing the repetition task and more.

4. In the next chapter, I will provide a detailed description of some of these techniques.

5. The ERP techniques measure the electrical activity recorded from neural tissue evoked by controlled stimuli (Reber and Reber 2001, 253).

6. For a further example in this direction, see the classical Newell et al. 1958, 151.

7. For example, let's consider the following quotation from one of the most important contemporary cognitive psychologists (Mandler 2007, 221): "In the long run, it seems inevitable that at the core of cognitive science establishment will be psychology (to tell us how the mind works) and neuroscience (to tell us how the brain does it)." Unfortunately, probably because of the historical character of his book, Mandler assumes it as a *matter of fact* and thus does not explain the reasons why these two disciplines should be put together (unless by a priori assuming that the mind must be conceived as what the brain does [3 and 189], of course).

8. It is important to stress that, by virtue of the identity relation, the notion of reduction here assumed does not imply per se the elimination of all of the psychological variables and terms and does not indicate the necessity to see physiology or neurology as the complete and exhaustive basis of human behavior (Mandler 2007, 207; Crane 2001, 53). As the philosopher Lewis pointed out (1966, 101), IT says that a mental-state ascription has the same reference as a certain neural-state ascription but does not say that these ascriptions have the same sense. This is because the former is whatever state occupies a specific causal role, whereas the latter is the attribute of *being-in* that occupies this causal role.

9. More exactly, upon the heuristic version the philosopher Bechtel proposed.

10. See, for example, Polger 2004; Gozzano 2007.

11. I here refer to the proposals the psychologist Place made in a 1956 paper and the philosopher Smart in a 1959 paper (both of which, in turn, were strongly influenced by the logical empiricist positions of the philosopher Feigl). These proposals are very similar to each other except for subtle differences that I do not consider necessary to discuss here. They probably are the most quoted and discussed versions of the IT in philosophical literature.

12. It is important to note that Gray appears to be quite skeptical about the validity of IT applied to the conscious mental states. This is because he argues that IT makes it very difficult to respond to certain important questions "about the necessary features of the processes to which consciousness is linked, and about the Darwinian survival value of consciousness" (1971, 254).

13. Because neither of these two authors explicitly argues for any version of the IT, it is not clear if they conceive it in terms of types or tokens.

14. After all, we can find many examples of patently wrong claims assumed as fundamental or respectable truths in the history of science (see phlogiston theory or the Ptolemaic model of the heavens).

15. According to the historical reconstruction Bechtel (2010) proposed, although some of the supporters of the early versions of the modern IT "sought to incorporate what was known about the brain in developing their accounts, they were limited by the paucity of tools for linking human mental activities to the brain. (This was a major reason the neurosciences ended up playing such a minor role in the first decades of cognitive science)" (359). In fact, if we take a look at Place's 1956 paper and Smart's 1959 paper, we can see how their proposals are logical and theoretical and do not refer to any empirical study in neuroscience (which is quite surprising for Place, because he argues explicitly that his proposal must be considered as a scientific hypothesis that "cannot be dismissed on logical grounds" [1956, 44]). In contrast, today supporters of this theory (and thus of the HIT) have attended to a great increase in the neuroscientific methodologies and discoveries in the past two decades and have seen how "like identity theorists, those who embrace the techniques of cognitive neuroscience identify cognitive mechanisms with brain mechanisms . . ." (360).

16. Another problem of the studies about the TVSH is that of the population validity mentioned above. In fact, most of the empirical evidence adduced in its support comes from the analysis of a single patient, Dee Flechter (D. F.). For an exhaustive examination of this interesting case, see Goodale and Milner 2004.

17. A rough sketch of the same argument can be found in the last chapter of the historical book by the cognitive psychologist Mandler (2007, 238, my italics): "Today psychology and neuroscience interface is a two-way street with psychological phenomena motivating the search for their physiological basis and *the latter leading to a confirmation of the psychological concepts.*"

18. It can be interpreted in a weak form (if we follow the logic underlying the function-to-structure deduction) or in a strong form (if we follow the logic underlying the structure-to-function induction) (Henson 2006, 220).

19. In the last quotation taken from Henson, the examples used in favor of his principle refer to visual perception research, as well as those made by Bechtel in Bechtel and Mundale 1999, 190–201, and in McCauley and Bechtel 2001, 745–52, in favor of the HIT discussed above.

20. However, it is important to stress that these two positions are independent of each other. In fact, Henson's position is an empirical assumption about the use of neurophysiological data in research, whereas Bechtel's position is a philosophical and methodological position about the mind-brain relation.

Chapter Five

A Reevaluation of Damasio's Somatic Marker Hypothesis

In the previous chapters I proposed a description and a discussion of four different approaches to experimental psychology. More precisely, I dealt with:

- Two variants of introspective psychology (Wundtian and Jamesian) in chapter 1.
- Two variants of behavioristic psychology (Watsonian and Tolmanian) in chapter 2.
- Cognitive psychology (CP) in chapter 3.
- Cognitive neuroscience (CN) in chapter 4.

Although I am sure to have omitted many issues and authors pertaining to these approaches, I think I have been able to point out the commonalities and differences among them. In particular, I believe I have succeeded in specifying how certain metaphysical and epistemological assumptions can influence the preference for certain methods and kinds of data over others in experimental practice. However, it is a fact that, even in a single experiment, researchers tend to adopt many different methods and thus to deal with various kinds of data.

Personally, I am in favor of adopting multiple ways and tools of analysis and of comparing among them. Experimental psychology, like other scientific disciplines, should try to integrate the results coming from various research methods and cannot be based on a single one. But I think also that many researchers do not pay much attention to which approach a technique or datum pertains. In this sense, they do not appear always to be fully aware of what the choice of a certain method can imply for their inquiry.[1]

This can lead to misconceptions and difficulties at both the empirical and theoretical level, especially when a comparison among many results is required. A possible risk in such a situation could be the dismissal of important sources of information only because they are incompatible with others that are assumed to be more decisive. For example, let's briefly reconsider the case for CP discussed in chapter 3. Although in their experimental practice cognitivists make great use of verbal reports, they tend to underestimate their utility because of the postulation that the mental is introspectively inaccessible. In this situation, it is clear that the behavioral data can be a priori considered to be more relevant than the introspective and verbal ones and thus preferable as empirical evidence for testing a certain theory. The same can be said of the CN approach discussed in chapter 4, where the behavioral and neural data appear to be a priori considered much more reliable and decisive than the verbal and introspective ones.

Similar examples are quite common in psychological research. In this and the two following chapters, I'll provide a sort of *case study* of one of them, the *Somatic Marker Hypothesis (SMH)*. I will proceed in two ways: On the one hand, I will assess the theory from a logical point of view, that is, in the light of the theoretical and philosophical discussion proposed in the first four chapters. On the other, I will evaluate its empirical content by proposing a retesting of it. I have stated previously the need for such empirical retesting: I aim to show through an empirical example how certain (not always explicit) theoretical and philosophical claims can affect both the choice of methods and the interpretation of data.

In this chapter, I will present the SMH and I will critically discuss its theoretical and philosophical underpinnings, the way it has been empirically assessed, and I'll introduce my three replication studies.

DAMASIO'S WORK ON EMOTIONS AND DECISION MAKING

The SMH is a neuropsychological theory that aims to explain how emotions determine decision-making processes and choice behavior. According to it, an emotion has two main features:

(a) A certain number of *changes in the body* (Naqvi et al. 2006, 261). More precisely, it is assumed that emotions are represented in the brain as transient modifications in the activity pattern of the somato-sensory structures (Tranel and Damasio 2000, 125).
(b) A *mental image*, that is, a certain perception or thought (Bennett and Hacker 2003, 212).

(a) and (b) are postulated to be strictly connected (Damasio 1994, 145; Damasio 1999, 282). In this sense, an emotion is defined as a specific somatic modification (a) in response to a certain perceptual stimulus or abstract thought (b).

For example, an emotion does not arise only if we concretely see a grizzly bear during a walk in the woods, but also if we imagine we can meet one during a trip in the woods. Something similar happens when we are deliberating to make a decision: we have different options at our disposal that are represented in the form of mental images. These images trigger bodily changes having a positive or negative valence: those associated with *negative changes* are considered to be disadvantageous choices, whereas those associated with *positive changes* are valued as advantageous (Dunn et al. 2006, 241). As we can see, the bodily modifications operate as sorts of *biological alarms* alerting us that certain options considered are advantageous and other disadvantageous. In this sense, these modifications lead us to prefer some of them instead of others. In this way, emotions are said to constrain the process of deliberation and to allow us to choose the best options among those at our disposal, particularly in situations of choice under uncertainty (Damasio 1996, 1415; Tranel and Damasio 2001, 125). Because emotions are conceived as so entrenched in the body, they can be called *somatic markers (SM)* (Damasio 1999, 41).

The ventral-medial prefrontal cortex (VMPC) has a central role in the SMH. In fact, this cerebral area is assumed to provide the neural substrate for the learning associations between the events comprising a certain situation and the bodily signals elicited by them. These associations are defined as *dispositional*: They do not hold the exact representation of the facts and emotional states experienced by the person in a certain situation, but rather the potential to reactivate the same bodily modifications through evoking activity in the proper cortical and sub-cortical cerebral areas (Damasio 1996, 1414–15). In other words, a *dispositional representation* of a certain mental image does not contain an image as such. Rather, it contains "the firing patterns which trigger the momentary reconstruction of an approximate representation . . . of the mental image considered" (Damasio 1994, 102).

As we can see, the VMPC performs a learning and memory function (Tranel and Damasio 2000, 125). More precisely, this cerebral area is postulated to be the repository of knowledge acquired through the associations between events and bodily changes mentioned above, and also of the cognitive processes through which this knowledge is acquired (Damasio 1994, 218). It is important to stress that both the knowledge acquired and the learning and memory processes of its acquisition are postulated to work at an implicit and unconscious level, that is, they do not reach the threshold of consciousness in any way (Damasio 1994, 167; Damasio 1999, 55, table 2.1). Further, because these functions are localized in the VMPC, its lesion causes difficulties in learning from past experiences and thus insensitivity to the future consequences of an action (Bechara et al. 1994, 7). In other words, this lesion is considered to be responsible for the loss of the "ability to choose the most advantageous course of action . . . , despite otherwise intact mental capacities" (Damasio 1994, 56).

As I just said, an important feature of the SMH is that a person does not consciously feel when she deliberates on a decision to make. In fact, the emotional signals can be detected only through instruments measuring the physiological activity of the person, and thus they are assumed unconsciously to influence the decision-making reasoning and to drive behavior. In other words, the SMH says that, when a person has to make a decision, certain physiological processes activate before she is able to report the results of her conscious reasoning verbally and select certain options as possible choices and eliminate others (Bechara et al. 1997, 1293). In this sense, the cognitive processes (such as memory and learning) involved in the productions of the anticipatory SMs also are considered to work unconsciously (Damasio 1994, 214; Bechara et al. 2005, 160, box 1). For this reason, persons are said to choose advantageously before consciously knowing which are the best and the worst options at their disposal.

It is implicit in such a description that Damasio and colleagues conceive decision making as distinguishable in two evaluation processes: one unconscious and emotional, which precedes the other, which is conscious and rational (Bechara et al. 1997, 1293; Naqvi and Bechara 2004, 113). In this sense, the good functioning of the former is postulated to be mandatory for the good functioning of the latter. This means that the SM system prepares "the ground for conscious, cognitive processing. Without such a preparation, the realization of what is bad would either never arrive, or would arrive too late and be too little" (Damasio 1994, 222). For this reason, (unconscious) emotions must be considered as causally necessary for decision making (Dunn et al. 2006, 245).

Later in this chapter I will discuss in detail the philosophical and theoretical underpinnings of the SMH. For now, I want only to anticipate a central issue I think clearly emerges from what I have shown: The consciousness-unconsciousness dichotomy on which the SMH is based is nothing but the cognitivistic one discussed in chapter 3, with the difference that Damasio and coworkers conceive the mental to be identical to the neurobiological as showed in chapter 4.

THE IOWA GAMBLING TASK (IGT)

Almost all of the empirical evidence in favor of the SMH comes from a series of studies using a neuropsychological test invented by Damasio and coworkers. Such a test is known as the *Iowa Gambling Task (IGT)* and simulates real-life decision making in the way it factors uncertainty of premises and outcomes, as well as reward and punishment (Bechara et al. 1996, 215). It is worth noting that the IGT was developed primarily to assess the decision-making difficulties of *patients with an impairment in the VMPC (VMPS)*. Thus, Damasio and colleagues' data are mainly based on the comparison between clinical groups composed of VMPS and control groups of healthy participants.

The IGT involves four decks of cards (A, B, C, and D) equal in appearance and size (Bechara et al. 1996, 220). The goal is to maximize profit on a loan of play money ($2,000). Participants are asked to make a series of one hundred card selections, but they are not told ahead of time how many card selections they are allowed to make. The participants can select the cards one at a time from any deck, and they are free to switch from any deck to another as often as they wish. The choice to select from one deck or another is largely influenced by schedules of reward or punishment. These schedules are pre-programmed and known to the examiners but not to the participants. They are arranged in such a way that every time participants select a card from decks A and B they get $100 (or a few more) and every time they select a card from decks C and D they get $50 (or a few more) (reward).

However, in each of the four decks participants can sometimes encounter, along with the reward, an unpredictable money loss (punishment). The punishment is set to be higher in the high-paying decks A and B, lower in the low-paying decks C and D. In decks A and B, participants encounter a total loss of $1,250 every ten cards chosen and in decks C and D a total loss of $250 every ten cards chosen. In the long term, decks A and B are considered *disadvantageous and risky* because they result in an overall loss and decks C and D are considered *advantageous and safe* because they result in an overall gain.

However, it is worth noting that, although disadvantageous in terms of profits, decks A and B are different in terms of frequency distribution of reward/punishment cards. In fact, in deck A punishment is frequent but of small magnitude, whereas in deck B it is infrequent but of big magnitude. The same is for the advantageous decks C and D: In deck C punishment is frequent but of small magnitude, whereas in deck D it is infrequent but of big magnitude. Thus, in terms of frequency distribution of reward/punishment cards, deck A is the same as deck C and deck B is the same as deck D.

Three features are assessed during the performance of the task and then compared:

(a) The behavioral performance, that is, the number of cards selected from the advantageous decks (C and D) and from the disadvantageous decks (A and B) (Bechara et al. 1994, 10–13; Bechara et al. 1997).

(b) The anticipatory Skin Conductance Responses (SCRs)[2] generated four to five seconds prior to turning a card from any given deck, that is, during the time period participants ponder from which deck to choose a card (Bechara et al. 1996, 221; Bechara et al. 1997).
(c) The participants' verbal reports about what they have understood and understand of the task and the strategy they have used and use for solving it. This aspect is assessed by interrupting the game briefly after ten cards chosen and by asking them two questions: "(i) Tell me all you know about what is going on in this game. (ii) Tell me how you feel about this game" (Bechara et al. 1997, 1293).[3]

For each of the previous features the following predictions are made:

- For (a): Participants of the control group will choose many more cards from the advantageous decks (C and D) than from the disadvantageous ones (A and B) throughout the task. Conversely, participants from the clinical group will choose many more cards from the disadvantageous decks (A and B) than from the advantageous ones (C and D) throughout the task.
- For (b): Participants of the control group will show an increase in the magnitude of the SCRs occurring four to five seconds before selecting a disadvantageous deck (A or B) significantly higher than before selecting an advantageous deck (C or D). Conversely, participants from the clinical group will not show the increase of the SCRs occurring four to five seconds before selecting a disadvantageous deck (A and B) (Bechara et al. 2005, 160).
- For (c): Participants from both groups will be able to answer the questions about the IGT structure only after many selections of cards. That is, after having encountered a certain number of reward and reward/punishment cards, participants of the two groups will be able to express a certain level of knowledge of the IGT and thus of how to deal with it.

It is worth noting that for Damasio and coworkers, (b) is the crucial point of the IGT studies. In fact, the SMH says that the increase in the magnitude of the SCRs in front of the disadvantageous decks (A and B) (b) in the healthy participants will explain and predict both their preference for advantageous decks (C and D) (a) and their difficulty in answering the questions in the first phases of the task (c). In fact, the increase in the magnitude of the SCRs for the disadvantageous decks (A and B) will determine the normal participants' preference for the advantageous decks (C and D) many card selections before they will be able to answer the questions exhaustively.

It is also worth noting that such an increase indicates nothing but the activation of certain unconscious emotional responses (detected through the measurement of the SCRs) before certain stimuli. As I pointed out above, these responses cannot be felt consciously by participants and can be detected only through instruments. For this reason, healthy participants are said to be unaware of their choices. Thus, we can say that, according to the SMH, the emotional responses generated by normal participants are the SMs that allow *deciding advantageously before knowing the advantageous strategy* (that is, before being able to report verbally how the task works and thus to understand that decks C and D are more advantageous than decks A and B) (Bechara et al. 1997, 1293; Bechara et al. 2005, 159). Of course, this is not the case for the VMPS: Because of their cerebral lesion (and their consequent functional impairment), these patients cannot produce SCRs sufficiently high for *marking* decks A and B as risky; and, although they can have a good knowledge of the task at a certain point, they cannot avoid choosing the disadvantageous options.

From another point of view, neurons in the VMPC *individuate* the disadvantageous decks before participants become aware of how the task is structured and *mark* them as risky, causing an increase of the SCRs when participants are going to choose them. In this way, such bodily signals anticipate the intervention of the higher mental processes (for example, mathematical or inductive reasoning) and drive the participant to choose the advantageous decks. Instead, because of their impairment, patients cannot unconsciously evaluate decks A and B as risky and so they cannot avoid choosing them when they become aware of how the IGT is structured.

In conclusion, the IGT seems to be a good empirical test for assessing the processes at the basis of decision making. First, it allows us to assess how people learn the rules of a complex situation both in an implicit and an explicit way. In fact, at least in the first phases of the task, they appear to behave on the basis of an acquired implicit and unconscious knowledge; only after many trials do they come to an explicit and conscious knowledge of how the task works (Bechara et al. 1997, 1293; Bechara et al. 2005, 159; Dalgleish et al. 2006, 244). Second, the IGT permits us to assess not only whether people are able to make advantageous choices, but also whether they are able adequately to plan their choice behavior. Third, the IGT appears to be sufficiently structured and defined to allow both the observation of participants' behavior and the registration of various physiological measures, and the submission of self-report questionnaires or verbal questions.

SOME CONCEPTUAL ISSUES ABOUT DAMASIO'S THEORIZING

Before proposing the SMH, Damasio coauthored a methodological textbook titled *Lesion Analysis in Neuropsychology* (1989). In my opinion, this book is crucial for understanding the foundations of his research program and adherence to CN's assumptions discussed in chapter 4. In fact, three main assumptions are presented in this book:

1. The central role of neural data for understanding cognition. This follows from the fact that Damasio places much reliance on the lesion method as a way of testing the psychological theories. That is, "given a pre-existing theory about the operation of the normal brain and how it would mediate the performance of an experimental task, the lesion . . . can be seen as a probe to test the validity of the theories, that is, a means to decide if the account of brain organization and operation provided by a given model is or is not falsifiable" (7).
2. The postulation that CN is a bridging discipline between CP and neurobiology. That is, he argues that, for refining the lesion method, advances in both the conceptualization regarding the brain tissue and the neural functioning and the theoretical formulations about the cognitive processes are required (9–10).
3. The assumption that the anatomy and physiology of the nervous system strongly constrain the mental/cognitive architecture and thus that the partitioning into little components of the former implies the partitioning of the latter. Thus, in contrast with CP's assumptions but in accordance with CN's assumptions, Damasio postulates that the nervous system's organization is not conceivable as a mere hardware implementation apparatus for mental/cognitive processes. This is because its specification severely restricts the range of representations and algorithmic operations that it can implement. In this sense, it is not likely to implement representations or algorithms other than those the nervous system's anatomy embodies and is destined to operate (58).

It is clear that (3) is nothing but another formulation of the principle of localization of (mental) functions interpreted according to the type identity theory discussed in chapter 4. In this view, (3) is necessary for justifying both (2) (the assumption that the mental terms used in CP's theories refer to cerebral or physiological functions) and (1) (the detection of the cerebral or physiological activity as an important independent variable of the experimental design).

In his popular book *Descartes' Error* (1994), Damasio does not seem to have modified the point of view he articulated in 1989. Thus, we can say that the SMH exposed in it is based on (1), (2), and (3). This is clear in the following excerpt: "Because of the brain's design, the requisite broad-based knowledge (for decision-making) depends on numerous systems located in relatively separate brain regions rather than in one region. A large part of such knowledge is recalled in the form of images at many brain sites rather than a single site. . . . Probably the relative simultaneity of activity at different sites binds the separate parts of the mind together" (Damasio 1994, 84). In this sense, we can conclude that the SMH is a paradigmatic example of CN's antimentalistic approach as characterized in chapter 4.[4]

Adopting such an approach has different implications for both theory and methodology. At the theoretical level, it leads us to assume that each mental term directly refers to a certain (not necessarily specified) cerebral or neurophysiological feature and thus that all the psychological descriptions are at last neurological descriptions. In my opinion, such a commitment to the type identity theory discussed in chapter 4 is clearly evident in the following quotation[5] (Damasio 1999, 51): "Emotions are complicated collections of chemical and neural responses forming a pattern."

At the methodological level, it implies that the objective/third-person or intersubjective methods (behavioral and physiological) must be considered the most adequate for dealing with the mental. This is because in principle, in virtue of the postulated identity, for giving an exhaustive comprehension of how a certain mental state or process works should be enough to assess the (cor)relations between the neural or physiological variables (detectable through instruments) and the behavioral variables directly observable (H. Damasio and A. R. Damasio 1989, 7; Tranel and Damasio 1996, 119).

However, these methods are clearly not sufficient when a theory specifies that a certain nervous system's activity is identical with a conscious or an unconscious mental state. In such a situation, the appeal to the subjective/first-person methods seems to be unavoidable. In this sense, it is clear why the VMPS's behavior and verbal reports at the IGT represent the best (perhaps the only) empirical evidence for assessing the conscious-unconscious distinction hypothesized by the SMH. In fact, their inability to choose the *advantageous decks* and their ability to make exhaustive verbal reports about how the task works are explained very well by the postulation of two different neural and cognitive evaluational systems, one unconscious (via SMs) and the other conscious (via overt reasoning) (Damasio 1994, 40; Bechara et al. 1997, 1293; Bechara et al. 2005, 159).

In summary, we can see that, although supporters of CN's antimentalistic approach (such as Damasio and colleagues) consider the subjective/first-person (or introspective) verbal reports less reliable than the objective/third-person (or intersubjective) methods, their use is unavoidable for assessing the degree of consciousness and explicit knowledge of the task. As we will discuss in the following chapters, the very methodological problem of the SMH is whether the questions Damasio and coworkers asked the participants of their experiments are adequate and sufficiently sensible tools for this aim (for a spirited tit for tat on this issue, see Bechara et al. 2005 and Maia and McClelland 2005). In other words, the point is whether the methods for assessing consciousness that Damasio and coworkers used are reliable and respect certain criteria of validity (for example, the four individuated in Newell and Shanks 2014, 3–4, and discussed in chapter 3 of this book).

A further problematic point of Damasio and colleagues' theoretical framework is that, although he declares himself to be unsympathetic to the lack of concreteness (or *disembodiment*) of CP's constructs (Damasio 1994, 250), his conceptualization of the two evaluational systems appears to owe a strong debt to cognitivism. In fact, as in many cognitivistic models, the unconscious evaluational system is conceived as arranged for the procedural or implicit knowledge, or *know how* (in other words, the ability to act or to do something); whereas the conscious one is for the declarative or explicit knowledge, or *know that* (in other words, the ability to say or verbally describe something).[6]

The only (but crucial) difference between Damasio and colleagues' proposal and a cognitivistic one is that the first emphasizes that the unconscious system is localized in the VMPC and the conscious system in other parts of the brain. In chapter 3 we have seen that, although the distinction between *know how* and *know that* seems to be acceptable at a first look, it is quite problematic, because researchers do not share clear criteria to distinguish the former from the latter.[7]

This could present a difficulty for the SMH, especially in evaluating the empirical data coming from the healthy participants at the IGT. For example, which of the two systems should be considered the leading one if a participant would produce high SMs and make the correct choices and, at the same time, would be able to give an exact verbal description of how the IGT works (on this point see Dalgleish et al. 2006, 245–49)? I think this issue is strictly connected to another communality between Damasio and coworkers' SMH and the cognitivistic theorizing.

In chapter 3 I argued that one of the main tenets of CP is that the psychological determinants of behavior are unconscious and that people can access introspectively only a minimal part of their mind. I pointed out that an implication of this tenet is the denial (or, at least, the strong limitation) of the causal efficacy of the conscious and subjective/first-person processes and contents and thus, at the methodological level, of the reliability of verbal reports.[8]

Now, as I said above, the SMH (like many cognitivistic models) postulates that the *know how unconscious system* has primacy over the *know that conscious system* and that the functioning (or malfunctioning) of the former causally determines the functioning (or malfunctioning) of the latter. In my opinion, this can be seen as another formulation of the cognitivistic tenet mentioned above, with the difference that the unconscious determinants that Damasio and colleagues proposed are observable because they are concretely conceived and those proposed by CP unobservable because they are abstractly conceived. This means that the same considerations made for the cognitivistic models can apply to the SMH: The unconscious evaluation system is the fundamental determinant of the choice behavior, and the role of the conscious one must be conceived to be very limited. I think that this picture has some problematic issues that deserve to be analyzed. In the following pages I will focus on them by proposing an empirical replication, two variants of Damasio and colleagues' studies and a critical discussion of his theoretical and methodological assumptions.

DIFFERENCES BETWEEN DAMASIO'S AND MY STUDIES

My three studies replicate those proposed in Bechara et al. 1994, Bechara et al. 1996, and Bechara et al. 1997, except for some features I present here.

The Composition of the Experimental Groups

In Bechara et al. 1994 (10), Damasio and coworkers provide a comparison between a group of forty-four healthy participants (twenty-one women and twenty-three men) and a group of six VMPs (two women and four men). Further, they compare the performances of the VMPs with a group of nine patients (three women and six men) suffering from other kinds of brain damage. Such a comparison is conducted to assess whether the performance of the VMPs on the IGT is specific to VMPC damage and not merely caused by other sorts of brain impairment.

In Bechara et al. 1996 (216), they compare a group of twelve healthy participants (six women and six men) with a group of seven VMPs (three women and four men). In Bechara et al. 1997 (1293), they compare a group of ten healthy participants (the number of women and men is not reported) with a group of six VMPs (three women and three men). It is important to point out that the overall number of VMPs Damasio and coworkers tested in the three articles here considered is nine and not nineteen. This is because four VMPs of the 1994 research participated also in the 1996 one (Bechara et al. 1996, 216) and six VMPs of the 1994 and 1996 studies were tested also in the 1997 study (Bechara et al. 1997, 1294, note 3).

In my first study, I provide a within-subjects analysis of eleven healthy participants (seven men and four women). In my second study, I provide a within-subjects analysis of eleven healthy participants (six men and five women). In my third study, I provide a within-subjects analysis of eleven healthy participants (six men and five women).

The Behavioral Dependent Measures

In Damasio and colleagues' studies, only one behavioral measure is considered: the number of cards chosen from the four decks (A, B, C, and D) throughout the task.[9] In my studies, I also consider the number of cards chosen, but I add the reaction time (RT) as an additional behavioral measure. RT is generally defined as the time between the presentation of a stimulus and the subject's response to it (Uttal 1998, 174; Reber and Reber 2001, 601). It is important to note that, if for the number of cards chosen from each deck all one hundred selections are considered, for the RT only ninety selections are assessed. This is because the RTs correspondent to the first selection and to the stops made after ten cards for asking some questions (see above) could be measured.

The Physiological Dependent Measures

In Bechara et al. 1996 and Bechara et al. 1997, Damasio and coworkers consider the SCRs generated by a participant before the choice of a card from a deck. In my studies, I add other physiological indexes and I consider all of them—not only when generated *four seconds before* the selection of each card but also when generated *four seconds after* such a selection: This is simply to assess whether the emotional signals produced by participants' bodies could have not only an anticipatory value (as Damasio and colleagues postulated), but could be an effect of the detection of a certain stimulus. What follows is a brief list of the additional physiological indexes:

- BVP (Blood Volume Pulse) is a measure of the blood volume changes in a limb or segment of tissue (Andreassi 2000, 306). It represents the pumping action of the heart as represented in local blood vessels.
- EMG (Electromyography) is a measure used to record the electrical potentials associated with the contraction of muscle fibers (Andreassi 2000, 168; Tassinary and Cacioppo 2000, 176).
- PULS (Heart Rate) is a measure of the heart activity, and it is based on the number of beats per unit of time (in my studies, per minute) (Andreassi 2000, 263).
- TEMP (Temperature) is a measure of the changes in skin temperature (Andreassi 2000, 61; Peek 2003, 381).

The Verbal Data

In Bechara et al. 1997 (1293), Damasio and coworkers briefly interrupt the game after twenty cards' selections made by the participants and asked the two questions above. These questions are then repeated at each ten-card interval and the responses audiotaped. However, the use of these questions has been strongly criticized in an article written by the psychologists Maia and McClelland (2004, 16075). In this paper, they point out that the questions Damasio and colleagues asked during the task are too broad and vague to be an adequate measure of participants' degree of explicit knowledge and learning and thus fail to identify what participants consciously know about the IGT (Newell and Shanks 2014, 12).

In support of this claim, Maia and McClelland propose a replication study where a sample of healthy participants is asked more sensitive questions than those proposed in Bechara et al. 1997 (1293) at each ten-card interval (Maia and McClelland 2004, 16076). They conclude that, by using these questions, participants show much more explicit knowledge in the first phases of the task than Damasio and colleagues' results suggest. This means asserting that the IGT in the early stages involves an unconscious evaluation system can no longer be endorsed confidently. As Newell and Shanks stated clearly in their review on the role of the unconscious in decision making, "performance in tasks such as the IGT which is routinely cited as evidence for unawareness can be readily explained by conscious acquisition of deck knowledge" (2014, 15). Thus, Maia and McClelland's results seem to undermine the utility of postulating the SMs as causally necessary for decision making, because participants at the IGT appear to be able to decide through conscious deliberation (Dunn et al. 2006, 249).

As I will discuss in detail in chapter 7, I consider Maia and McClelland's criticisms very well aimed and their results empirically tenable. Further, it is worth noting that their questions seem fully to satisfy the four criteria (Reliability, Relevance/Information, Immediacy, and Sensitivity) for the construction of a reliable test of consciousness individuated in Newell and Shanks 2014 (3–4) and discussed in chapter 3. However, Maia and McClelland's questions asked during the task require quite a long time to be answered. Such a time does not seem to be compatible with the measurement of physiological indexes; for this reason, I choose to not repropose their questions in my studies.

Thus, although I accept Maia and McClelland's findings and conclusions, during the task I briefly interrupt the game at each ten-card interval and I ask participants the three following questions: "(1) In your opinion, are there some differences among the decks? What are the differences you have found?" "(2) Which is your favorite deck? Why?" (3) "Supposing you had to choose cards only from one deck from here to the end of the game, which deck would you choose and why?" Further, at the end of the task, I submit an evaluation questionnaire to participants (see appendix A).

The Instructions

The original sheet of instructions for participants is translated from Italian (see appendix A). In this translation, I decided to omit points 9 and 10 because I believe they can give the participants important hints for solving the task. Then, point 6 is maintained only in my first study because I consider it an important independent variable for the second and third studies.

MY THREE STUDIES

First Study

It is worth noting that, although the IGT is used in many studies, few of them have included physiological measures (Dunn et al. 2005, 249). For this reason, my three studies primarily aim to replicate Damasio and coworkers' research by assessing the same behavioral dependent measure and the same physiological dependent measure. Further, differently from Damasio and coworkers studies, I assess an additional behavioral dependent measure and four additional physiological dependent measures.

I hypothesize that my results can support those of Damasio and colleagues if both of these conditions occur throughout the task:

1. Participants will choose more cards from the advantageous (C and D) than from the disadvantageous decks (A and B).
2. Participants will generate higher anticipatory SCRs before the disadvantageous (A and B) than before the advantageous decks (C and D).

It is worth noting, however, that the lack of results for (2) could be considered as empirical evidence in contrast with Damasio and colleagues' results but not necessarily as a disconfirmation of his SMH per se. In fact, because such a theory points out that *certain signals arise from the body for giving a value mark to the four decks* and thus determine participants' preference for the advantageous decks (C and D), it could be supported also by the detection of an increase in the physiological measures different from the SCRs. Thus, Damasio and colleagues' theory also could be supported if both of the following conditions occur throughout the task:

1. Participants will choose more cards from the advantageous (C and D) than from the disadvantageous decks (A and B).
2. Participants will generate higher anticipatory responses for at least one of the additional physiological dependent measures considered before the disadvantageous (A and B) than before the advantageous decks (C and D).

As we can see, in my first study the detection of the physiological measures different from the SCRs aims to replicate and widen Damasio and colleagues' results and thus evaluate their theory, not assess other new ones. For this purpose, I refer to the behavioral measures we have seen above—the number of cards chosen from each deck and the reaction times (RTs).

By considering the first, I hypothesize that:

- Participants will choose more cards from decks B and D than from decks A and C, because the former have many more reward cards than the latter ones. In other words, participants will prefer a certain deck more on the basis of its frequency distribution than on the basis of its magnitude in the amount of money of the reward/punishment cards.

By considering the second, instead, I do not formulate a specific hypothesis to test. Rather, I decide only to observe whether significant differences appear in the RT among the decks.

Finally, by considering the questions asked of the participants at each ten-card interval and those asked at the post-experiment questionnaire, I make the following hypotheses:

- Participants who will give the best answers to the questions asked during and after the task performance will choose more cards from the advantageous (C and D) than from the disadvantageous decks (A and B). Conversely, participants who will give the worst answers to the questions asked during and after the task performance will choose more cards from the disadvantageous (A and B) than from the advantageous decks (C and D) or they will choose the same number of cards from each of the four decks.

Second Study

As I pointed out above, the second study has the same experimental design and variables as the first study. Thus, all of the aims and hypotheses formulated for the first are valid for the second study. However, in the second study, I introduce a further independent variable. In fact, I change point 6 of Damasio and colleagues' instruction sheet in order to invite or induce the participants to develop a deliberate and conscious play strategy. More precisely, I hypothesize that:

- Participants who will develop a defined play strategy will choose more cards from the advantageous (C and D) than from the disadvantageous decks (A and B). On the contrary, the participants who will not develop any coherent play strategy will choose more cards from the disadvantageous (A and B) than from the advantageous decks (C and D) (or they will choose the same number of cards from each of the four decks).
- Participants who will develop a defined play strategy will provide good answers to the questions asked during and after the task performance. Conversely, participants who will not develop any coherent play strategy will provide poor answers to the questions asked during and after the task performance.

Third Study

Like the second study, the third study has the same experimental design and variables as the first study. Thus, all of the aims and hypotheses formulated for the first (and for the second) are also valid for the third study. However, in the third study, I introduce a further independent variable. In my instructions, I add a point more than in Damasio and colleagues' and my first study's instructions—point 7 (see appendix A), where participants are invited to pay attention to their bodily sensations throughout the task, in particular when they have to choose a certain deck.

Here I do not formulate a specific hypothesis. Rather, I decide only to observe whether significant differences occur in every physiological measure for each different deck and, if so, how these differences will be related to the behavioral measures.

The Task

All three studies: The task is a computer program version of the IGT described above. It was kindly provided to me by one of its authors and Damasio's coworkers, Antoine Bechara.

The Experimental Design

All three studies: The design consists of four phases:

1. *Pre-experimental phase: Instructions*: Participant is asked to sit down, and an examiner in front of her reads the instructions. After the participant

listens to the instructions, the examiner asks her if she has understood the instructions and if she wants a second reading.

2. *Experimental phase: Task*: Participant is asked to sit in front of a computer screen and she is prepared for the measurement of her electrophysiological activity by an examiner. Then the participant is told to begin to play the IGT on the computer by choosing the decks she prefers with a mouse placed on her right. After the participant selects ten cards, an examiner interrupts her and asks her the three questions listed above. These questions are then repeated at each ten-card interval until the end of the task, and the responses are audiotaped.
3. *Post-experimental phase: Questionnaire submission*: After having performed the IGT, participant is asked to complete a paper-and-pencil questionnaire (see appendix B).
4. *Post-experimental phase: Debriefing*: After having completed the paper-and-pencil questionnaire, the participant is informed in detail of what the study has been about and of any deception or withholding of information that may have been a necessary element for solving the IGT.

NOTES

1. On this point, see Dennett 2009, Thagard 2009, and Bechtel 2010.

2. That is, they are the changes in the electrical activity of the skin surface (Andreassi 2000, 196; Reber and Reber 2001, 292).

3. It is worth noting that Damasio and coworkers assessed all three features only in Bechara et al. 1997. In Bechara et al. 1994, they considered only (a) and in Bechara et al. 1996 only (b).

4. Thus, at last, we can agree with the neuroscientist Bennett and the philosopher Hacker's analysis according to which Damasio and colleagues' hypothesis is nothing but a stimulus-response theory working at the neural level rather than at the behavioral level (2003, 212, note 16).

5. But other similar quotations can be found throughout Damasio's work. For example, consider this one: "Innate knowledge is based on dispositional representations in hypothalamus, brain stem, and limbic system. . . . Acquired knowledge is based on dispositional representations in higher-order cortices and throughout many gray-matter nuclei beneath the level of the cortex" (Damasio 1994, 104–5).

6. On these tricky distinctions, see also Rossetti and Revonsuo 2000.

7. On this point applied to the distinction between implicit and explicit learning, see Shanks and St. John 1994; St. John and Shanks 1997; Frensch and Ruenger 2003. See also chapter 3 of this book.

8. A clear formulation of this claim can be found in Wegner 2005.

9. For details, see Bechara et al. 1994, 11, fig. 2; Bechara et al. 1996, 221, fig. 3, and Bechara et al. 1997, 1294, fig. 1.

Chapter Six

Retesting the Somatic Marker Hypothesis

In this chapter I will report the results of my replication studies,[1] the *behavioral data* (those data coming from the observation of behavior not considered in Damasio's studies [number of choices from the four decks and reaction times, or RTs]), the *physiological data* (those data coming from the registration of those physiological measures not considered in Damasio's studies), and the *qualitative data* (those data coming from the questions asked throughout the task and the questionnaire submitted at the end of the task).[2]

A REPLICATION OF DAMASIO'S STUDIES[3]

I here report the results of my studies aimed at replicating those of Damasio and colleagues. Thus, I consider a behavioral measure (the number of cards chosen from the decks) and a physiological measure (the SCRs before the choice of decks).

First Study—Behavioral Measure

By following the analysis reported in Bechara et al. 1994 (12), I compare the number of cards chosen from each deck by participants and I run a one-way repeated measures analysis of variance (ANOVA) with a four-level variable (decks). The test of within-subjects effects indicates a significant effect of the variable decks ($F (3,30) = 3.40$, $p < .05$): The pair-wise comparisons result in a significant difference in the number of cards selected between deck A ($M = 0,21$, $SD = 0,06$) and deck D ($M = 0,32$, $SD = 0,10$) (CI.95 = –.20 [lower] –.11 [upper], $p < .05$).

For the reasons discussed above, I cannot replicate the factorial analysis of variance (ANOVA 2 × 4) with a two-level variable (decks) and a four-level variable (periods) similar to that proposed in Bechara et al. 1997 (1295, note 9).[4] Thus, I run a one-way analysis of variance (ANOVA) with a two-level variable (decks) for each learning period.

The test of within-subjects effects indicates no significant difference in the number of cards chosen either in PP ($F(1, 10) = .10$, $p > .05$) or in PH ($F(1, 10) = .01$, $p > .05$) or H ($F(1, 10) = 1.31$, $p > .05$). Rather, in C, the test of within-subjects effects indicates a significant difference for the variable decks ($F(3, 30) = 1.55$, $p > .05$): The pair-wise comparisons result in a significant difference in the mean number of cards between advantageous (M = 0,62, SD = 0,15) and disadvantageous (M = 0,38, SD = 0,15) decks (CI.95 = –.45 [lower] –.04 [upper]).

Further, for providing a more fine-grained analysis of the number of cards selected in the four learning periods, I run a one-way analysis of variance (ANOVA) with a four-level variable (decks) for each learning period. Also in this case, the test of within-subjects effects indicates no significant difference in the number of cards chosen either in PP ($F(3, 30) = 2.81$, $p > .05$) or in PH ($F(2.61, 26.07) = 2.58$, $p > .05$) or H ($F(3, 30) = 3.66$, $p > .05$). Rather, in C, the test of within-subjects effects indicates a significant difference in the number of cards chosen: The pair-wise comparisons result in a significant difference in the mean number of cards between deck A (M = 0,16, SD = 0,08) and deck C (M = 0,28, SD = 0,11) (CI.95 = –.24 [lower] -.00 [upper]) and between deck A (M = 0,16, SD = 0,08) and deck D (M = 0,34, SD = 0,15) (CI.95 = –.31 [lower] -.06 [upper]).

First Study—Physiological Measure

By following the analysis reported in Bechara et al. 1996 (221), I try to assess whether participants in my first study produce somatic marker responses (measured through SCRs) before the choice of one of the decks. Thus, I run a one-way repeated measures analysis of variance (ANOVA) with a four-level variable (decks A, B, C, and D). The test of within-subjects effects indicates no significant effect of the variable decks ($F(2.73, 27.30) = .68$, $p > .05$).

Then, I run a one-way repeated measures analysis of variance (ANOVA) with a two-level variable (advantageous decks [C+D] and disadvantageous decks [A+B]). The test of within-subjects effects indicates no significant effect of the variable decks ($F(1, 10) = .04$, $p > .05$).

Further, by following the analysis reported in Bechara et al. 1997, I run a factorial repeated measures analysis of variance (ANOVA 2 × 4) with a two-level variable (decks) and a four-level variable (periods). ANOVA's results indicate neither a significant main effect of the variable decks (F (1, 10) = .08, p > .05), nor a significant main effect of the variable periods (F (2.565, 25.65) = .945, p > .05), nor a significant interaction effect between the variables decks and periods on the SCRs (F (3, 30) = .47, p > .05).

Second Study—Behavioral Measure

By following the analysis reported in Bechara et al. 1994 (12), I compare the number of cards chosen from each deck by participants and I run a one-way repeated measures analysis of variance (ANOVA) with a four-level variable (decks). The test of within-subjects effects indicates a significant effect of the variable decks (F (3,30) = 5.16, p < .05): The pair-wise comparisons result in a significant difference in the number of cards selected between deck A (M = 0,17, SD = 0,05) and deck B (M = 0,27; SD = 0,06) (CI.95 = –.16 [lower] –.05 [upper], p < .05) and between deck A (M = 0,17, SD = 0,05) and deck D (M = 0,32, SD = 0,09) (CI.95 = –.23 [lower] -.06 [upper], p < .05). The Bonferroni post-experiment tests confirm such a significant difference in the number of cards selected between deck A and deck B (CI.95 = –.18 [lower] –.02 [upper], p < .05) and between deck A and deck D (CI.95 = –.27 [lower] –.24 [upper], p < .05).

Then, by following the distinction in four learning periods proposed in Bechara et al. 1997, I run a one-way analysis of variance (ANOVA) with a two-level variable (decks) for each learning period.

The test of within-subjects effects indicates neither a significant effect in PP (F (1, 10) = 2.66, p > .05) nor in PH (F (1, 10) = .09, p > .05). However, there is a significant effect in H (F (1, 10) = 10.13, p < .05) and in C (F (1, 10) = 5.11, p < .05). For H, the pair-wise comparisons result in a significant difference in the mean number of cards between disadvantageous (M = 0,38, SD = 0,13) and advantageous (M = 0,62, SD = 0,13) decks (CI.95 = –.42 [lower] –.07 [upper]); for C, the pair-wise comparisons result in a significant difference in the mean number of cards between disadvantageous (M = 0,36, SD = 0,20) decks and advantageous (M = 0,64, SD = 0,20) decks (CI.95 = –.54 [lower] –.00 [upper]).

To provide a more fine-grained analysis of the number of cards selected in the four learning periods, I run a one-way analysis of variance (ANOVA) with a four-level variable (decks) for each learning period. The test of within-subjects effects indicates neither a significant effect in PP (F (3, 30) = 1.02, p > .05), nor in C (F (3, 30) = 1.94, p > .05). However, there is a significant effect in PH (F (3, 30) = 4.00, p < .05) and in H (F (3, 30) = 4.04, p < .05). For PH, the pair-wise comparisons result in a significant difference in the mean number of cards between deck A (M = 0,19, SD = 0,06) and deck B (M = 0,30, SD = 0,10) (CI.95 = –.19 [lower] –.015 [upper]), between deck A (M

= 0,19, SD = 0,06) and deck D (M = 0,30, SD = 0,09) (CI.95 = –.19 [lower] –.03 [upper]) and between deck C (M = 0,21, SD = 0,08) and deck D (M = 0,30, SD = 0,09) (CI.95 = –.18 [lower] -.01 [upper]); for H, the pair-wise comparisons result in a significant difference in the mean number of cards between deck A (M = 0,15, SD = 0,08) and deck D (M = 0,35, SD = 0,12) (CI.95 = –.31 [lower] –.10 [upper]) and between deck B (M = 0,23, SD = 0,11) and deck D (M = 0,35, SD = 0,12) (CI.95 = –.22 [lower] –.02 [upper]).

Second Study—Physiological Measure

By following the analysis reported in Bechara et al. 1996 (221), I run a one-way repeated measures analysis of variance (ANOVA) with a four-level variable (decks). The test of within-subjects effects indicates no significant effect of this variable ($F(3, 30) = 1.34$, $p > .05$).

Then, I run a one-way repeated measures analysis of variance (ANOVA) with a two-level variable (decks). The test of within-subjects effects indicates no significant effect of this variable ($F(1, 10) = 1.83$, $p > .05$).

Further, by following the analysis reported in Bechara et al. 1997, I run a factorial repeated measures analysis of variance (ANOVA 2 × 4) with a two-level variable (decks) and a four-level variable (periods). ANOVA's results indicate neither a significant main effect of the variable decks ($F(1, 9) = 1.82$, $p > .05$), nor a significant main effect of the variable periods ($F(1.445, 13.00) = 2.21$, $p > .05$), nor a significant interaction effect between the variables decks and periods ($F(1.36, 12.23) = 2.27$, $p > .05$).[5]

Third Study—Behavioral Measure

By following the analysis reported in Bechara et al. 1994 (12), I compare the number of cards chosen from each deck by participants by running a one-way repeated measures analysis of variance (ANOVA) with a four-level variable (decks). The test of within-subjects effects indicates a significant effect of this variable ($F(3, 30) = 4.11$, $p < .05$): The pair-wise comparisons result in a significant difference between deck A (M = 0,18, SD = 0,05) and deck B (M = 0,26, SD = 0,08) (CI.95 = –127 [lower] -.012 [upper], $p < .05$) and between deck A (M = 0,18, SD = 0,05) and deck D (M = 0,33, SD = 0,12) (CI.95 = –.245 [lower] –.034 [upper], $p < .05$).

Then, by following the distinction in four periods proposed in Bechara et al. 1997, I run a one-way analysis of variance (ANOVA) with a two-level variable (decks) for each learning period. The test of within-subjects effects indicates neither a significant effect in PP ($F(1, 10) = 3.38$, $p > .05$), for PH ($F(1, 10) = .26$, $p > .05$), nor in H ($F(1, 10) = 4.24$, $p > .05$) nor in C ($F(1, 10) = 4.11$, $p > .05$).

Further, to provide a more fine-grained analysis of the number of cards selected in the four learning periods, I run a one-way analysis of variance (ANOVA) with a four-level variable (decks) for each learning period. The test of within-subjects effects indicates no significant effect for PH (F (1.55, 15.48) = 1.49, p > .05) and C (F (2.11, 21.065) = 1.15, p > .05). However, there is a significant effect in PP (F (3, 30) = 6.94, p < .05) and in H (F (3, 30) = 4.53, p < .05). For PP, the pair-wise comparisons result in a significant difference in the mean number of cards between deck A (M = 0,18, SD = 0,10) and deck B (M = 0,41, SD = 0,15) (CI.95 = –.36 [lower] –.10 [upper]), between deck B (M = 0,41, SD = 0,15) and deck C (M = 0,24, SD = 0,13) (CI.95 = .00 [lower] .34 [upper]) and between deck B (M = 0,41, SD = 0,15) and deck D (M = 0,17, SD = 0,09) (CI.95 = .09 [lower] .38 [upper]); for H, the pair-wise comparisons result in a significant difference in the mean number of cards between deck B (M = 0,18, SD = 0,11) and deck D (M = 0,41, SD = 0,21) (CI.95 = -.41 [lower] –.04 [upper]) and between deck C (M = 0,20, SD = 0,09) and deck D (M = 0,41, SD = 0,21) (CI.95 = –.395 [lower] –.025 [upper]).

Third Study—Physiological Measure

By following the analysis reported in Bechara et al. 1996 (221), I run a one-way repeated measures analysis of variance (ANOVA) with a four-level variable (decks). The test of within-subjects effects indicates no significant effect of this variable (F (3, 30) = 1.60, p > .05).

Then, I run a one-way repeated measures analysis of variance (ANOVA) with a two-level variable (decks). The test of within-subjects effects indicates no significant effect of this variable (F (1, 10) = 4.07, p > .05).

Further, by following the analysis reported in Bechara et al. 1997 (1294), I run a factorial repeated measures analysis of variance (ANOVA 2 × 4) with a two-level variable (decks) and a four-level variable (periods). ANOVA's results indicate neither a significant main effect of the variable decks (F (1, 8) = 1.30, p > .05), nor a significant main effect of the variable periods (F (1.14, 9.13) = 1.55, p > .05), nor a significant interaction effect between the variables decks and periods (F (1.54, 12.32) = .76, p > .05).[6]

HOW THE PARTICIPANTS OF THE THREE STUDIES BEHAVE AND CHOOSE AT THE IGT

I here report the *behavioral data* not considered by Damasio and colleagues in their studies.

First Study

Number of cards chosen from disadvantageous (A + B) and advantageous (C + D) decks throughout the task: The test of within-subjects effects indicates no significant effect for the variable considered (F (1, 10) = 2.60, p > .05).

Number of cards chosen from low punishing (B + D) and high punishing (A + C) decks throughout the task: The test of within-subjects effects indicates a significant effect for the variable considered (F (1, 10) = 7.92, p < .05). The pair-wise comparisons result in a significant difference in the mean number of cards chosen between high punishing (A + C) (M = 43,55, SD = 7,61) and low punishing decks (B + D) (M = 56,45, SD = 7,61) (CI.95 = – 23.13 [lower] – 2.69 [upper], p < .05).

RTs throughout the task: The test of within-subjects effects indicates no significant effect for the variable considered (F (3, 30) = .98, p > .05).

RTs according to four learning periods: ANOVA's results indicate a significant main effect for the variable decks (F (1, 10) = 6.84, p < .05). The pair-wise comparisons result in a significant difference between disadvantageous and advantageous decks (CI.95 = –.310 [lower] .025 [upper], p < .05). Further, ANOVA's results indicate also a significant main effect of the variable periods (F (1.38, 13.81) = 4.40, p < .05). The pair-wise comparisons result in a significant difference between PP (M = 6.22) and H (M = 5.34) (CI.95 = .09 [lower] 1.68 [upper], p < .05) and PH (M = 5.82) and H (M = 5.34) (CI.95 = .03 [lower] .94 [upper], p < .05). ANOVA's results indicate no significant interaction effect between the variables decks and periods (F (3, 30) = 2.73, p > .05).

Second Study

Number of cards chosen from disadvantageous (A + B) and advantageous (C + D) decks throughout the task: The test of within-subjects effects indicates a significant effect for the variable considered (F (1, 10) = 5.95, p < .05). The pair-wise comparisons result in a significant difference in the mean number of cards between advantageous (A + B) (M = 0,44, SD = 0,08) and disadvantageous (C + D) decks (M = 0,56, SD = 0,08) (CI.95 = –.23 [lower] –.01 [upper]).

Number of cards chosen from low punishing (B + D) and high punishing (A + C) decks throughout the task: The test of within-subjects effects indicates a significant effect for the variable considered (F (1, 10) = 6.49, p < .05). The pair-wise comparisons result in a significant difference in the mean number of cards chosen between high punishing (A + C) (M = 41,18, SD = 11,48) and low punishing (B + D) decks (M = 58,82, SD = 11,48) (CI.95 = –33.06 [lower] – 2.21 [upper], p < .05).

RTs throughout the task: The test of within-subjects effects indicates no significant effect for the variable considered (F (1.64, 16.40) = .37, p > .05).

RTs according to four learning periods: ANOVA's results indicate neither a significant main effect for the variable decks (F (1, 9) = .23, p > .05), nor a significant main effect for the variable periods (F (1.305, 11.75) = 1.775, p > .05), nor a significant interaction effect between the variables decks and periods (F (3, 27) = 1.52, p > .05).

Third Study

Number of cards chosen from disadvantageous (A + B) and advantageous (C + D) decks throughout the task: The test of within-subjects effects indicates no significant effect for the variable considered (F (1, 10) = 2.88, p > .05).

Number of cards chosen from low punishing (B + D) and high punishing (A + C) decks throughout the task: The pair-wise comparisons result in a significant difference in the mean number of cards chosen between decks (A + C) (M = 41,55, SD = 8,86) and decks (B + D) (M = 58,45, SD = 8,86) (CI.95 = –28.81 [lower] – 5.01 [upper], p <.05).

RTs throughout the task: The test of within-subjects effects indicates no significant effect of the variable considered (F (3, 30) = 1.66, p > .05).

RTs according to four learning periods: ANOVA's results indicate neither a significant main effect of the variable decks (F (1, 8) = .24, p > .05), nor a significant main effect of the variable periods (F (1.48, 11.81) = .74, p > .05), nor a significant interaction effect between the variables decks and periods (F (3, 24) = .68, p > .05).

Comparison among Studies

I here report the results of the comparisons among my three studies for the behavioral measures considered (the number of cards chosen and the RTs).

- *Decks A, B, C, D (throughout the task)*: The test of within-subjects effects indicates neither a significant effect for the variable deck A (F (2, 20) = 1.64, p > .05), nor a significant effect for the variable deck B (F (1.39, 13.89) = .29, p > .05), nor a significant effect for the variable deck C (F (2, 20) = .14, p > .05), nor a significant main effect for the variable deck D (F (2, 20) = .04, p > .05).
- *Decks (A + B) and (C + D) (throughout the task)*: The test of within-subjects effects indicates neither a significant effect for the variable disadvantageous decks (A + B) (F (2, 20) = .08, p > .05), nor a significant effect for the variable advantageous decks (C + D) (F (2, 20) = .08, p > .05).

- *Decks A, B, C, D (by considering the four learning periods)*:
  - PP The test of within-subjects effects indicates neither a significant effect for the variable deck A (F (2, 20) = 3.095, p > .05), nor a significant effect for the variable deck B (F (2, 20) = 3.46, p > .05), nor a significant effect for the variable deck C (F (2, 20) = 1.13, p > .05), nor a significant main effect for the variable deck D (F (2, 20) = .80, p > .05).
  - PH The test of within-subjects effects indicates neither a significant effect for the variable deck A (F (2, 20) = .92, p > .05), nor a significant effect for the variable deck B (F (2, 20) = .44, p > .05), nor a significant effect for the variable deck C (F (2, 20) = .088, p > .05), nor a significant main effect for the variable deck D (F (2, 20) = .22, p > .05).
  - H The test of within-subjects effects indicates neither a significant effect for the variable deck A (F (2, 20) = 1.49, p > .05), nor a significant effect for the variable deck B (F (2, 20) = 1.45, p > .05), nor a significant effect for the variable deck C (F (2, 20) = .83, p > .05), nor a significant main effect for the variable deck D (F (2, 20) = .585, p > .05).
  - C The test of within-subjects effects indicates neither a significant effect for the variable deck A (F (2, 20) = .81, p > .05), nor a significant effect for the variable deck B (F (2, 20) = .09, p > .05), nor a significant effect for the variable deck C (F (2, 20) = .01, p > .05), nor a significant main effect for the variable deck D (F (2, 20) = .05, p > .05).

Decks (A + B) and (C + D) (by considering the four learning periods):

- PP The test of within-subjects effects indicates neither a significant effect for the variable disadvantageous decks (A + B) (F (2, 20) = 1.63, p > .05), nor a significant effect for the variable advantageous decks (C + D) (F (2, 20) = 1.63, p > .05).
- PH The test of within-subjects effects indicates neither a significant effect for the variable disadvantageous decks (A + B) (F (2, 20) = .21, p > .05), nor a significant effect for the variable advantageous decks (C + D) (F (2, 20) = .21, p > .05).
- H The test of within-subjects effects indicates neither a significant effect for the variable disadvantageous decks (A + B) (F (2, 20) = .85, p > .05), nor a significant effect for the variable advantageous decks (C + D) (F (2, 20) = .85, p > .05).
- C The test of within-subjects effects indicates neither a significant effect for the variable disadvantageous decks (A + B) (F (2, 20) = .04, p > .05), nor a significant effect for the variable advantageous decks (C + D) (F (2, 20) = .04, p > .05).

Decks (A + C) and (B + D) (throughout the task): The test of within-subjects effects indicates neither a significant effect for the variable high punishing decks (A + C) ($F(2, 20) = .23$, $p > .05$), nor a significant effect for the variable low punishing decks (B + D) ($F(2, 20) = .23$, $p > .05$).

RTs: ANOVA's results indicate neither a significant main effect for the variable study ($F(2, 20) = 1.71$, $p > .05$), nor a significant main effect for the variable decks ($F(3, 30) = .60$, $p > .05$), nor a significant interaction effect between the variable study and decks ($F(2.15, 21.48) = 1.41$, $p > .05$).

RTs (by considering the four learning periods): The test of within-subjects effect indicates neither a significant effect for the variable PP ($F(2,20) = 1.75$, $p > .05$), nor a significant effect for the variable PH ($F(2,20) = 1.84$, $p > .05$), nor a significant effect for the variable H ($F(2,20) = .96$, $p > .05$), nor a significant effect for the variable C ($F(2,20) = .36$, $p > .05$).

HOW PARTICIPANTS OF THE THREE STUDIES BODILY RESPOND TO THE IGT[7]

I here report the *physiological data* not considered by Damasio and colleagues in their studies.

First Study

This study shows no significant effects of any sort to be reported for any of the following measures: BVP before, BVP after (in four learning periods), EMG before, EMG after, EMG before-after, EMG before (in four learning periods), EMG after (in four learning periods), PULS before, PULS after, SCR after, SCR before-after, SCR after (in four learning periods), TEMP before, TEMP before-after, TEMP before (in four learning periods), TEMP after (in four learning periods).

BVP after: ANOVA's results indicate a significant main effect of the variable decks ($F(3,30) = 3.19$, $p < .05$): The pair-wise comparisons result in a significant difference in the BVPs between deck A ($M = 54,05$, $SD = 0,24$) and deck B ($M = 53,95$, $SD = 0,23$) (CI.95 = .007 [lower] .184 [upper]) and between deck A ($M = 54,05$, $SD = 0,24$) and deck C ($M = 53,95$, $SD = 0,26$) (CI.95 = .01 [lower] .19 [upper], $p < .05$).

BVP before-after: ANOVA's results indicate a significant main effect of the variable decks ($F(3, 30) = 2.94$, $p < .05$): The pair-wise comparisons result in a significant difference in the BVPs between deck A ($M = 54.01$, $SD = .07$) and deck B ($M = 53.94$, $SD = .06$) (CI.95 = .01 [lower] .13 [upper], $p < .05$) and between deck A ($M = 54,01$, $SD = .07$) and deck D ($M = 53,95$, $SD = .08$) (CI.95 = .02 [lower] .115[(upper], $p < .05$).

BVP before (in four learning periods): ANOVA's results indicate a significant main effect of the variable periods (F (3, 30) = 8.99, p < .05): The pair-wise comparisons result in a significant difference between PP and PH (CI.95 = –.313 [lower] –.088 [upper], p < .05), PP (M = 53,76, SD = .08) and H (M = 54,96, SD = .07) (CI.95 = –.344 [lower] -.055 [upper], p < .05) and PP (M = 53,76, SD = .08) and C (M = 53.98, SD = .07) (CI.95 = –.321 [lower] –.122 [upper], p < .05).

PULS before-after: ANOVA's results indicate a significant main effect of the variable time (F (1, 10) = 18.2, p < .05): The pair-wise comparisons result in a significant difference in the PULSs between the time before (M = 77.80, SD = 3.66) and the time after (M = 77.26, SD = 3.70) (CI.95 = .255 [lower] .815 [upper], p < .05).

PULS before (in four learning periods): ANOVA's results indicate a significant main effect of the variable periods (F (1.52, 15.17) = 4.85, p < .05): The pair-wise comparisons indicate a significant difference between PP (M = 82.18, SD = 4.33) and PH (M = 77.24, SD = 3.90) (CI.95 = .26 [lower] 9.63 [upper], p < .05) and PP (M = 82.18, SD = 4.33) and H (M = 76.87, SD = 3.59) (CI.95 = .69 [lower] 9.95 [upper], p < .05).

PULS after (in four learning periods): ANOVA's results indicate a significant main effect of the variable periods (F (1.28, 12.835) = 4.88, p < .05): The pair-wise comparisons result in a significant difference between PP (M = 81.87, SD = 4.58) and PH (M = 76.59, SD = 3.93) (CI.95 = .455 [lower] 10.10 [upper], p < .05) and PP (M = 81.87, SD = 4.58) and H (M = 76.55, SD = 3.62) (CI.95 = .24 [lower] 10.41 [upper], p < .05).

Second Study

This study shows no significant effects of any sort to be reported for any of the following measures: BVP before, BVP after, BVP before-after, BVP before (in four learning periods), BVP after (in four learning periods), EMG before, EMG after, EMG before-after, EMG before (in four learning periods), EMG after (in four learning periods), PULS before, PULS after, PULS before (in four learning periods), PULS after (in four learning periods), SCR after, SCR before-after, SCR before (in four learning periods), SCR after (in four learning periods), TEMP before, TEMP after, TEMP before-after, temp before (in four learning periods), TEMP after (in four learning periods).

PULS before-after: ANOVA's results indicate a significant main effect of the variable time on the PULSs (F (1, 10) = 7.67, p. < .05): The planned contrasts reveal that the PULSs at time before (M = 71.34, SD = 6.84) are significantly higher than those at time after (M = 70.91, SD = 6.80). The pair-wise comparisons confirm such a conclusion (CI.95 = –.766 [lower] –.083 [upper], p. < .05).

Third Study

This study shows no significant effects of any sort to be reported for any of the following measures: BVP before, BVP after, BVP after-before, BVP before (in four learning periods), BVP after (in four learning periods), EMG before, EMG after, EMG before (in four learning periods), EMG after (in four learning periods), PULS before, PULS after, SCR after, SCR before-after, SCR before (in four learning periods), SCR after (in four learning periods), TEMP before, TEMP after, TEMP before-after, TEMP before (in four learning periods), TEMP after (in four learning periods).

EMG before-after: ANOVA's results indicate a significant interaction effect between the variable decks and the variable time (F (1.67, 16.69) = 4.23, p. < .05).

PULS before-after: ANOVA's results indicate a significant main effect of the variable time: The planned contrasts reveal that the PULSs before the choice of a deck (M = 84.78, SD = 2.98) are significantly higher than those after the choice of the deck (M = 84.32, SD = 2.99) (F (1, 10) = 17.38, p < .05). The pair-wise comparisons confirm such a conclusion (CI.95 = .22 [lower] .71 [upper], p < .05).

PULS before (in four learning periods): ANOVA's results indicate a significant main effect of the variable periods (F (3, 24) = 14.15, p < .05): The pair-wise comparisons reveal a significant difference between PP (M = 91.78, SD = 2.69) and PH (M = 85.94, SD = 3.20) (CI.95 = 3.02 [lower] 8.65 [upper], p < .05), PP (M = 91.78, SD = 2.69) and H (M = 85.04, SD = 3.64) (CI.95 = 2.57 [lower] 10.91 [upper], p < .05) and PH (M = 85.94, SD = 3.20) and H (M = 84.36, SD = 3.12) (CI.95 = 3.63 [lower] 11.21 [upper], p < .05).

PULS after (in four learning periods): ANOVA's results indicate a significant main effect of the variable periods (F (3, 24) = 14.15, p > .05): The pair-wise comparisons result in a significant difference between PP (M = 91.39, SD = 2.87) and PH (M = 85.20, SD = 3.26) (CI.95 = 3.36 [lowe]) 9.04 [upper], p < .05), PP (M = 91.39, SD = 2.87) and H (M = 84.88, SD = 3.57) (CI.95 = 3.05 [lower] 9.90 [upper], p < .05), and PH (M = 85.20, SD = 3.26) and C (M = 83.99, SD = 3.08) (CI.95 = 3.70 [lower] 11.11 [upper], p < .05).

Comparison among Studies

This comparison shows no significant effects of any sort to be reported for any of the following measures: PULS before, PULS after, SCR after, SCR before-after, TEMP before, TEMP after, TEMP before-after.

BVP before: ANOVA's results indicate a significant main effect of the variable study (F (1.05, 10.52) = 17.03, p < .05): The pair-wise comparisons result in a significant difference between study 1 (M = 53.94, SD = 0.07) and study 2 (M = 51.40, SD = 0.53) (CI.95 = 1.26 [lower] 3.83 [upper], $p < .05$), between study 1 (M = 53.94, SD = 0.07) and study 3 (M = 53.21, SD = 0.08) (CI.95 = .464 [lower] 1.006 [upper], $p < .05$) and between study 2 (M = 51.40, SD = 0.53) and study 3 (M = 53.21, SD = 0.08) (CI.95 = –2,945 [lower] –.678 [upper], $p < .05$).

BVP after: ANOVA's results indicate a significant main effect of the variable study (F (1.04, 10.41) = 17.895, $p < .05$): The pair-wise comparisons reveal a significant difference between study 1 (M = 53.98, SD = 0.07) and study 2 (M = 51.31, SD = 0.55) (CI.95 = 1.33 [lower] 4.00 [upper], $p < .05$), between study 1 (M = 53.98, SD = 0.07) and study 3 (M = 53.25, SD = 0.08) (CI.95 = .50 [lower] 1.025 [upper], $p < .05$) and between study 2 (M = 53.98, SD = 0.07) and study 3 (M = 53.25, SD = 0.08) (CI.95 = –3.07 [lower] –.795 [upper], $p < .05$).

BVP before-after: ANOVA's results indicate a significant main effect of the variable study (F (1.045, 10,45) = 17.58, $p < .05$): The pair-wise comparisons result in a significant difference between study 1 (M = 53.96, SD = 0.07) and study 2 (M = 51.36, SD = 0.54) (CI.95 = 1.302 [lower] 3.914 [upper], $p < .05$), between study 1 (M = 53.96, SD = 0.07) and study 3 (M = 53.23, SD = 0.08) (CI.95 = .459 [lower] 1.013[(upper], $p < .05$) and between study 2 (M = 51.36, SD = 0.54) and study 3 (M = 53.23, SD = 0.08) (CI.95 = –3.004 [lower] –.741[(upper], $p < .05$).

EMG before: ANOVA's results indicate a significant main effect of the variable study (F (2, 20) = 5.0, $p < .05$): The pair-wise comparisons result in a significant difference between study 2 (M = 16.56, SD = 2.76) and study 3 (M = 30.07, SD = 3.73) (CI.95 = –22.05 [lower] –4.98 [upper], $p < .05$).

EMG after: ANOVA's results indicate a significant main effect of the variable study (F (2, 20) = 4.80, $p < .05$): The pair-wise comparisons result in a significant difference between the study 2 (M = 30.2, SD = 3.76) and study 3 (M = 16.59, SD = 2.77) (CI.95 = –22.05 [lower] –4.83 [upper], $p < .05$).

EMG before-after: ANOVA's results indicate a significant main effect of the variable study (F (2, 20) = 4.9, $p < .05$): The pair-wise comparisons result in a significant difference between study 2 (M = 16.57, SD = 2.77) and study 3 (M = 30.05, SD = 3.75) (CI.95 = -22.05 [lower] –4.91 [upper], $p < .05$).

PULS before-after: ANOVA's results indicate a significant main effect of the variable time (F (1, 10) = 41.26, $p < .05$): The pair-wise comparisons results a significant difference in the PULSs between before (M = 77.97, SD = 2.37) and after (M = 77.49, SD = 2.36) (CI.95 = .310 [lower] .639 [upper], $p < .05$).

HOW PARTICIPANTS OF THE THREE STUDIES EXPLICITLY REASON AND THINK DURING THE IGT[8]

I here report the *qualitative data* coming from my studies.

First Study

For the questions asked throughout the task, if a participant gives all correct responses, she obtains 30 points ([Q1 = 10] + [Q2 = 10] + [Q3 = 10] = 30). Thus, table 6.1 shows the results for each participant.

For the questions on the post-experiment questionnaire, if a participant gives all correct responses, she obtains 6 points ([Q1 = 1] + [Q2 = 1] + [Q3 = 1] + [Q4 = 0.5 + 0.5] + [Q5 = 0.5 + 0.5] + [Q6 = 1] = 6). Table 6.2 shows the results for each participant.

From the comparisons of the two total score ratios of each participant, we can say that:

- Participants 1 and 9 give excellent responses both to questions asked during the task performance and those on the post-experiment questionnaire.
- Participants 5 and 10 give good responses both to questions asked during the task performance and those on the post-experiment questionnaire.
- Participants 2, 7, and 11 give good responses to questions on the post-experiment questionnaire but poor responses to those asked during the task performance.
- Participants 4 and 8 give good responses to questions asked during the task performance but poor responses to those on the post-experiment questionnaire.

Table 6.1. Answers Given Throughout the Task

Participants	*Rates*	*Total Score*	*Total Score Ratio %*
1	([Q1 = 9] + [Q2 = 8] + [Q3 = 8])	25/30	83%
2	([Q1 = 5] + [Q2 = 3] + [Q3 = 3])	11/30	36%
3	([Q1 = 1] + [Q2 = 1] + [Q3 = 0])	2/30	6%
4	([Q1 = 4] + [Q2 = 4] + [Q3 = 5])	13/30	43%
5	([Q1 = 0] + [Q2 = 6] + [Q3 = 8])	14/30	46%
6	([Q1 = 0] + [Q2 = 8] + [Q3 = 3])	11/30	36%
7	([Q1 = 2] + [Q2 = 2] + [Q3 = 6])	10/30	33%
8	([Q1 = 5] + [Q2 = 5] + [Q3 = 5])	15/30	50%
9	([Q1 = 7] + [Q2 = 8] + [Q3 = 8])	23/30	77%
10	([Q1 = 0] + [Q2 = 9] + [Q3 = 7])	16/30	53%
11	([Q1 = 0] + [Q2 = 2] + [Q3 = 8])	10/30	33%

Table 6.2. Answers Given on the Post-Experiment Questionnaire

Participants	*Rates*	*Total Score*	*Total Score Ratio %*
1	([Q1 = 1] + [Q2 = 1] + [Q3 = 1] + [Q4 = 0.5 + 0] + [Q5 = 0 + 0] + [Q6 = 1])	4.5/6	75%
2	([Q1 = 0] + [Q2 = 1] + [Q3 = 0] + [Q4 = 0.5 + 0.5] + [Q5 = 0 + 0] + [Q6 = 1])	3/6	50%
3	([Q1 = 0] + [Q2 = 0] + [Q3 = 0] + [Q4 = 0 + + 0] + [Q5 = 0 + 0] + [Q6 = 1])	1/6	16%
4	([Q1 = 0] + [Q2 = 0] + [Q3 = 0] + [Q4 = 0 + + 0] + [Q5 = 0.5 + 0.5] + [Q6 = 0])	1/6	16%
5	([Q1 = 0] + [Q2 = 1] + [Q3 = 1] + [Q4 = 0.5 + + 0] + [Q5 = 0.5 + 0] + [Q6 = 0])	3/6	50%
6	([Q1 = 0] + [Q2 = 0] + [Q3 = 0] + [Q4 = 0 + + 0.5] + [Q5 = 0 + 0] + [Q6 = 1])	1.5/6	25%
7	([Q1 = 1] + [Q2 = 0] + [Q3 = 0] + [Q4 = 0.5 + + 0.5] + [Q5 = 0.5 + 0] + [Q6 = 0])	2.5/6	42%
8	([Q1 = 0] + [Q2 = 0] + [Q3 = 0] + [Q4 = 0 + + 0.5] + [Q5 = 0.5 + 0] + [Q6 = 0])	1/6	16%
9	([Q1 = 1] + [Q2 = 1] + [Q3 = 0] + [Q4 = 0.5 + + 0] + [Q5 = 0 + 0] + [Q6 = 1])	3.5/6	58%
10	([Q1 = 0] + [Q2 = 1] + [Q3 = 0] + [Q4 = 0.5 + + 0] + [Q5 = 0.5 + 0] + [Q6 = 1])	3/6	50%
11	([Q1 = 1] + [Q2 = 1] + [Q3 = 0] + [Q4 = 0.5 + + 0] + [Q5 = 0.5 + 0] + [Q6 = 1])	4/6	66%

- Participant 6 gives poor responses both to questions asked during the task performance and those on the post-experiment questionnaire.
- Participant 3 gives really poor responses both to the questions asked during the task performance and those on the post-experiment questionnaire.

Participants 1 and 9 choose more cards from advantageous (C + D) than from disadvantageous decks (A + B).[9] Participant 11 behaves more or less in the same way, although she chooses fewer cards from advantageous decks (C + D) than participants 1 and 9 do.[10] Conversely, participant 3 chooses more cards from the disadvantageous (A + B) than from advantageous decks (C + D).[11] And participants 2, 4, 5, 6, 7, 8, and 10 choose more or less the same number of cards from both advantageous (C + D) and disadvantageous (A + B) decks.

Table 6.3. Rotated Component Matrix(a) (DECKS)

	Component				
	1	2	*3*	*4*	*5*
1	.301	.020	.727	.063	.057
2	–.475	.284	.201	.515	—.340
3	.376	–.310	–.118	.184	—.053
4	.044	–.040	–.183	.749	.122
5	.076	.093	.049	.150	.770
6	.277	.027	–.683	.022	.031
7	.109	–.720	.257	.104	.110
8	–.385	–.071	–.016	–.046	.652
9	.087	–.153	.315	.569	.057
10	.234	.752	.165	.022	.137
11	*.765*	*.177*	*.101*	*.005*	*—.131*

Notes: Extraction Method: Principal Component Analysis.
Rotation Method: Varimax with Kaiser Normalization.
A rotation converged in nine iterations.

Principal Component Analysis

I run a component analysis on all of the behavioral and physiological measures taken for each subject, but I choose to report only the results of the behavioral measures (the number of cards chosen from each deck and the reaction times [RTs]). This is because I think such data are the most relevant for assessing the relation between the participants' level of comprehension of the task and their performance at it. Tables 6.3 and 6.4 report these data.

Table 6.4. Rotated Component Matrix(a) (RT)

	Component			
	1	2	*3*	4
1	.272	.436	.368	.332
–2	.127	.500	–.509	.145
–3	.059	–.177	–.661	.007
–4	.822	–.030	–.101	.018
–5	.076	.066	.684	.207
–6	.687	.132	.056	.333
–7	.188	.181	.124	.618
–8	.281	.626	.309	.113
–9	.456	–.073	.314	–.574
10	.088	–.194	.133	.629
11	–.209	.768	.056	–.172

Notes: Extraction Method: Principal Component Analysis.
Rotation Method: Varimax with Kaiser Normalization.
A rotation converged in eight iterations.

Then, I choose to focus on the performances of participant 1 (who gives the *best answers* both to questions asked during the task and on the questionnaire and chooses more cards from advantageous than from disadvantageous decks) and of participant 3 (who gives the *worst answers* both to questions asked during the task and on the questionnaire and chooses more cards from disadvantageous than from advantageous decks). My hypothesis is that there is a different trend in the number of cards chosen from each deck and in the reaction times throughout the task for participants 1 and 3. In other words, from the component analysis I expect to find that participants 1 and 3 tend to load the same component in a completely different fashion.

As table 6.3 shows, for the variable decks, component 3 is highly loaded by participant 1 (.73) and negatively loaded by participant 3 (-.12). This indicates that, unlike participant 1 (who clearly prefers the advantageous), participant 3 does not seem to prefer one or more decks throughout the task.[12]

Rather, as table 6.4 shows, for the variable RTs, component 3 is fairly loaded by participant 1 (.37) and negatively loaded by participant 3 (-.66). As we can see in the following table, participant 1 takes much more time to make her choices than participant 3 does (at least in the first half of the task performance).

Second Study

For the questions asked throughout the task, if a participant gives all correct responses, she obtains 30 points ([Q1 = 10] +[Q2 = 10] + [Q3 = 10] = 30). Thus, table 6.5 reports the results for each participant.

Table 6.5. Answers Given Throughout the Task

Participants	*Rates*	*Total Score*	*Total Score Ratio %*
1	([Q1 = 3] + [Q2 = 4] + [Q3 = 2])	9/30	30%
–2	([Q1 = 6] + [Q2 = 5] + [Q3 = 5])	16/30	53.3%
–3	([Q1 = 5] + [Q2 = 3] + [Q3 = 4])	12/30	40%
–4	([Q1 = 8] + [Q2 = 8] + [Q3 = 7])	23/30	76%
–5	([Q1 = 1] + [Q2 = 0] + [Q3 = 0])	1/30	3%
–6	([Q1 = 3] + [Q2 = 4] + [Q3 = 4])	11/30	36%
–7	([Q1 = 1] + [Q2 = 6] + [Q3 = 5])	12/30	40%
–8	([Q1 = 5] + [Q2 = 5] + [Q3 = 3])	13/30	50%
–9	([Q1 = 8] + [Q2 = 6] + [Q3 = 8])	22/30	43.3%
10	([Q1 = 3] + [Q2 = 3] + [Q3 = 3])	9/30	30%
11	([Q1 = 5] + [Q2 = 8] + [Q3 = 5])	18/30	60%

For the questions on the post-experiment questionnaire, if a participant gives all correct responses, she obtains 6 points ([Q1 = 1] + [Q2 = 1] + [Q3 = 1] + [Q4 = 0.5 + 0.5] + [Q5 = 0.5 + 0.5] + [Q6 = 1] = 6). Table 6.6 reports the results for each participant.

From the comparisons of the two total score ratios of each participant, we can say that:

- Participant 4 gives excellent responses both to questions asked during the task performance and those on the post-experiment questionnaire.
- Participants 2 and 11 give good responses both to questions asked during the task performance and those on the post-experiment questionnaire.
- Participants 8 and 9 give good responses to questions asked during the task performance but poor responses to those on the post-experiment questionnaire.

Table 6.6. Answers Given on the Post-Experiment Questionnaire

Participants	*Rates*	*Total Score*	*Total Score Ratio %*
1	([Q1 = 1] + [Q2 = 0] + [Q3 = 0] + [Q4 = 0.5 + + 0] + [Q5 = 0 + 0] + [Q6 = 1])	1.5/6	25%
2	([Q1 = 0] + [Q2 = 1] + [Q3 = 0] + [Q4 = 0.5 + + 0] + [Q5 = 0.5 + 0.5] + [Q6 = 1])	3/6	50%
3	([Q1 = 1] + [Q2 = 0] + [Q3 = 0] + [Q4 = 0 + + 0.5] + [Q5 = 0 + 0] + [Q6 = 0])	1.5/6	25%
4	([Q1 = 1] + [Q2 = 0] + [Q3 = 1] + [Q4 = 0.5 + + 0.5] + (Q5 = 0.5 + 0.5] + (Q6 = 1])	5/6	83.3%
5	([Q1 = 0] + [Q2 = 0] + [Q3 = 0] + [Q4 = 0 + + 0] + [Q5 = 0.5 + 0.5] + [Q6 = 0])	1/6	16.6%
6	([Q1 = 0] + [Q2 = 0] + [Q3 = 0] + [Q4 = 0.5 + + 0.5] + [Q5 = 0.5 + 0.5] + [Q6 = 0])	2/6	33.3%
7	([Q1 = 0] + [Q2 = 0] + [Q3 = 1] + [Q4 = 0 + + 0] + [Q5 = 0 + 0] + [Q6 = 1])	2/6	33.3%
8	([Q1 = 1] + [Q2 = 0] + [Q3 = 0] + [Q4 = 0.5 + + 0.5] + [Q5 = 0 + 0] + [Q6 = 0])	2/6	33.3%
9	([Q1 = 1] + [Q2 = 1] + [Q3 = 0] + [Q4 = 0 + + 0] + [Q5 = 0 + 0] + [Q6 = 1)]	2/6	33.3%
10	([Q1 = 0] + [Q2 = 0] + [Q3 = 0] + [Q4 = 0.5 + + 0] + [Q5 = 0 + 0] + (Q6 = 1])	1.5/6	25%
11	*([Q1 = 1] + [Q2 = 0] + [Q3 = 0] + [Q4 = 0.5 + + 0.5] + [Q5 = 0 + 0] + [Q6 = 1])*	*3/6*	*50%*

- Participants 1, 3, 6, 7, and 10 give poor responses both to questions asked during the task performance and those on the post-experiment questionnaire.
- Participant 5 gives really poor responses both to questions asked during the task performance and those on the post-experiment questionnaire.

Participants 7 and 11 choose more cards from advantageous (C + D) than from disadvantageous decks (A + B).[13] Participants 2 and 6 behave more or less in the same manner, although they choose fewer cards from advantageous decks (C + D) than participants 7 and 11 do.[14] And participants 1, 3, 4, 5, 8, 9, and 10 choose more or less the same number of cards from both advantageous (C + D) and disadvantageous decks (A + B).[15]

Principal Component Analysis

As in the first study, in the second I run a component analysis of all of the behavioral and physiological measures taken for each subject, but I choose to report only the results of the behavioral measures (the number of cards chosen from each deck and the reaction times [RTs]).

Thus, I choose to focus on the performances of participant 11 (who gives the *best answers* both to questions asked during the task and on the questionnaire and chooses more cards from advantageous than from disadvantageous decks) and of participant 5 (who gives the *worst answers* both to questions asked during the task and on the questionnaire and chooses more or less the same number of cards from disadvantageous and from advantageous decks). My hypothesis is that there is a different trend in the number of cards chosen from each deck and in the reaction times throughout the task for participants 11 and 5. In other words, from the component analysis I expect to find that participants 11 and 5 tend to load the same component in a completely different fashion.

As table 6.7 shows, for the decks, component 4 is highly loaded by participant 11 (.73) and negatively loaded by participant 5 (-.02). This indicates that participants 5 and 11 behave quite differently throughout the task (in particular, in choosing the cards from advantageous deck C and from the disadvantageous decks).

Rather, as table 6.8 shows, component 1 is highly loaded by participant 11 (V11 = .81) and negatively loaded by participant 5 (V5 = -.245). In fact, as we can see from the following tables, participant 5 tends to take more time in her choices throughout the task than does participant 11 (who shows more or less the same RT throughout the task, except in the first twenty selections, where she takes more time to choose).

Table 6.7. Rotated Component Matrix(a) (DECKS)

	Component				
	1	*2*	*3*	*4*	*5*
1	.774	–.001	.126	–.044	.021
2	–.044	–.756	.151	–.051	.068
3	.489	.456	–.098	–099	–.303
4	.450	.304	.119	–.074	.575
5	–.552	.501	.393	–.016	.086
6	–.125	–.154	.033	–.071	.778
7	–.007	.012	.769	.149	.179
8	–.058	.353	–.585	.045	.080
9	–.332	–.211	–.432	.344	.359
10	.032	.121	.010	–.762	.156
11	.021	.349	.118	.730	.066

Notes: Extraction Method: Principal Component Analysis.
Rotation Method: Varimax with Kaiser Normalization.
A rotation converged in sixteen iterations.

Third Study

For the questions asked throughout the task, if a participant gives all correct responses, she obtains 30 points ([Q1 = 10)] + [Q2 = 10] + [Q3 = 10] = 30). Table 6.9 reports the results for each participant.

Table 6.8. Rotated Component Matrix(a) (RT)

	Component				
	1	*2*	*3*	*4*	*5*
1	–.047	.141	–.143	.033	.806
2	.062	–.182	.269	.648	.387
3	.131	.680	.073	–.144	.308
4	.805	–.049	–.136	.022	.027
5	–.245	–.097	–.667	–.083	.035
6	.196	.445	–.099	.407	–.397
7	.366	.053	.639	.128	–.197
8	.017	–.089	.100	–.738	.101
9	–.118	.678	–.127	.114	–.022
10	.335	.543	.466	–.028	–.106
11	.806	.127	.154	.017	–.085

Notes: Extraction Method: Principal Component Analysis.
Rotation Method: Varimax with Kaiser Normalization.
A rotation converged in nine iterations.

Table 6.9. Answers Given Throughout the Task

Participants	*Rates*	*Total Score*	*Total Score Ratio %*
1	([Q1 = 7] + [Q2 = 7] + [Q3 = 7])	21/30	70%
2	([Q1 = 0] + [Q2 = 0] + [Q3 = 0])	0/30	0%
3	([Q1 = 2] + [Q2 = 6] + [Q3 = 8])	16/30	53.3%
4	([Q1 = 5] + [Q2 = 4] + [Q3 = 3])	12/30	40%
5	([Q1 = 5] + [Q2 = 3] + [Q3 = 3])	11/30	36.6%
6	([Q1 = 9] + [Q2 = 9] + [Q3 = 9])	27/30	90%
7	([Q1 = 1] + [Q2 = 3] + [Q3 = 7])	11/30	36.6%
8	([Q1 = 7] + [Q2 = 6] + [Q3 = 7])	20/30	66.6%
9	([Q1 = 0] + [Q2 = 1] + [Q3 = 2])	3/30	10%
10	([Q1 = 1] + [Q2 = 0] + [Q3 = 0])	1/30	3%
11	([Q1 = 6] + [Q2 = 1] + [Q3 = 2])	9/30	30%

For the questions on the post-experiment questionnaire, if a participant gives all correct responses, she obtains 6 points ([Q1 = 1] + [Q2 = 1] + [Q3 = 1] + [Q4 = 0.5 + 0.5] + [Q5 = 0.5 + 0.5] + [Q6 = 1] = 6). Table 6.10 reports the results for each participant.

From the comparisons of the total score ratios of each participant, we can say that:

- Participants 1, 6, and 8 give excellent responses both to questions asked during the task performance and those on the post-experiment questionnaire.
- Participants 4, 5, 7, and 11 give good responses to questions on the post-experiment questionnaire but poor responses to those asked during the task performance.
- Participant 3 gives good responses to questions asked during the task performance but poor responses to those on the post-experiment questionnaire.
- Participants 2, 9, and 10 give poor responses both to questions asked during the task performance and those on the post-experiment questionnaire.

Participants 3, 4, 6, 7, and 8 choose more cards from advantageous than from disadvantageous decks.[16] And participants 1, 2, 5, 9, 10, and 11 choose more or less the same number of cards from both advantageous and disadvantageous decks.[17]

Table 6.10. Answers Given on the Post-Experiment Questionnaire

Participants	*Rates*	*Total Score*	*Total Score Ratio %*
1	([Q1 = 1] + [Q2 = 1] + [Q3 = 1] + [Q4 = 0.5 + + 0] + [Q5 = 0 + 0] + [Q6 = 1])	4.5/6	75%
2	([Q1 = 0] + [Q2 = 0] + [Q3 = 1] + [Q4 = 0 + + 0] + [Q5 = 0 + 0.5] + [Q6 = 0])	1.5/6	25%
3	([Q1 = 0] + [Q2 = 1] + [Q3 = 0] + [Q4 = 0 + + 0] + [Q5 = 0 + 0] + [Q6 = 0])	1/6	16.6%
4	([Q1 = 1) + [Q2 = 1) + [Q3 = 0) + [Q4 = 0 + + 0) + [Q5 = 0.5 + 0.5) + [Q6 = 0])	3/6	50%
5	([Q1 = 1] + [Q2 = 0] + [Q3 = 0] + [Q4 = 0.5 + + 0.5] + [Q5 = 0.5 + 0.5] + [Q6 = 1])	3/6	50%
6	([Q1 = 1] + [Q2 = 1] + [Q3 = 1] + [Q4 = 0 + + 0] + [Q5 = 0 + 0] + [Q6 = 1])	4/6	66.6%
7	([Q1 = 0] + [Q2 = 1] + [Q3 = 0] + [Q4 = 0.5 + + 0.5] + [Q5 = 0.5 + 0.5] + [Q6 = 1])	4/6	66.6%
8	([Q1 = 0] + [Q2 = 1] + [Q3 = 1] + [Q4 = 0.5 + + 0] + [Q5 = 0.5 + 0] + [Q6 = 1])	4/6	66.6%
9	([Q1 = 0] + [Q2 = 0] + [Q3 = 0] + [Q4 = 0 + + 0] + [Q5 = 0 + 0] + [Q6 = 0])	0/6	0%
10	([Q1 = 0] + [Q2 = 0] + [Q3 = 0] + [Q4 = 0 + + 0.5] + [Q5 = 0 + 0.5] + [Q6 = 0])	0.5/6	8.33%
11	([Q1 = 1] + [Q2 = 1] + [Q3 = 1] + [Q4 = 0.5 + + 0] + [Q5 = 0 + 0] + [Q6 = 1])	3.5/6	58.33%

Principal Component Analysis

As in the first and the second studies, I run a component analysis on all of the behavioral and physiological measures taken for each subject, but I choose to report only the results of behavioral measures (the number of cards chosen from each deck and the reaction times [RTs]).

At this point, I choose to focus on the performances of participant 8 (who gives the *best answers* both to questions asked during the task and on the questionnaire and chooses more cards from advantageous than from disadvantageous decks) and of participant 6 (who gives the *worst answers* both to questions asked during the task and on the questionnaire and chooses more or less the same number of cards from disadvantageous and advantageous decks). My hypothesis is that there is a different trend in the number of cards chosen from each deck and in the reaction times throughout the task for participants 6 and 8. In other words, from the component analysis I expect to

Table 6.11. Rotated Component Matrix(a) (DECKS)

	Component				
	1	*2*	*3*	*4*	*5*
1	.312	.135	.160	.738	.193
2	–.074	–.164	.146	.028	.735
3	–.739	.241	.097	.019	–.156
4	.364	.619	.187	–.053	.085
5	.218	–.613	–.067	–.082	.143
6	.248	.093	.593	–.440	–.039
7	.730	.099	.119	–.002	–.089
8	–.193	–.028	–.094	.742	–.194
9	.125	.165	–.103	–.062	.765
10	–.078	.680	–.429	.008	.128
11	*–.062*	*–.023*	*.828*	*.122*	*.080*

Notes: Extraction Method: Principal Component Analysis.
Rotation Method: Varimax with Kaiser Normalization.
A rotation converged in seven iterations.

find that participants 6 and 8 tend to load the same component in a completely different fashion.

As table 6.11 shows, for the decks, component 5 is highly loaded by participant 9 (.765) and negatively loaded by participant 8 (-.19). This indicates that participants 8 and 9 behave quite differently throughout the task (in particular, in choosing the cards from the advantageous deck C and from the disadvantageous decks).

Table 6.12. Rotated Component Matrix(a) (RT)

	Component				
	1	*2*	*3*	*4*	*5*
1	–.117	.169	–.174	.779	.228
2	.034	–.051	–.775	–.169	.154
3	–.055	.099	.031	.078	.777
4	–.239	.703	–.015	.006	.131
5	–.248	–.461	.205	.268	–.283
6	.717	.076	–.176	.007	–.110
7	.073	–.160	.235	.690	–.128
8	–.041	–.013	.667	–.179	.439
9	.709	–.193	.098	–.070	.130
10	.405	.545	.202	.113	–.144
11	–.339	.474	.092	–.001	–.443

Notes: Extraction Method: Principal Component Analysis.
Rotation Method: Varimax with Kaiser Normalization.
A rotation converged in fifteen iterations.

Rather, as table 6.12 shows, for the RT, the component 1 is highly loaded by participant 9 (= .71) and negatively loaded by participant 8 (-.04). In fact, although participants 8 and 9 tend to take more or less the same time making their choices throughout the task, participant 9 takes more time than participant 8 does in the same phases of the task (for example, from the 10th and 20th and from the 70th and 80th selections).

Comparison among Studies

By considering the results of qualitative analyses of the three studies, I distinguish three different levels of comprehension of the IGT structure both for the questions asked throughout the task and for the questions asked on the post-experiment questionnaire for each participant:

- High Level (H.L.): if a participant gets a score between 100% and 56%.
- Medium Level (M.L.): if a participant gets a score between 55% and 42%.
- Low Level (L.L.): if a participant gets a score between 41% and 0%.

Tables 6.13 and 6.14 report the analysis of the level of comprehension for each study. I consider all of the possible different combinations between the level reached for the questions asked during the task performance and the level reached for the questions asked on the post-experiment questionnaire.

By using the data presented in the previous tables, I perform a number of calculations. First, for each study I calculate the proportion of participants reaching a certain degree (low or high) of comprehension of the IGT by summing up all of the total ratios except that called *L.L. 10 Stops & L.L. Post-Experiment.* That is, for each study I calculate the sum of all of the ratios without L.L. 10 Stops & L.L. Post-Experiment, Σ ([H.L. 10 Stops &

Table 6.13. Level of Comprehension for Each Study (I)

	First Study	*Second Study*	*Third Study*
H.L. 10 Stops & H.L. Post-Experiment	1, 9	4	1, 8, 6
H.L. 10 Stops & M.L. Post-Experiment	None	11	None
H.L. 10 Stops & L.L. Post-Experiment	None	9	None
M.L. 10 Stops & M.L. Post-Experiment	5, 10	2	None
M.L. 10 Stops & H.L. Post-Experiment	None	None	None
M.L. 10 Stops & L.L. Post-Experiment	4, 8	8	3
L.L. 10 Stops & L.L. Post-Experiment	3, 6	1, 3, 5, 6, 7, 10	2, 9, 10
L.L. 10 Stops & H.L. Post-Experiment	11	None	7, 11
L.L. 10 Stops & M.L. Post-Experiment	2, 7	None	4, 5

Table 6.14. Level of Comprehension for Each Study (II)

	First Study (Ratio %)	*Second Study (Ratio %)*	*Third Study (Ratio %)*
H.L. 10 Stops and H.L. Post-Experiment	18.18%	9.1%	27.27%
H.L. 10 Stops and M.L. Post-Experiment	None	9.1%	None
H.L. 10 Stops and L.L. Post-Experiment	None	9.1%	None
M.L. 10 Stops and M.L. Post-Experiment	18.18%	9.1%	None
M.L. 10 Stops and H.L. Post-Experiment	None	None	None
M.L. 10 Stops and L.L. Post-Experiment	18.18%	9.1%	9.1%
L.L. 10 Stops and L.L. Post-Experiment	18.18%	54.5%	27.27%
L.L. 10 Stops and H.L. Post-Experiment	9.1%	None	18.18%
L.L. 10 Stops and M.L. Post-Experiment	18.18%	None	18.18%

H.L. Post-Experiment] + [H.L. 10 Stops & M.L. Post-Experiment] + [H.L. 10 Stops & L.L. Post-Experiment] + [M.L. 10 Stops & M.L. Post-Experiment] + [M.L. 10 Stops & H.L. Post-Experiment] + [M.L. 10 Stops & L.L. Post-Experiment] + [L.L. 10 Stops & H.L. Post-Experiment] + [L.L. 10 Stops & M.L. Post-Experiment]). The results show that 81.82% of participants in the first study, 45.50% of participants in the second study, and 72.73% of participants in the third study reach a certain degree of conscious and explicit knowledge of the IGT.

Second, for each study I calculate the proportion of participants reaching a low level of knowledge of the task by summing up all of the ratios containing at least one L.L. That is, I calculate the sum of all of the ratios with only L.L.s, Σ ([H.L. 10 Stops & L.L. Post-Experiment] + [M.L. 10 Stops & L.L. Post-Experiment] + [L.L. 10 Stops & L.L. Post-Experiment] + [L.L. 10 Stops & H.L. Post-Experiment] + [L.L. 10 Stops & M.L. Post-Experiment]). The results show that 63.64% of participants in the first study, 72.70% of participants in the second study, and 72.72% of participants in the third study reach a low level of conscious and explicit knowledge of the IGT.

Third, for each study, I calculate the proportion of participants reaching a medium-high level of knowledge of the task by summing up all of the ratios not containing any L.L. That is, I calculate the sum of all of the ratios without any L.L., Σ ([H.L. 10 Stops & H.L. Post-Experiment] + [H.L. 10 Stops & M.L. Post-Experiment] + [M.L. 10 Stops & M.L. Post-Experiment] + [M.L. 10 Stops & H.L. Post-Experiment]). The results show that 36.36% of participants in the first study, 27.30% of participants in the second study, and 27.27% of participants in the third study reach a medium-high level of conscious and explicit knowledge of the IGT.

NOTES

1. This means that I will consider the same kinds of measures and observations as Damasio and colleagues.

2. For some general considerations on the methodology and the statistical analyses used in Damasio's studies, see appendix C, section I.

3. For some critical considerations on the methodology and the statistical analyses used to assess the behavioral data in Damasio's studies, see appendix C, section II.

4. Such an analysis is *similar* (but not identical) because the ANOVA run in Bechara et al., 1997 (1295, note 9) is a factorial ANOVA 2 × 2 × 4 with two two-level variables (a between-group variable [groups] and a within-group variable [decks], and a within-group and four-level variable [periods]).

5. In this analysis, I exclude participant 7 because during C she makes her choices only from advantageous decks (C and D). Thus, the ANOVA is run on only 10 participants.

6. In this analysis, I exclude participant 9 because during C she makes her choices only from advantageous decks (C and D). Thus, the ANOVA is run on only 10 participants.

7. For some considerations on the methodology and the statistical analyses used to assess the physiological data in my studies, see appendix C, section III.

8. For some considerations on the methodology used to assess the qualitative data in my studies, see appendix C, section IV.

9. More precisely, participant 1 makes 34% of her choices from decks A + B and 66% from decks C + D, whereas participant 9 makes 25% from decks A + B and 75% from decks C + D.

10. More precisely, participant 11 makes 41% of her choices from decks A + B and 59% from decks C + D.

11. More precisely, participant 3 makes 55% of her choices from decks A + B and 45% from decks C + D.

12. In fact, according to table 6.3, participant 3 chooses more or less the same percentage of cards from all of the decks.

13. More precisely, participant 7 makes 26% of her choices from decks A + B and 74% from decks C + D, whereas participant 11 makes 31% of her choices from decks A + B and 69% from decks C + D.

14. More precisely, participant 2 makes 44% of her choices from decks A + B and 56% from decks C + D, whereas participant 6 makes 42% from decks A + B and 58% from decks C + D.

15. It is worth noting that only participant 3 choose more cards from the disadvantageous (A + B) than from the advantageous decks (C + D).

16. More precisely, participant 3 makes 43% of her choices from decks A + B and 57% from decks C + D, participant 4 makes 38% from decks A + B and 62% from decks C + D, participant 6 makes 17% from decks A + B and 83% from decks C + D, participant 7 makes 41% from decks A + B and 59% from decks C+ D, and participant 8 makes 43% from decks A + B and 57% from decks C + D.

17. However, it is worth noting that participants 2, 5, and 9 choose more cards from disadvantageous (A + B) than from advantageous decks (C + D).

Chapter Seven

Doubts on the Somatic Marker Hypothesis

A FURTHER COMPARISON BETWEEN DAMASIO'S EXPERIMENTS AND MY THREE STUDIES

Although the Somatic Marker Hypothesis (SMH) is based on the distinction between an *unconscious and emotional evaluational system* (via Somatic Markers [SMs]) and a *conscious and rational one* (via overt reasoning), it is clear that it focuses mainly on the features of the former rather than on those of the latter. We can say that Damasio and colleagues' first aim is to provide evidence for justifying the postulation of an unconscious system as necessary for decision making. In this sense, a full justification of this postulation requires that both of these empirical conditions must be satisfied:

1. *Behavioral condition*: Participants[1] at the Iowa Gambling Task (IGT) must make more selections from the advantageous (C and D) than from the disadvantageous (A and B) decks.
2. *Neurophysiological condition*: Participants at the IGT must produce higher anticipatory SCRs before the disadvantageous (A and B) than before the advantageous (C and D) decks.

As we can see, (1) is causally connected to (2): Participants tend to behave advantageously (that is, to make more selections from advantageous decks [C and D]) because of the SMs' activation before the selection of disadvantageous decks (A and B). Thus, only if (1) or (2) were satisfied, the appeal to the SM for explaining the participants' choices at the IGT would not be justified.

It is worth noting that the SMH would be confirmed also in case both conditions (1) and (2) did not apply. That is, if participants tended to choose more or less the same percentage of cards from each deck and, at the same time, they did not produce any anticipatory SCRs, this would mean that they failed to produce any SM and so to express their preference for advantageous decks (C and D). This is because "in the absence of a SM, options and outcomes become virtually equalized and the process of choosing will depend entirely on logic operations over many option-outcome pairs. The strategy is necessary slower and may fail to take into account previous experience" (Damasio 1996, 1415).

It is clear that my data do not support the SMH in any case. In fact, about (1), we can see that my participants neither prefer advantageous decks (C and D) to disadvantageous ones (A and B) nor do they consider all decks as *virtually equalized.* Rather, they express a preference for certain decks but not in the way Damasio and colleagues predicted. In fact, in all three of my studies, participants do not tend to choose advantageous decks (C and D)[2] and avoid disadvantageous ones (A and B).[3]

About (2), two controversial features can be noted in the Damasio and colleagues' experimental methodology. The first is that, in their studies, they use the SCRs as the only physiological measure for the SM. This can be considered a tricky point. In fact, in their exhaustive critical review of the SMH (2006), the psychologists Dunn, Dalgleish, and Lawrence point out that Skin Conductance Response (SCR) is generally not considered to be particularly sensitive in discriminating between a positive and a negative valence (251). For this reason, they argue that such a measure may not be the best physiological index for *detecting* the SM and thus, for better testing the SMH, the detection of other different physiological indexes should be required. By following this suggestion, in my studies I provide an analysis of other measures (BVPs, EMGs, PULSs, TEMPs) as alternatives and in addition to SCRs. However, I do not find any higher anticipatory physiological activation before the choice of disadvantageous (A and B) than before advantageous (C and D) decks.

The second controversial feature is that, probably because of the postulated *anticipatory nature* of the SM, in their studies using the physiological measure (1996, 1997) Damasio and colleagues register only the SCRs produced by participants four to five seconds before the choice of any deck. However, this point seems implicitly to imply that participants should also show a decrease in the SCRs immediately after their choices. More precisely, a significant increase in the SCRs four to five seconds before the selection of a disadvantageous deck (A or B) followed by a significant decrease immediately after this selection is certainly an important proof to validate the SMH. Unfortunately, I have not found any study by Damasio and colleagues or other researchers considering this feature. In my studies, I consider this point and I find a significant increase followed by a significant decrease after the choice only for the PULSs.

As a general conclusion I can say that, according to my data, the SMs cannot be considered to drive the normal participants' behavior at the IGT. Thus, the question is: What can explain it? The answer can be put this way: Although my main aim is to assess the validity of the SMH, in chapter 5 I make a prediction about the number of cards selected throughout the task alternative to that proposed by Damasio and colleagues. That is, I argue that, in all three of my studies, participants would choose more cards from the decks with a high number of reward cards and a low number of reward/punishment cards (B and D) than from the decks with a low number of reward cards and a high number of reward/punishment cards (A and C), setting aside the amount of money they could have won from each deck. I find a confirmation of this prediction in all three of my studies. This could suggest that normal participants' behavior is explainable not because of the SMs that *emotionally mark* those decks that make them lose huge amounts of money in the long term (that is, decks A and B). Rather, it is explainable because participants try to avoid the decks with a high frequency of reward/punishment cards (that is, decks A and C). However, to confirm or disconfirm this hypothesis, other studies are required.

THE CRUCIAL ROLE OF REACTION TIMES AS DEPENDENT BEHAVIORAL MEASURES

In the IGT, participants are presented with four stimuli (the four decks A, B, C, and D), and they must make one hundred selections from them on the basis of their preference. In such a case, the measurement of the RTs does not deal simply with the time between the presentation of a stimulus and the participants' response to it. Rather, the RTs can be said to measure something more complex, that is, the minimum time to respond to a certain stimulus plus the time required to choose a certain stimulus from among the other ones plus the time to make the selection of the stimulus chosen (Uttal 1998, 174; Reber and Reber 2001, 601).

As we can see, the RTs can be used as an indirect measure of the mental processes underlying the choice behavior. For example, if higher RTs were found for a certain deck than for the other ones, this could indicate that participants are trying (perhaps consciously?) to calculate the number of reward/punishment cards present in such a deck or to assess how many selections must be done until they encounter a reward/punishment card. However, it must be said that the RT data coming from my studies are quite difficult to interpret. The main reason for this difficulty is that the differences detected in RTs are circumscribed only to part of the first study's results. More precisely, by considering the four learning periods of the first study, we can see a significant main effect of the variable decks (the RTs for the advantageous decks [C + D] are higher than those for the disadvantageous decks [A + B], [C + D] > [A + B]) and a significant main effect of the variable periods (the RTs are higher in the PP than in the H [PP > H], and the RTs are higher in the PH than in the H [PH > H]). Thus, this means that, if the data are analyzed considering the four learning periods:

(a) Participants take more time to choose the advantageous decks (C + D) than to choose the disadvantageous decks (A + B).
(b) Participants are quicker to make their selections in the H than in the PP and PH ([PP > H] and [PH > H]). However, they take the same time to make their selections in the PP, PH, and C (PP = PH = C) and to make their selections in the H and C (H = C).

Such results can be interpreted to be due to the fact that, in the pre-experimental phase of the first study, participants are not asked explicitly either to develop a play strategy (as in the second study) or to pay attention to their bodily sensations or changes that the decks can induce throughout the task (as in the third study). That is, the fact that in the first study participants do not receive any suggestion about the behavior to assume in the task seems to explain (a) and (b) quite well.

However, I think the empirical evidence at our disposal to support such a conclusion is not sufficient. First, we must consider that there is no difference in the RTs between disadvantageous (A + B) and advantageous decks (C + D) throughout task, that is, not considering the four learning periods. Thus, the results reported in (a) could be an artifact due to the factorial repeated measures analysis of variance run for these data. Second, although (b) is certainly an interesting result, no clear evidence shows that this depends on the absence of any suggestion in the pre-experimental phase. In fact, by comparing the RTs of each period of every study, no differences are found. This seems to suggest that the lack of instructions given in the pre-experimental phase had no effect on the RTs.

THE PHYSIOLOGICAL MEASURES AS THE MAIN WAY TO DETECT THE SOMATIC MARKER

Among the physiological measures in addition to the SCRs, I find some results only for the BVPs, the EMGs, and the PULSs. I will consider each of them.[4]

For the BVP, it is important to say that such a measure is not used extensively in psychophysiological research (Andreassi 2000, 301). So, my considerations cannot rest on a large body of literature. Probably, the most important area of research using the BVP regards the distinction between orienting (OR) and defensive (DR) responses (Hugdahl 1995, 192). Both OR and DR are definable as attentive responses made to a certain stimulus in the environment, but the latter differ from the former because they are usually elicited by stimuli having an inherent emotional valence (Hugdahl 1995, 140; Reber and Reber 2001, 495). The increases in the BVP responses are generally correlated with the OR; the decreases, with the DR. Further, the OR seems to habituate with a continued stimulus's presentation; the DR seem to be immune to this effect (Andreassi 2000, 324).

By following the results of the research on the OR-DR distinction, I can comment on the results of my studies. In my first study, we can see that participants produce higher BVP responses for deck A than for the other decks (B, C, and D) (for BVP After, A > B and A > C and for BVP Before-After, A > B and A > D). This seems to indicate that participants in the first study are more habituated to deck A than to decks B and C. Further, we can see that participants in the first study also show lower levels of BVP responses before the choice of any decks in the PP than in the following learning periods (PH, H, and C). This can indicate that participants habituate to the task's stimuli after the first ten selections. Finally, we can see that, in all conditions considered (Before, After, and Before-After), participants in the second study show lower levels of BVP responses than those in the first and the third study. Such a result could be an effect of the instructions given in the pre-experimental phase to participants of the second study. That is, because in such a phase they are induced to develop a strategy for playing the IGT, these participants seem to be less habituated to the task's stimuli than those in the other two studies. In other words, the development of a play strategy seems to induce the participants in the second study to *fend off* in front of stimuli having an inherent emotional valence (such as the four decks [A, B, C, and D] are).

For the EMG, it must be said that it is generally considered to be the measure of the control of motor behavior because it records the electrical potentials associated with muscular activities (Andreassi 2001, 165). Now, because all participants in my three studies are told to stay as still as possible during the IGT and the task does not necessitate any complex movement to be performed, the increases or decreases in the EMG responses cannot be interpreted as due to differences in the observable movements but rather to other factors. In the third study, a factor influencing the different levels of EMG could be the instructions given in the pre-experimental phase. In fact, in such a study, participants are asked to pay attention to the *bodily signals* induced by the decks throughout the task. Such instructions seem to lead participants to be more controlled before the choice of deck A than before the choice of the other three decks (B, C, and D) and after the choice of any of the four decks (A, B, C, and D). Such an effect of the instructions over the control of motor behavior seems to be confirmed by the fact that participants in the third study show higher levels of muscular contraction than those in the second study.

For the PULS, we can see that participants in all three studies tend to produce higher responses before the selection of any deck than after such a selection. In other words, heartbeats accelerate immediately before any participant makes a choice followed by a deceleration immediately after. In general, PULS acceleration is associated with stimulus rejection and the defensive response (DR) (Andreassi 2000, 285). As we have seen for BVP, a DR is usually elicited by stimuli having an inherent emotional valence, and participants could feel all four decks (A, B, C, and D) (and not only some of them) in this way. This could be due to the fact that all four stimuli contain a certain number of reward/punishment cards. Thus, whichever deck they select, participants expect to choose a reward/punishment card and so to lose a certain amount of money. Such an expectation seems to induce a certain level of arousal (defined as a dimension of activity based on the level of sensory excitability, hormonal levels, and muscular readiness correlated with the acceleration of the PULS) (Öhman et al. 2000, 534–35; Reber and Reber 2001, 51) in participants. However, this arousal dissolves immediately after the selection of a deck (correlated with a deceleration of the heart rates). In this sense, we can say that the participants in all three of the studies show a certain arousal due to the choice they have to make, not to the deck they want to select. It is interesting to note that, for the condition by considering the four learning periods, participants in the first and third studies show a high increase in the PULS responses, especially in PP. This means that, in the first ten selections, participants in the first and third studies show higher levels of arousal than participants in the second study. As for the PULS seen above, such a result could be an effect of the instructions given in the pre-experimental phase to the participants in the second study. That is, because in that phase they are induced to develop a strategy for playing the IGT, these participants seem to be more ready initially to deal with the task than those in the other two studies. However, this does not seem to keep them from having a high level of arousal throughout the task like the participants in the first and third studies.

As we can see, the four decks of IGT are *emotionally laden stimuli* able to elicit physiological responses (like DRs) of a certain sort. However, none of the responses registered in my three studies seems to indicate the presence of a physiological response anticipating (and thus influencing) participants' choices like an SM.

THE EFFICACY OF EXPLICIT THINKING AND REASONING FOR DEALING WITH THE IGT

In Bechara et al. 1997, Damasio and colleagues attempt to integrate three different kinds of data:

1. Behavioral (as in Bechara et al. 1994)
2. Physiological (as in Bechara et al. 1996)
3. Verbal and introspective

The reason for introducing (3) in the 1997 article was due to Damasio and colleagues' attempt to distinguish between the unconscious and emotional system (via SMs) and the conscious and rational one (via overt reasoning) and to show the primacy (and the necessity) of the former over the latter. As I said in chapter 5, the psychologists Maia and McClelland (2004) have argued that (3) is the main problematic and controversial methodological aspect of Bechara et al. 1997, because the two questions used to assess the level of knowledge of the participants are too vague and broad to be understood clearly by participants. Instead of these questions, in their reexamination they use the following questionnaire (16076, fig. 1):

> Q1. Rate, on a scale of –10 to +10, how good or bad you think deck A is, where –10 means that it is terrible and +10 means that is excellent.
>
> Q2. Okay; why did you rate deck B with . . . ?
>
> (Repeat questions Q1 and Q2 for decks B through D.)
>
> Q3. In answering the questions that follow, consider the following definitions. Your "winning amount" for a trial is the amount you won on that trial. Your "loss" on a trial is the amount you lost on that trial. Your "net result" for a trial is the amount you won minus the amount you won minus the amount you lost on that trial. Do you understand these definitions and the differences between the three terms? (If not, explain again using example.)
>
> Okay, now suppose you were to select 10 cards from deck A.
>
> Q3.1. What would you expect your average net result to be?
>
> Q3.2. What would you expect your average winning amount to be?
>
> Q3.3. In how many of the 10 trials would you expect to get a loss (not necessarily a net loss)?
>
> Q3.4. For those trials in which you would get a loss, what would you expect the average loss to be?
>
> (Repeat question Q3 for decks B through D.)
>
> Q4. Okay, now tell me, on a scale of 0 to 100, how much you think that you know what you should do in this game in order to win as much money as possible (or, if you can't win, to avoid losing money as much as possible). 0 means that you have no idea of what you should do and feel that you still need to ex-

plore the game more and 100 means that you know exactly what you should do and have no doubts that that would be the best strategy.

Q5. Now suppose I told you that you could only select cards from one of the decks until the end of the game, but that you were allowed to choose now the deck from which you would draw your cards. Which of the four decks would you pick?

Such a questionnaire is submitted to the participants following the same procedure presented in Bechara et al. 1997 (1293), that is, after the first twenty selections and then every ten selections made. Maia and McClelland define it as a *test of awareness* because it permits us to identify the three levels of *conscious knowledge* (verbally reportable knowledge about the IGT) (16076):

- Level 0. Participants do not have any conscious knowledge specifying a preference for one of the two advantageous decks (C and D).
- Level 1. Participants have conscious knowledge specifying a preference for one of the two advantageous decks (C and D), but they do not have any conscious knowledge about the outcomes of the decks that could provide a basis for such a preference.
- Level 2. Participants have conscious knowledge specifying a preference for one of the two advantageous decks (C and D) and they have conscious knowledge about the outcomes of the decks that could provide a basis for such a preference.

Their results show that, in virtually all cases, normal participants reach Level 1 when they behave advantageously (that is, when they choose decks C and D). Further, in a large number of cases, participants also reach Level 2 when they behave advantageously. In summary, every time participants choose cards from the advantageous decks, they seem to possess conscious and verbally reportable knowledge regarding the task that can provide a basis for their behavior (16075). Thus, Maia and McClelland conclude that these data do not support the SMH. In fact, why do we need to attribute a priority to the unconscious and emotional evaluational system when it is clear that participants have both a "conscious access to the relative goodness or badness of the decks, and . . . an explicit, reportable knowledge that could provide the basis for such judgment and behaviour" (16078)? In other words, Maia and McClelland's results cast doubts upon the validity of one of the core notions of the SMH: the distinction between the two evaluational systems and the primacy of the unconscious over the conscious one.

Beyond the validity of their results, it is worth noting that Maia and McClelland's criticisms of Damasio and colleagues' results touch on an important methodological issue. In fact, they point out that their introspective (or at least *subjective* and *qualitative*)[5] methods do not appear to be sufficiently powerful to uncover all knowledge that participants have about the IGT and the mental processes they use to solve it (16075).

I completely agree with this point, and in chapter 5 I argued the reasons why, in my opinion, Damasio and colleagues do not consider the introspective reports to be *scientifically reliable*. Nonetheless, I think that Maia and McClelland's study can be criticized for two reasons. First, it is a very partial replication of Damasio and colleagues' 1997 experiment: In fact, it does not consider the VMPF patients' performance[6] or the physiological measures (Bechara et al. 2005, 160). Second, in my opinion, the questionnaire they use is very articulated and takes a lot of time to be answered at each ten-card interval. For these reasons, in my studies I take five different physiological measures (SCRs included), I ask only three brief questions (as opposed to those of Damasio and colleagues) at each ten-card interval, and I submit a questionnaire to the participants at the end of the experiment.

In spite of these criticisms and the differences between Maia and McClelland and my studies,[7] I think that my results can be considered quite compatible with theirs. Specifically, they support Maia and McClelland's conclusion according to which it is not possible to establish which are the best and the worst decks a priori. This is because "each participant has nothing but his or her own experience to go by (during the IGT), so we follow the general practice . . . in considering advantageous behavior to be behavior that follows the net outcomes experienced up until the trial in which a decision is being made" (Maia and McClelland 2004, 16076). This means that the definition of *advantageous* or *disadvantageous deck* cannot be a priori established because any deck, in a certain moment of the game, could be advantageous or disadvantageous. Such a conclusion seems to be supported by my behavioral and subjective data. In fact, my participants appear to consider advantageous a deck more on the basis of its frequency distribution of reward and reward/punishment cards than on the basis of the amount of money it can make them win or lose. In this sense, deck B does not seem to be disadvantageous for my participants, at least not in the way Damasio and colleagues assumed.

If we look at the verbal reports, we can see that many participants correctly recognize the features of such a deck-stimulus, but their evaluation of its *being advantageous (or disadvantageous)* does not seem to depend only upon such features but also upon other factors related to the participant's subjective point of view (such as her feelings, expectations, beliefs, motivations, kinds of reasoning, play strategies used, etc.). Further, the verbal reports of my participants seem to indicate—in accordance with Maia and McClelland (2004, supporting text) and against Damasio and colleagues (Bechara et al.

1997) (that, all along IGT, knowledge is not progressive but rather revisable and changeable). For example, in certain situations, both my participants and Maia and McClelland's participants seem to possess the right hunch but then wrongly revise it, or understand everything about the task but then go back to believe something wrong or to be uncertain about what they learn.

Another point to note about my qualitative analyses is that the first study has more participants reaching both a minimum and a medium-high level of conscious knowledge about the IGT than the second and third studies. The second study has more participants reaching a low level of knowledge than the first and third studies. These results are quite surprising and counterintuitive, because one could think that the additional instructions given in the second and third studies should serve as a motivation for acquiring a certain conscious knowledge of the IGT.

A possible explanation of these results could be that the additional instructions given in the second and third studies could influence participants' verbal reports of what they learn. That is, instead of simply reporting about the IGT structure and what they learn (as participants in the first study do), participants in the second and third studies tend to talk about the play strategy they use to solve the task or about the sensations they feel before the decks. These details about the play strategy and their feelings seem to lead participants to make many mistakes responding to the questions they have to face. It is worth noting that this does not mean that they do not learn anything about the task: It simply means that the instructions seem to undermine the clarity and correctness of their responses.

CONCLUDING REMARKS

An important point emerging from Maia and McClelland's article and my studies is that, for dealing with IGT, participants appeal to many cognitive abilities pertaining to the conscious and rational evaluational system (such as reasoning, mathematical skills, and so on) starting from the first phases of the game. In this sense, it is not clear if the IGT is the best task to test the SMH.[8] This is because it requires managing many variables whose weight appears to be very difficult to discern.[9] Thus, also in case of positive detection of an SM (as in Damasio and colleagues' studies), it remains controversial whether the SMH can be considered to be able to give an exhaustive account of a complex activity such as decision making. Such a controversial point can be seen as strictly connected to the methodological choices Damasio and colleagues made. That is, the *objective methods* he assumes to be decisive appear to be quite inadequate to explain decision-making behavior if taken alone and seem to necessitate an integration with the *verbal introspective (subjective and qualitative) ones*. This indicates that subjectivity plays a crucial role in the IGT and thus it requires well-developed and proper methods to be evaluated seriously.

NOTES

1. It does not matter if they belong to a clinical or a (healthy) control group.
2. In fact, C is selected as well as all of the other decks (A, B, and D), and D is selected more only than deck A in each study.
3. In fact, A is less selected more only than deck D in each study and deck B is selected more only than deck A in the second and third studies.
4. Before proceeding with the discussion, it is important to note that some of the results here discussed regard the distinction in four learning periods. As I said above, such a distinction seems to be more controversial than it appears at first. In my opinion, it has two main problems. The first deals with the disproportion in the number of cards selected from each deck in every learning period present in Bechara et al. 1997. I discuss this point and I propose a way to solve it in chapter 6 of this book. The second deals with the reliability of self-account verbal reports Damasio and colleagues used along with the behavioral and physiological measures for making the distinction. As I said in chapter 5, the psychologists Maia and McClelland (2004) criticize the use of these reports made by Damasio and colleagues' in their work and, in a replication study, they find that normal participants possess much more conscious and explicit knowledge in the first phases of the task (that is, in PP and PH) than Damasio and colleagues' results suggest. I agree with their criticisms, and in the next section I will examine more closely the relevance of the self-account verbal reports for the IGT and the SMH. In this section, I want to point out that, in spite of its problems, the distinction in four learning periods as proposed in Bechara et al. 1997 (1294, note 1), can be useful because it allows us to examine the participants' performance and physiological activity in different moments of the task. In other words, such a distinction permits us to assess the temporal factor in the IGT.
5. I here refer to those methods based on verbal reporting.
6. Of course, this is a limitation of my studies too.
7. It is important to stress that Maia and McClelland's data are quantitative and thus provide an objective/third-person measure of the degree of knowledge of the participants at the IGT. Rather, my verbal reports' data are qualitative (although they can be prepared to be used quantitatively). This is certainly a serious limitation of my studies.
8. In this sense, it seems that the IGT could work better as a test to assess conscious reasoning than to evaluate unconscious reasoning.
9. It can be said that the virtues of the IGT (its being inartificial and lifelike in comparison with most of the neuropsychological tests [Damasio 1994, 12]) are probably what increase its number of variables to the detriment of the experimental control.

Chapter Eight

Concluding Considerations

In the first four chapters of this book I described and discussed four different notions of mind on which the so-called *mental terms* (such as memory, learning, knowledge, and perception) can be interpreted. In other words, these terms can be defined:

(a) *Mentalistically*, in the sense proposed in chapter 1. Thus, *mental terms here refer to properties and features of the conscious mind.*
(b) *Antimentalistically*, in the sense proposed in chapter 2. Thus, *mental terms here refer to concrete and observable experimental operations.*
(c) *Mentalistically*, in the sense proposed in chapter 3. Thus, *mental terms here refer to properties and features of the unconscious mind.*
(d) *Antimentalistically*, in the sense proposed in chapter 4. Thus, *mental terms here refer to cerebral and physiological functions.*

In the last four chapters I presented a conceptual and empirical reexamination of the SMH the neurologist Damasio and his colleagues proposed. As I said in chapter 5, I have chosen to deal with it because it touches most of the theoretical and methodological issues seen in the first part. In fact, although Damasio and coworkers emphasize the neurobiological details of the SMH, it is clear that their theory is formulated in psychological terms. Thus, the question is: How can this mentalistic vocabulary be interpreted on the basis of the four different notions listed above?

Let us start by considering the term unconscious (or nonconscious) as an example to analyze this point. Such a term is very important in the SMH because "in normal individuals, non-conscious biases guide behaviour before conscious knowledge does. Without the help of such biases, overt knowledge may be insufficient to ensure advantageous behaviour" (Bechara et al.

1997, 1293). I think the notion of nonconscious used here has nothing of the mentalistic or antimentalistic in the way indicated above. In this quotation, Damasio and colleagues simply say that SMs are not felt consciously by normal participants at the IGT, but they are only detectable through measuring SCRs. I think that is not controversial. However, in the SMH, we can find another use of this notion when we argue that an SM is acquired through the processes of memory and learning (Tranel and Damasio 1996, 125; Bechara and Damasio 2005, 351).

Such processes are said to be unconscious because, at least during the first half of the IGT, participants do not seem to be able to report verbally either how they use them in the task or the contents they acquire through them. That is, participants (unconsciously) acquire a certain amount of (implicit) knowledge that produces adequate SMs driving them to avoid the disadvantageous options (decks A and B) and to choose the advantageous ones (decks C and D). Thus, the notion of unconscious seems to be used mentalistically here, that is, to indicate the postulation of terms such as knowledge, memory, and learning. In other words, these terms seem to be defined as in (c).

However, it is rather controversial if Damasio and colleagues conceive the notion of unconscious in this way. In their studies, they tend to use the mental terms to refer to the functions of certain cerebral areas or physiological processes. This is quite clear when they describe the decision-making process on the basis of SMH. They argue that a situation that requires making a decision activates *two different (parallel but interacting) chains of events*. In the former, the sensory representation of the situation itself (or the facts evoked by it) activates neural systems holding *non-declarative dispositional knowledge* related to the person's previous emotional experience of similar situations. The ventro-medial prefrontal cortex (VMPC) is among the structures holding such a dispositional knowledge, the activation of which, in turn, activates autonomic and neurotransmitter nuclei, among other regions. The ensuing nonconscious bodily signals then act as covert biases upon the cerebral circuits supporting the processes of cognitive evaluation and reasoning. In the latter chain of events, the representation of a certain decision-making situation generates the overt recall of pertinent facts (for example, different options and outcomes pertaining to a certain course of action) and the application of reasoning strategies to these facts and options (Bechara et al. 1997, 1294).

In brief, Damasio and coworkers argue for the existence of a dissociation between a specific neural system for the *non-declarative dispositional knowledge* responsible for the SMs (in other words, the *unconscious and emotional evaluational system*) and other (unspecified here) nervous system areas devoted to the *overt reasoning* and to the *declarative (or conscious) knowledge* (in other words, the *conscious and rational evaluational system*) (1293). As we can see, Damasio and colleagues seem to use the *principle of localization of (mental) functions* (interpreted both narrowly and broadly) discussed in chapter 4. For this reason, their position about the definition of mental terms seems to be that presented in (d).

It is important to stress that, although the acceptance of this position does not imply per se the dismissal of the introspective reports as a reliable method of inquiry, it can lead researchers to underestimate them or, at worst, to consider them *unscientific* or *lacking scientificity*. In fact, once an identity relation is postulated between a certain mental state and a certain neurophysiological state, why should we look for something more than the observation of certain behaviors and the detection of certain nervous system activities? In chapter 4, I expressed my doubts about the theoretical plausibility of (d); and in chapters 5, 6, 7, and 8, I proposed a test of its empirical validity by replicating Damasio and colleague's studies using the IGT. It must be said that my studies are not an exact replication of their work, because I considered only samples of normal participants and not of VMPC patients. Of course, this is clearly an important limitation of my work. However, also notice that many of Damasio and colleagues' inferences and conclusions from his studies are based on the results of the control groups composed of normal participants.[1] For this reason, I think that a reexamination of Damasio and colleagues' studies focusing only on normal participants should provide some interesting information.

In chapters 6 and 7, I noted that my behavioral and physiological data do not replicate those of Damasio and colleagues. More precisely, my participants neither express a preference for the advantageous decks C and D (thus, they do not behave advantageously in the way Damasio and colleagues postulated) nor produce high anticipatory SCRs before the choice of the disadvantageous decks A and B (thus, no SM has been detected). In this sense, my results allow us to reject the hypothesis that the SM is the "major factor in the interaction between environmental conditions and human decision processes" (Bechara and Damasio 2005, 368).

It is worth noting that the SMH is based on a general (and rather vague, in my opinion) claim according to which a certain number of physiological or neural variables play a causal role in participants' choices. Thus, in spite of the falsification of the SMH, someone could still point out that we can detect such variables and relate them to participants' behavior. For example, among my results, I find that all participants tend to choose many more cards from the decks with a high number of reward cards and a low number of reward/punishment cards (B and D) than from the decks with a low number of reward cards and a high number of rewards/punishment cards (A and C). Now, if they had produced higher *anticipatory SCRs* (or other physiological responses) before the latter cards than before the former, I could have found empirical support to assume that some physiological or neural variables play a causal role in participants' behavior. However, none of my physiological data seem to support such a conclusion. Thus, lacking detection of any difference in the physiological activation among the four decks of the IGT, my participants' preference for certain decks does not seem to be explainable by assuming that memory, knowledge, or other mental terms refer to certain neural or physiological variables (d).

Thus, to what do these terms refer? We have three options at our disposal: (a), (b), and (c). Let us start with (b) and (c). The problem of defining the mental terms according to (b) or (c) can be seen as a variant of the old dispute between supporters of the intervening variables and supporters of the hypothetical constructs discussed in chapter 2. If we choose (b), all mental terms postulated for explaining the behavioral performances at IGT must be defined operationally. This means that such terms must be related precisely and objectively to the procedures of the experimental setting and to the behavior directly observable resulting from such procedures. For example, an operational definition of the term *learning* can be the following: "a relatively permanent change in response potentiality which occurs as a result of reinforced practice" (Reber and Reber 2001, 390). Such a definition seems to apply quite well in the explanation of my behavioral data. In fact, because the IGT's stimuli (decks A, B, C, and D) provide schedules of reinforcement and reinforcement-punishment, participants show *a certain change in their response potentiality*, that is, they make more selections from decks B and D (containing few reward-punishment cards) than from decks A and C (containing many reward-punishment cards). In other words, the IGT participants make more selections from the *reinforcing decks* than from the *reinforcing/punishing ones*.

As we can see, to define the term learning we do not need to appeal to mental states or to theoretical entities of any sort but only to observable events (Lehaey 1992, 324–25; Lundin 1996, 7). This means that a definition of mental terms according to (b) does not allow psychologists to make any abstract inference from their experiments. I think that this is not a bad thing per se because it can put some healthy limitations on psychologists' theories and inferences. However, as I said in chapter 2, it is worth noting that many mental terms seem to resist a full operational characterization, because they appear to carry a surplus meaning irreducible to a limited number of observable events (MacCorquodale and Meehl 1948, 104; Marx 1963, 42; Lehaey 1992, 385–86; Reber and Reber 2001, 486). In this sense, in reference to the IGT studies, terms such as memory and knowledge do not appear to be as easy to operationalize as learning.

For example, it is clear that some participants *know* that the number of rewards/punishment cards in deck C is lower than in deck A and they also *remember* that they have encountered a big loss of money from deck B when they have chosen it at a certain moment. Now, how can we define *knowing* and *remembering* in terms of observable operations by maintaining all of their meaning? Further, even if someone provided such operational reductions, the need to limit psychology's subject matter only to the things that have an empirical reference is not clear (Schultz and Schultz 1996, 287). As we saw in chapter 3, the appeal to memory and knowledge to explain and describe participants' behavior at the IGT appears to be reasonable and legitimate without defining such terms according to (b).

It is easy to see how (c) can avoid the difficulties of (b). In fact, because the mental terms refer to theoretical entities, psychologists are allowed to make abstract inferences from their experiments and so they can legitimately postulate *real mental factors as causally relevant for the behavior*. For example, to give an account of my participants' behavioral performances at the IGT, I can appeal to memory defined as the mental process of retaining information about stimuli, ideas, images, and so forth after all of these things are no longer present (Reber and Reber 2001, 423). In this sense, I can explain why participants choose few cards from decks A and C: After a certain number of selections (and of trial-and-errors), they have acquired the information that these decks make them lose many times. Thus, in such a view, the memory process and the information acquired through it have to be considered as important causal factors in the participants' preference for decks B and D.

In my opinion, compared to (b) and (d) (the two antimentalistic views), (c) has the advantage of proposing an objective/third-person psychology without limiting it only to the things that have a concrete (operational or physiological) reference. This means that, according to (c), psychology can be said to be an autonomous discipline, with mind as its proper subject matter. However, it is worth noting that the mentalism proposed in (c) has a lot in common with the antimentalism proposed in (b). In fact, the observation of behavior and the rebuttal of the first-person perspective are central features of both (b) and (c).

In chapter 3, we saw that the refusal of the subjective view leads us to assume that mind (or, at least, most of it) must be considered unconscious. In other words, according to (c), all mental processes and states are supposed to be inaccessible to (any form of) introspection (Crane 2003, 213). This means that memory, attention, emotion, and all mental entities we can postulate to explain my participants' behavior at the IGT must be considered to be unconscious in principle (in this sense, they are similar to the entities postulated according to (d), with the crucial difference that they do not have a physiological or cerebral reference).

This is certainly quite an odd and counterintuitive conclusion, especially if we think that participants' verbal reports can give some important clues about the mental processes they use to perform the task. In fact, as I pointed out in chapters 6 and 7, the results of my qualitative analyses seem to give some indications that participants possess a certain amount of reliable *conscious knowledge* they use during the task to solve it.Thus, it seems possible to infer from these data that participants can use certain mental processes consciously and also be aware of the contents they deal with. However, it must be said that, in spite of their informativeness, my results show a lack of reliability because of their qualitative nature. In fact, the data coming from the questions asked during the IGT and the questionnaire completed at its end are quite raw, and they must be cleaned up to be treated quantitatively. In other words, they can be assessed only by considering each participant individually and not all of the participants together. In summary, in such a form, these data do not seem to be generalizable in any way and they do not appear to provide a solid empirical ground to test psychological theories.

Nonetheless, this can be seen as a methodological limitation of my work but it does not lead to dismissing the self-account reports as a method for studying the mental per se. As argued clearly by the psychologist Ericsson and the economist Simon in their seminal book *Protocol Analysis. Verbal Reports as Data* (1985), "a single invalid verbal report should not force us to discard analysis of verbal reports generally" (9).

According to them, verbal reports can be considered as a kind of behavior that can be recorded and observed like any other kind of behavior and used to test psychological theories (2). Their accuracy and reliability depend on the procedures used to collect and analyze them (27). To do this work, throughout their book Ericsson and Simon propose an articulated methodology for individuating and avoiding the common risks coming from the subjective data (for example, at page 20, they describe the possible errors implicit in the comprehension of *the why-questions* [such as *why did you buy this book?*] by the participants and how they can influence their responses) and for dealing with them in an objective/third-person way (for a detailed account on this point, see 261–373). It is important to note that Ericsson and Simon's proposal finds its foundations in a defined information-processing model composed of different parts (a recognition memory, a long-term memory, a short-term memory, an attention process, a fixation process and an automation process) (13–15) typical of cognitive psychology's research.

For Ericsson and Simon, such a model must be considered a necessary framework either for interpreting the verbal data obtained from experimental participants and for relating them to other kinds of behavior (10). Leaving aside the details of their model, it seems clear that Ericsson and Simon do not conceive its different cognitive processes to be unconscious in principle. Rather, deciding whether a certain mental process or content is unconscious seem to be an empirical question that can be answered only by appealing to different types of verbalizing procedures (109–68). However, accepting verbal reports as a reliable source of data implies accepting that we have access (or at least a certain degree of access that can be assessed through research) to our mental processes and contents: In other words, that we are able to introspect (Locke 2009, 24–25). This means that dismissing a priori the possibility of defining the mental terms as in (a) seems to be unfounded.

In conclusion, *what consequences can be drawn from my analysis of the mentalism versus antimentalism debate?* I believe I see two. The first can appear quite trivial, but I am sure it is not: There is no room for an antimentalistic psychology of any sort. In this work I hope to have been able to show that the mental appears to be difficult to reduce to something different from it and that such an irreducibility does not preclude the construction of a rigorous and sound scientific psychology in any way. Because of my adherence to such a position, when I have exposed some arguments in chapters 4 and 5 on the occasion of conferences and workshops, I have been criticized for being unsympathetic to CN and unable to see the important results this enterprise reached. This is patently false. In fact, the target of my criticisms is not CN per se but the (more or less explicit) reductionistic outlook assumed by many (most?) of its practitioners and supporters. Personally, I think that assuming this outlook can lead to confusions and misunderstandings[2] in the interpretation of the experimental data and thus obscure rather than clarify the relationships between mind and the nervous system.

Second, I want to stress is that if we accept mentalism in psychology, we must apply ourselves to provide a more adequate and precise[3] definition and description of the mental and its properties and of the methods for dealing with it. I believe this task is more or less the same as the task of explication the philosopher Carnap discusses brilliantly in chapter 1 of his 1950 book. Very briefly, this task is to transform more or less inexact and undefined concepts (the *explicanda*) into more exact and defined ones (the *explicata*) that can fulfill the conditions of similarity to the explicanda: exactness, fruitfulness, and simplicity (Carnap 1950, 3–8). In this sense, I think that the most urgent problem to face is to give a substantial theoretical revision (and thus an explication) of the distinction between conscious and unconscious mind discussed in chapter 3 by taking seriously our ability to introspect and to consciously determine our behavior.

In my opinion this is a very big challenge, because it could put into question the ideal of a completely naturalized and physicalistic psychology, which for same people simply means to *abandon science*. I think that such a risk must be run because the game is worth it. In fact, the game we are here to play is to understand, paraphrasing the title of a famous Cole Porter song, *what is this thing called mind.*

NOTES

1. About this point, it is important to remember that the number of VMPCs tested by Damasio and colleagues in Bechara et al. 1994, Bechara et al. 1996, and Bechara et al. 1997 is quite limited (according to my calculations, only nine participants). For a discussion of the composition and the peculiarities of Damasio and colleagues' and my experimental groups, see chapter 5 of this book and Appendix C.
2. For an exhaustive discussion of the misinterpretations of neuroscientists and an interesting (perhaps controversial) proposal of foundation for an antireductionistic CN, see Bennett and Hacker 2003.
3. I mean a definition that can be shared among most researchers.

Appendix A

Instructions for Participants

- Instructions for subject (original instructions)[1]

1. In front of you on the screen are four decks of cards: A, B, C, and D.
2. When we begin the game, I want you to select one card at a time by clicking on a card from any deck you choose.
3. Each time you select a card, the computer will tell you that you won some money. I don't know how much money you will win. You will find out as we go along. Every time you win, the green bar gets bigger.
4. Every so often, when you click on a card, the computer will tell you that you won some money as usual, but then it will say that you lost some money as well. I don't know when you will lose or how much. You will find out as we go along. Every time you lose, the green bar gets smaller.
5. You are absolutely free to switch from one deck to the other at any time, and as often as you wish.
6. The goal of the game is to win as much money as possible and avoid losing as much money as possible.
7. You won't know when the game will end. Simply keep on playing until the computer stops.
8. I am going to give you $2,000 credit, the green bar, to start the game. The red bar is a reminder of how much money you have to pay back before we see whether you won or lost.
9. The only hint I can give you, and the most important thing to note, is this: Out of these four decks of cards, some are worse than others, and to win you should try to stay away from bad decks. No matter how much you find yourself losing, you can still win the game if you avoid the worst decks.

10. Also note that the computer does not change the order of the cards once the game begins. It does not make you lose at random, or make you lose money based on the last card you picked.

- Istruzioni per il partecipante (first study)

1. Grazie per aver accettato di partecipare a questa ricerca. La prova che ti propongo è un gioco d'azzardo da svolgere al computer. All'inizio del gioco ti è data la somma virtuale di 2.000 dollari che può aumentare o diminuire secondo i guadagni e le perdite cui andrai incontro voltando delle carte.
2. Sullo schermo di fronte a te ci sono 4 mazzi di carte: A, B, C e D.
3. Seleziona una carta alla volta cliccando sul mazzo che preferisci. Dopo ogni selezione attendi che sullo schermo compaia la scritta "Scegli una carta" con la quale ti viene dato il permesso di continuare.
4. Ogni volta che selezionerai una carta il computer ti dirà che hai vinto dei soldi. Ogni volta che vinci la barra verde aumenta di lunghezza.
5. Può capitare che, quando cliccherai su una carta, il computer, oltre a dirti che hai vinto dei soldi, ti dica anche che ne hai perduti una parte. Ogni volta che perdi la barra verde diminuirà di lunghezza.
6. Sei assolutamente libero di passare da un mazzo all'altro in qualsiasi momento e ogni volta che desideri.
7. *Lo scopo del gioco è vincere quanto più denaro possibile e cercare di perderne il meno possibile.*
8. Gioca fino a quando il programma non si fermerà automaticamente. In genere la partita dura circa mezz'ora/quaranta minuti.
9. Ora ti mostrerò come funziona il gioco con una breve simulazione.

- Istruzioni per il partecipante (second study)

1. Grazie per aver accettato di partecipare a questa ricerca. La prova che ti propongo è un gioco d'azzardo da svolgere al computer. All'inizio del gioco ti è data la somma virtuale di 2.000 dollari che può aumentare o diminuire secondo i guadagni e le perdite cui andrai incontro voltando delle carte.
2. Sullo schermo di fronte a te ci sono 4 mazzi di carte: A, B, C e D.
3. Seleziona una carta alla volta cliccando sul mazzo che preferisci. Dopo ogni selezione attendi che sullo schermo compaia la scritta "Scegli una carta" con la quale ti viene dato il permesso di continuare.
4. Ogni volta che selezionerai una carta il computer ti dirà che hai vinto dei soldi. Ogni volta che vinci la barra verde aumenta di lunghezza.

5. Può capitare che, quando cliccherai su una carta, il computer, oltre a dirti che hai vinto dei soldi, ti dica anche che ne hai perduti una parte. Ogni volta che perdi la barra verde diminuirà di lunghezza.
6. Sei assolutamente libero di passare da un mazzo all'altro in qualsiasi momento e ogni volta che desideri.
7. *Lo scopo del gioco è vincere quanto più denaro possibile e cercare di perderne il meno possibile. Per questo, nel corso del gioco, cerca di elaborare una strategia che ti permetta di raggiungere questo scopo.*
8. Gioca fino a quando il programma non si fermerà automaticamente. In genere la partita dura circa mezz'ora/quaranta minuti.
9. Ora ti mostrerò come funziona il gioco con una breve simulazione.

- Istruzioni per il partecipante (third study)

1. Grazie per aver accettato di partecipare a questa ricerca. La prova che ti propongo è un gioco d'azzardo da svolgere al computer. All'inizio del gioco ti è data la somma virtuale di 2.000 dollari che può aumentare o diminuire secondo i guadagni e le perdite cui andrai incontro voltando delle carte.
2. Sullo schermo di fronte a te ci sono 4 mazzi di carte: A, B, C e D.
3. Seleziona una carta alla volta cliccando sul mazzo che preferisci. Dopo ogni selezione attendi che sullo schermo compaia la scritta "Scegli una carta" con la quale ti viene dato il permesso di continuare.
4. Ogni volta che selezionerai una carta il computer ti dirà che hai vinto dei soldi. Ogni volta che vinci la barra verde aumenta di lunghezza.
5. Può capitare che, quando cliccherai su una carta, il computer, oltre a dirti che hai vinto dei soldi, ti dica anche che ne hai perduti una parte. Ogni volta che perdi la barra verde diminuirà di lunghezza.
6. Sei assolutamente libero di passare da un mazzo all'altro in qualsiasi momento e ogni volta che desideri.
7. Lo scopo del gioco è vincere quanto più denaro possibile e cercare di perderne il meno possibile.
8. *Ti chiedo inoltre di cercare di fare attenzione alle tue sensazioni corporee: per esempio, cerca di contare l'aumento o la diminuzione dei battiti cardiaci e di osservare se succede qualcosa nel tuo corpo che tu puoi rilevare (aumento della sudorazione) mentre scegli un mazzo piuttosto che un altro.*
9. Gioca fino a quando il programma non si fermerà automaticamente. In genere la partita dura circa mezz'ora/quaranta minuti.
10. Ora ti mostrerò come funziona il gioco con una breve simulazione.

NOTE

1. Professor Antoine Bechara sent me these instructions along with the IGT version for Windows XP Professional.

Appendix B

Experimenter's Sheet and Post-Experiment Questionnaire

- Experimenter's Sheet (with the questions to ask during the task)
  Data Esperimento, .../.../...
  Sigla partecipante:
  Età:
  Genere: M F
  Nazionalità:
  Occupazione:
  Se studente, indicare presso quale scuola o facoltà:
  Disposizione mazzi

A = 100 120 80–150 ...	B = 100 80 110 ...
C = 50 60 40–50 ...	D = 50 40 45 ...

Domande e risposte dopo ogni 10 selezioni

1. Secondo te, ci sono differenze tra i mazzi? Se sì, quali sono le differenze che hai trovato?
   Stop 10
   Stop 20
   Stop 30
   Stop 40
   Stop 50
   Stop 60
   Stop 70
   Stop 80
   Stop 90
   Stop 100
2. Quale è il mazzo o i mazzi che preferisci? Perché?
   Stop 10
   Stop 20
   Stop 30
   Stop 40
   Stop 50
   Stop 60
   Stop 70
   Stop 80
   Stop 90
   Stop 100
3. Se ti dicessi che da qui fino alla fine del gioco devi scegliere le carte da un solo mazzo, quale sceglieresti e perché?
   Stop 10
   Stop 20
   Stop 30
   Stop 40
   Stop 50
   Stop 60
   Stop 70
   Stop 80
   Stop 90
   Stop 100

Post-Experiment Questionnaire

1. Secondo te ci sono differenze tra i mazzi?
   Sì
   No

Se hai risposto di no, passa alla domanda successiva. Se hai risposto di sì, quali sono le differenze che hai trovato?

____

____

____

____

2. C'è un mazzo o ci sono dei mazzi che preferisci rispetto agli altri?
   Sì
   No
   Se hai risposto di no, passa alla domanda successiva. Se hai risposto di sì, qual è il mazzo o quali sono i mazzi che preferisci? E perché?

____

____

____

____

3. Assegna a ciascun mazzo un punteggio da 0 a 10 a seconda di quanto lo ritieni vantaggioso ai fini del gioco (0 = per niente vantaggioso, 10 = massimamente vantaggioso)
   A = B = C = D =

4a. Considera le somme vinte e le perdite ottenute nel corso del gioco. Pensa a quante volte si guadagna (ossia aumenta la somma che avevi all'inizio del gioco) con il mazzo A e il mazzo B nel corso del gioco. Quali tra le seguenti affermazioni ti sembra la più corretta?
   (1) con il mazzo A si guadagna circa tante volte quante con il mazzo B
   (2) con il mazzo A si guadagna circa la metà delle volte rispetto al mazzo B
   (3) con il mazzo B si guadagna circa la metà delle volte rispetto al mazzo A
   (4) con il mazzo A si guadagna circa un quarto delle volte rispetto al mazzo B
   (5) con il mazzo B si guadagna circa un quarto delle volte rispetto al mazzo A

4b. Considera le somme vinte e le perdite ottenute nel corso del gioco. Pensa a quante volte si guadagna (ossia aumenta la somma che avevi all'inizio del gioco) con il mazzo C e il mazzo D nel corso del gioco. Quali tra le seguenti affermazioni ti sembra la più corretta?
   (1) con il mazzo C si guadagna circa tante volte quante con il mazzo D
   (2) con il mazzo C si guadagna circa la metà delle volte rispetto al mazzo D

(3) con il mazzo D si guadagna circa la metà delle volte rispetto al mazzo C
(4) con il mazzo C si guadagna circa un quarto delle volte rispetto al mazzo D
(5) con il mazzo D si guadagna circa un quarto delle volte rispetto al mazzo C

5a. Considera le somme vinte e le perdite ottenute nel corso del gioco. Pensa a quanti soldi si guadagnano (ossia aumentano la somma che avevi all'inizio del gioco) con il mazzo A e il mazzo B nel corso del gioco. Quali tra le seguenti affermazioni ti sembra la più corretta?
(1) con il mazzo A si guadagnano circa tanti soldi quanti con il mazzo B
(2) con il mazzo A si guadagnano circa la metà dei soldi rispetto al mazzo B
(3) con il mazzo B si guadagnano circa la metà dei soldi rispetto al mazzo A
(4) con il mazzo A si guadagnano circa un quarto dei soldi rispetto al mazzo B
(5) con il mazzo B si guadagnano circa un quarto dei soldi rispetto al mazzo A

5b. Considera le somme vinte e le perdite ottenute nel corso del gioco. Pensa a quanti soldi si guadagnano (ossia aumentano la somma che avevi all'inizio del gioco) con il mazzo C e il mazzo D nel corso del gioco. Quali tra le seguenti affermazioni ti sembra la più corretta?
(1) con il mazzo C si guadagnano circa tanti soldi quanti con il mazzo D
(2) con il mazzo C si guadagnano circa la metà dei soldi rispetto al mazzo D
(3) con il mazzo D si guadagnano circa la metà dei soldi rispetto al mazzo C
(4) con il mazzo C si guadagnano circa un quarto dei soldi rispetto al mazzo D
(5) con il mazzo D si guadagnano circa un quarto dei soldi rispetto al mazzo C

6. Durante il gioco, ritieni di avere usato una o più strategie? Prova a descriverla o a descriverle.

____

____

____

____

Ritieni che la strategia o le strategie che hai utilizzato siano state efficaci ai fini del gioco? Spiega perché.

____

____

____

____

Appendix C

Considerations on Methodology and Statistics

Here I will make some critical considerations about the methodology and the statistical analyses Damasio and colleagues used in their studies.

SECTION I—GENERAL CONSIDERATIONS

As I have already pointed out above, Damasio and colleagues report and discuss the empirical evidence in favor of the SMH in three articles: Bechara et al. 1994, Bechara et al. 1996, and Bechara et al. 1997. They use the IGT as a test of the participants' performances. Each article can be described as follows:

- Bechara et al. 1994 considers only a behavioral measure, to say, the number of cards selected from each deck (A, B, C, and D) throughout one hundred selections. It reports the results of a two-way repeated measures analysis of variance (ANOVA 2 × 4) with a two-level between-group variable (groups) and a four-level within-group variable (decks) (10-3).
- Bechara et al. 1996 considers only a physiological measure, that is, the SCRs generated before selecting a card from a given deck (216). It reports the results of a two-way repeated measures analysis of variance (ANOVA 2 × 4) with a two-level between-group variable (groups) and a four-level within-group variable (decks) (221-22).
- Bechara et al. 1997 considers the same behavioral measure as the 1994 article and the same physiological measure as the 1996 article. However, differently from these two articles, it does not consider participants' performance at the task throughout one hundred selections. Rather, it considers the number of cards selected from the so-called *advantageous decks* (C +

D) and from the so-called *disadvantageous decks* (A + B) in four different periods of the task. These periods are assessed on the basis of the answers given to the questions asked during the task (Bechara et al. 1997, 1294, fig. 1) and for this reason they are called *learning periods*:

- Pre-punishment (PP), ranging from the first to the tenth selection, where participants do not express any knowledge of how IGT works.
- Pre-hunch (PH), ranging from the eleventh to the fiftieth selection, where participants do not express any knowledge of how IGT works.
- Hunch (H), ranging from the fifty-first to the eightieth selection, where participants report some preference for certain decks (saying that they *like* or *dislike* certain decks) and try to guess which decks are risky or safe, but are not sure of their answers.
- Conceptual (C), ranging from the eighty-first to the one-hundredth selection, where participants are able to accurately report how IGT works and report which decks are advantageous and which not.

Bechara et al. 1997 reports the results of a three-way repeated measures analysis of variance (ANOVA 2 × 2 × 4) with two two-level variables (a between-group variable [groups] and a within-group variable [decks]) and a four-level and within-group variable (periods) for both the number of cards chosen and the SCRs (1295, notes 9 and 10).

If we consider only the results of the control group, we can see that:

- In Bechara et al. 1994:
  - Deck A is less selected than decks C and D (A < [C = D]) and as well as deck B (A = B).
  - Deck B is less selected than decks C and D (B < [C = D]) and as well as deck A (B = A).
  - Deck C is more selected than decks A and B (C > [A = B]) and as well as deck D (C = D).
  - Deck D is more selected than decks A and B (D > [A = B]) and as well as deck C (D = C).

Although this is not reported in Damasio and colleagues' article, it is clear that, if we take together the advantageous (C + D) and the disadvantageous decks (A + B), the former are statistically significantly selected more than the latter ([C + D] > [A + B]). As we can see, their results are very clear-cut: Throughout one hundred selections, normal controls express a preference for the advantageous decks (C and D, taken both together and separately) and avoid disadvantageous decks (A and B, taken together and separately).

- In Bechara et al. 1996:
  - The *anticipatory SCRs* for deck A are higher than those for decks C and D (A > [C = D]) and as well as those for deck B (A = B).
  - The *anticipatory SCRs* for deck B are higher than those for decks C and D (B > [C = D]) and as well as those for deck A (B = A).
  - The *anticipatory SCRs* for deck C are lower than those for decks A and B (C < [A = B]) and as well as those for deck D (C = D).
  - The *anticipatory SCRs* for deck D are lower than those for decks A and B (D < [A = B]) and as well as those for deck C (D = C).

Although this is not reported in Damasio and colleagues' article, it is clear that, if we take together the anticipatory SCRs for the disadvantageous decks (A + B) and those for the advantageous decks (C + D), the former are statistically significantly higher than the latter ([A + B] > [C + D]).

- In Bechara et al. 1997:
  - For the behavioral dependent variable (the number of cards selected):
    - The PP and PH show no significant difference between the number of selections made from the disadvantageous decks (A + B) and those made from the advantageous decks (C + D).[1]
    - The H and C show a significant difference between the number of selections made from the advantageous decks (C + D) and that from the disadvantageous decks (A + B) ([C + D] > [A + B]) (1295, note 9).
  - For the physiological dependent variable (the SCRs):
    - In the PP the anticipatory SCRs associated with the advantageous (C + D) or disadvantageous decks (A + B) are not different[2] (1294, fig. 1).
    - In the PH, H, and C the anticipatory SCRs for the disadvantageous decks (A + B) are higher than those for the advantageous decks (C + D).[3]

As we can see, the results reached in the 1997 article confirm those reached in the 1994 and 1996 articles.

In my study, I tried to run the same analyses used by Bechara et al. 1994 and Bechara et al. 1997 for the behavioral measure and those used by Bechara et al. 1996 in Bechara et al. 1997 for the physiological measure. However, when I tried to follow the analysis of the behavioral measure as proposed in Bechara et al. 1997, I found some methodological difficulties. In fact, as I pointed out above, in their article, Damasio and colleagues consider the numbers of selections from the advantageous (C + D) and from the disadvantageous decks (A + B) as subdivided in four learning periods:

PP: from 1 to 10 (so, Σ [A + B] + [C + D] = 10).
PH: from 11 to 50 (so, Σ [A + B] + [C + D] = 40).
H: from 51 to 80 (so, Σ [A + B] + [C + D] = 30).
C: from 81 to 100 (so, Σ [A + B] + [C + D] = 20).

This means that the number of cards participants can choose in each period is different. In fact, it is higher in the PH (forty selections) and lower in PP period (ten selections). More exactly, the number of selections at their disposal in each period is so distributed: PH > H > C > PP. For this reason, it would be better not to compare the raw data from each period because the number of cards that can be selected in each period depends on the *period size* (simply because it is different for each period). However, in spite of this problem, Damasio and colleagues compare the raw data from each period through a three-way analysis of variance (ANOVA) with two two-level variables (decks and groups) and a four-level variable (periods) (Bechara et al. 1997, 1294, fig. 1, and 1295, note 8). In my opinion, before running a repeated measures analysis of variance (ANOVA) considering the four learning periods, the raw data of each period need to be treated. More exactly, the calculus of means for each period is required, that is, to divide the sum of disadvantageous and advantageous decks for the period size:

PP: Σ (A + B) + (C + D)/10
PH: Σ (A + B) + (C + D)/40
H: Σ (A + B) + (C + D)/30
C): Σ (A + B) + (C + D)/20[4]

SECTION II—SOME CONSIDERATIONS ON THE METHODOLOGY AND STATISTICAL ANALYSES USED TO ASSESS THE BEHAVIORAL DATA IN DAMASIO'S STUDIES

Quite curiously, in none of the three articles here considered do Damasio and colleagues report having compared the total number of cards chosen from disadvantageous (A + B) and from advantageous (C + D) decks throughout task:

- Bechara et al. 1994 (10–13) compares the number of selections made from each deck (A, B, C, and D) throughout the task and the difference in the total number of selections made from the disadvantageous decks (A and B) minus the total number of selections from the advantageous decks (C and D) obtained from all of their experimental groups.

- Bechara et al. 1996 (221) considers only the anticipatory SCRs for each deck (A, B, C, and D) and does not report any data about the number of cards chosen by participants.
- Bechara et al. 1997 (1295, note 9) compares the number of cards chosen from disadvantageous (A + B) and advantageous (C + D) decks as subdivided in the four learning periods and not throughout the task.

For this reason, in all three of my studies, I perform such an analysis and I run a one-way repeated measures analysis of variance (ANOVA) with a two-level variable (decks [advantageous decks and disadvantageous decks]). I also run an one-way analysis of variance (ANOVA) with a two-level variable (decks) for the number of cards chosen from the low punishing (A + C) and the high punishing decks (B + D) throughout the task. Further, as I pointed out above, I consider reaction times (RTs) as a further behavioral measure and I run a one-way repeated measures analysis of variance (ANOVA) with a four-level variable (decks) and a factorial repeated measures analysis of variance (ANOVA 2 × 4) with a two-level variable (decks) and a four-level variable (periods).

Finally, I report some comparative analyses among the results of the three studies. Because the experimental structure and the measures considered in the three studies are the same and the only difference between them relies on certain points of the instructions, my aim is to assess whether these changes can be related to differences in the measures considered. To compare the number of cards chosen from the decks in the three studies, I consider the number of cards chosen in each study one-by-one (A, B, C, and D) and the number of cards chosen in each study according to the distinction between disadvantageous (A + B) and advantageous (C + D) decks. I run a one-way repeated measures analysis of variance (ANOVA) with a three-level variable (study) for each of the four decks (A, B, C, and D) and I run a one-way analysis of variance (ANOVA) with a three-level variable (study) for disadvantageous (A + B) and advantageous (C + D) decks.[5] Then, I compare the mean number of cards chosen in the three studies by considering the distinction in four learning periods proposed in Bechara et al. 1997. For such a comparison, the considerations made in chapter 6 apply here. Thus, I run a one-way analysis of variance (ANOVA) with a two-level variable (decks) for each learning period and a one-way analysis of variance (ANOVA) with a four-level variable (decks) for each learning period. Finally, I compare the number of cards chosen in each study by considering the distinction between high-punishing (A + C) and low-punishing (B + D) decks. Thus, I run a one-way repeated measures analysis of variance (ANOVA) with a three-level variable (study) for high-punishing (A + C) and low-punishing (B + D) decks.

To compare the RT in the three studies, I run a factorial repeated measures analysis of variance (ANOVA 3 × 4) with a three-level variable (study) and a four-level variable (decks) and a one-way repeated measures analysis of variance (ANOVA) with a three-level variable (study) for each learning period.[6]

SECTION III—SOME CONSIDERATIONS ON THE METHODOLOGY AND THE STATISTICAL ANALYSES USED TO ASSESS THE PHYSIOLOGICAL DATA IN MY STUDIES

As I said above, in my studies I consider a certain number of physiological measures in addition to the (supposed) *anticipatory SCRs* (or *before SCRs*) proposed in Damasio and colleagues' studies. I assess all of these measures not only before the participants' choice of a deck, as Damasio and coworkers do, but also after the participants' choice of a deck. In other words, for every measure, I consider a *before period* and an *after period*. As I said in chapter 5, this is to evaluate whether the emotional signals produced by participants' bodies could have not only an anticipatory value (as Damasio and colleagues postulated), but could be an effect of the detection of a certain stimulus.

In all three of my studies, the statistical model used for each physiological measure is the one-way repeated measures analysis of variance (ANOVA) with a four-level variable (decks). Further, I compare the before and the after period of each physiological measure through a factorial repeated measures analysis of variance (ANOVA 2 × 4) with a two-level variable (time) and a four-level variable (decks) as a statistical model. Finally, as well as for the behavioral measures presented above, I consider the four learning periods proposed in Bechara et al. 1997 as a repeated measures independent variable for all physiological measures. Thus, for each measure taken I run a factorial repeated measures analysis of variance (ANOVA 2 × 4) with a two-level variable (decks) and a four-level variable (periods).

In addition to behavioral measures, I report some comparative analyses among the results of the three studies. To compare all physiological measures before and after in the three studies I run a factorial repeated measures analysis of variance (ANOVA 3 × 4) with a three-level variable (study) and a four-level variable (decks). For the before-after measures I run a factorial repeated measures analysis of variance (ANOVA 2 × 3 × 4) with a two-level variable (time), a three-level variable (study), and a four-level variable (decks).[7]

Because of the many statistical analyses run, I choose to report here only the significant results. I believe this allows a clear picture of my results.

However, by introducing the results of every study, I will specify for which physiological measures I have not found any significant effect.

SECTION IV—SOME CONSIDERATIONS ON THE METHODOLOGY USED TO ASSESS THE QUALITATIVE DATA IN MY STUDIES

As I said above, in my studies I also assess how participants of the three studies explicitly reason and think during the IGT. Such an assessment is divided into two parts for each study: The first shows the results of a qualitative analysis dealing with the responses individual participants give to the questions asked when they are performing the task (they are stopped at each ten-card turn) and to those presented in the post-experiment questionnaire. The second shows the results of a component analysis comparing the participants' performances during the IGT among them and thus trying to infer communalities and differences. At the end of this assessment, I propose a comparison of results of the qualitative analyses of the three studies.

As I pointed out above, for each response given to the questions asked during the task and to those presented in the post-experiment questionnaire, I assign a score of 1 for a correct response and 0 for an incorrect response. This is the value of all responses except those given to questions 4 and 5 of the post-experiment questionnaire. Because both these questions are divided into two sub-questions, I assign each sub-response a score of 0,5 for a correct response and of 0 for an incorrect response. As we can see, the scores are ordered on a nominal scale because they are assigned on the basis of a dichotomic dependent variable (where 0 = incorrect and 0.5 and 1 = correct). For this reason (and because I do not apply any validation procedure either for the questions asked during the task performance or for the post-experiment questionnaire), I do not calculate a mean and I do not apply any statistical model on these data. Thus, such data must be considered as qualitative.

NOTES

1. It is important to note that, at a mere descriptive level, in the PP the number of selections made from disadvantageous decks (A + B) is more than that from advantageous decks (C + D) and in the PH the number of selections made from advantageous decks (C + D) is more than that from disadvantageous decks (A + B) (Bechara et al. 1997, 1294, fig. 1).

2. At a mere descriptive level, the SCRs for disadvantageous decks are reported to be higher than those for advantageous decks.

3. It is worth noting that, also in this case, this is exactly true only at a mere descriptive level. In fact, in note 8 at page 1295, Damasio and colleagues point out that "there was a significant increase in the magnitude of the SCRs during the Pre-Hunch Period . . . ($p < 0.01$)." However,

"although SCRs from the disadvantageous decks during the hunch or the conceptual period were generally (that is to say, at a mere descriptive level) higher than those from the advantageous decks, the difference did not reach statistical significance. However, Newman-Keuls tests comparing SCRs from the Hunch or the Conceptual Period to those from the pre-punishment period revealed significant differences in the case of the disadvantageous decks ($p < 0.01$) but not the advantageous decks. This suggests that SCR activity was sustained in the case of the disadvantageous decks, but may have been subsiding in the case of the advantageous decks."

4. It is worth noting that the sum of disadvantageous and advantageous decks (Σ [A + B] + [C + D]) will be equal to the period size whatever value (A + B) or (C + D) will have. This is because (A + B) and (C + D) are, respectively, the frequencies of disadvantageous decks and those of advantageous decks and the period size is the sum of those frequencies:

PP: $\Sigma (A + B) + (C + D)/10 = 10/10 = 1$
PH: $\Sigma (A + B) + (C + D)/40 = 40/40 = 1$
H: $\Sigma (A + B) + (C + D)/30 = 30/30 = 1$
C: $\Sigma (A + B) + (C + D)/20 = 20/20 = 1$

I cannot compare the means of different periods through a repeated measures analysis of variance (ANOVA). This is because the ratio of the sum of disadvantageous and advantageous decks (Σ [A + B] + [C + D]) to the period size is 1 for each period. That is, with respect to such a ratio, PP = PH = H = C. Thus, it is not possible to compare the number of cards selected from advantageous to disadvantageous decks among the four learning periods.

5. I cannot run a factorial repeated measures analysis of variance (ANOVA 3 x 4) with a three-level variable (study) and a four-level variable (decks) because:

First Study: $\Sigma (A + B + C + D)/10 = 1$
Second Study: $\Sigma (A + B + C + D)/10 = 1$
Third Study: $\Sigma (A + B + C + D)/10 = 1$

In other words, the comparison among the mean number of cards chosen in the three studies with a repeated measures analysis of variance (ANOVA) is not allowed because the ratio of the sum of all decks of each study is 1. That is, with respect to such a ratio, First Study = Second Study = Third Study. It is worth noting that this problem would be the same if we did not consider the ratios but rather the *rough number* of cards chosen from each deck. In fact:

First Study: $\Sigma (A + B + C + D) = 100$
Second Study: $\Sigma (A + B + C + D) = 100$
Third Study: $\Sigma (A + B + C + D) = 100$

The same considerations apply if we want to consider the distinction between disadvantageous (A+B) and advantageous decks (C+D). In fact:

First Study:	Σ ([A + B] + [C + D])/10 = 1 or Σ ([A + B] + [C + D]) = 100
Second Study:	Σ ([A + B] + [C + D])/10 = 1 or Σ ([A + B] + [C + D]) = 100
Third Study:	Σ ([A + B] + [C + D])/10 = 1 or Σ ([A + B] + [C + D]) = 100

6. In this sense, I choose to not perform the statistical analyses by considering the four learning periods as a further independent variable for the RT. That is, I do not run a factorial repeated measures analysis (ANOVA 3 × 4 × 4) with a three-level variable (study) and two four-level variables (decks and periods). In fact, I think that, because of the few number of participants for each study (n1 = 11, n2 = 11, n3 = 11), the introduction of a further four-level variable (periods) could compromise its statistical power and lead to a Type II Error. That is, it could lead to accepting the null hypothesis H0 when the alternative hypothesis H1 is true. In other words, such an error occurs when we believe there is no effect in the population when, in reality, there is (Piccolo 1998, 614–15; Ercolani et al. 2002b, 74 and 77; Field 2005, 748).

7. I choose to not perform the statistical analyses by considering the four learning periods as a further independent variable for all physiological measures for the same reasons exposed previously. Thus, I do not run a factorial repeated measures analysis (ANOVA 2 x 3 x 4 x 4) with a two-level variable (time), a three-level variable (study), and two four-level variables (decks and periods).

References

Achinstein, Peter. 1999. "Observation and Theory." In *A Companion to the Philosophy of Science*, edited by William H. Newton-Smith, 325–34. Oxford: Blackwell.

Amundson, Ron. 1983. "E. C. Tolman and the Intervening Variable: A Study in the Epistemological History of Psychology." *Philosophy of Science* 50: 268–82.

———. 1986. "The Unknown Epistemology of E. C. Tolman." *British Journal of Psychology* 77: 525–31.

Andreassi, John L. 2000. *Psychophysiology. Human Behaviour and Physiological Response*. Mahwah, NJ: Lawrence Erlbaum.

Baars, Bernard J., and Katherine McGovern. 1996. "Cognitive Views of Consciousness: What are the Facts? How Can We Think about Them?" In *The Science of Consciousness: Psychological, Neuropsychological and Clinical Reviews*, edited by Max Velmans, 63–94. London: Routledge.

Benjafield, John G. 1996. *A History of Psychology*. Boston: Allyn and Bacon.

Bechara, Antoine, and Antonio R. Damasio. 2005. "The Somatic Marker Hypothesis: A Neural Theory of Economic Decision." *Games and Economic Behaviour* 52: 336–72.

Bechara, Antoine, Antonio R. Damasio, Hanna Damasio, and Steven W. Anderson. 1994. "Insensitivity to Future Consequences Following Damage to Human Prefrontal Cortex." *Cognition* 50: 7–15.

Bechara, Antoine, Hanna Damasio, Daniel Tranel, and Antonio R. Damasio. 1997. "Deciding Advantageously Before Knowing the Advantageous Strategy." *Science* 275: 1293–94.

———. 2005. "The Iowa Gambling Task and the Somatic Marker Hypothesis: Some Questions and Answers." *Trends in Cognitive Sciences* 9: 159–62.

Bechara, Antoine, Daniel Tranel, Hanna Damasio, and Antonio R. Damasio. 1996. "Failure to Respond Autonomically to Anticipated Future Outcomes Following Damage to Prefrontal Cortex." *Cerebral Cortex* 6: 215–25.

Bechtel, William. 2005. "The Challenge of Characterizing Operations in the Mechanisms Underlying Behavior." *Journal of the Experimental Analysis of Behavior* 84: 313–25.

———. 2008. *Mental Mechanisms: Philosophical Perspectives on Cognitive Neuroscience*. London: Routledge.

———. 2010. "How Can Philosophy Be a True Cognitive Science Discipline?" *Topics in Cognitive Science* 2: 357–66.

Bechtel, William, and Robert N. McCauley. 1999. "Heuristic Identity Theory (or Back to the Future): The Mind-Body Problem against the Background of Research Strategies in Cognitive Neuroscience." In *Proceedings of the Twenty-First meeting of the Cognitive Science Society*, edited by M. Hanh and S. C. Stones, 67–72. Mahwah, NJ: Lawrence Erlbaum.

Bechtel, William, and Jennifer Mundale. 1999. "Multiple Realizability Revisited: Linking Cognitive and Neural States." *Philosophy of Science* 66: 175–207.

Bennett, Maxwell R., and Peter M. S. Hacker. 2003. *Philosophical Foundations of Neuroscience*. Oxford: Blackwell.

Bickle, John. 2006. "Multiple Realizability." *The Stanford Encyclopedia of Philosophy*. http://plato.stanford.edu/entries/multiple-realizability/.

Bickle, John, Peter Mandik, and Anthony Landreth. 2010. "The Philosophy of Neuroscience." *The Stanford Encyclopedia of Philosophy*. http://plato.stanford.edu/entries/neuroscience/.

Bird, Alexander. 1998. *Philosophy of Science*. London: UCL Press.

Blumenthal, Arthur L. 1975. "A Reappraisal of Wilhelm Wundt." *American Psychologist* 30; 1081–88.

Boring, Edwin G. 1929. *A History of Experimental Psychology*. Oxford: Appleton-Century.

Brandimonte, Maria A., Nicola Bruno, and Simona Collina. 2006. "Cognition." In *Psychological Concepts. An International Historical Perspective*, edited by Kurt Pawlik and Géry d'Ydewalle, 11–26. New York: Psychology Press.

Bruner, Jerome S. 1992. "Another Look at New Look 1." *American Psychologist* 47(6): 780–83.

Carnap, Rudolf. 1950. *Logical Foundations of Probability*. London: Routledge and Kegan Paul.

Castiglioni, Marco, and Antonella Corradini. 2011. *Modelli Epistemologici in Psicologia* (Epistemological models in psychology). Roma: Carocci.

Chalmers, David J. 2004. "How Can We Construct a Science of Consciousness?" In *The Cognitive Neuroscience*, 3rd ed., edited by Michael S. Gazzaniga, 1111–20. Cambridge: MIT Press.

Cohen, Neal J., and Larry R. Squire. 1980. "Preserved Learning and Retention of Pattern Analyzing Skill in Amnesia: Dissociation of Knowing How and Knowing That." *Science* 210: 207–9.

Colburn, Timothy R. 2000. *Philosophy and Computer Science*. London: M. E. Sharpe.

Coltheart, Max. 2006. "What Has Functional Neuroimaging Told Us about the Mind (So Far)?" *Cortex* 42(3): 323–31.

Crane, Tim. 2001. *Elements of Mind: An Introduction to the Philosophy of Mind*. Oxford: Oxford University Press.

———. 2003. *The Mechanical Mind. A Philosophical Introduction to Minds, Machines and Mental Representation*, 2nd ed. London: Routledge.

Damasio, Antonio R. 1994. *Descartes' Error: Emotion, Reason, and the Human Brain.* New York: Putnam.

———. 1996. "The Somatic Marker Hypothesis and the Possible Functions of the Prefrontal Cortex." *Proceedings of the Royal Society* 351: 1413–20.

———. 1999. *The Feeling of What Happens: Body and Emotion in the Making of Consciousness.* New York: Harcourt Brace.

Damasio, Hanna, and Antonio R. Damasio. 1989. *Lesion Analysis in Neuropsychology.* Oxford: Oxford University Press.

Danziger, Kurt. 1990. *Constructing the Subject: Historical Origins of Psychological Research.* Cambridge: Cambridge University Press.

Davies, Martin. 2005. "An Approach to Cognitive Science." In *The Oxford Handbook of Contemporary Analytic Philosophy*, edited by F. Jackson and M. Smith, 358–94. Oxford: Oxford University Press.

Dennett, Daniel C. 2009. "The Part of Cognitive Science that is Philosophy." *Topics in Cognitive Science* 1: 231–36.

Dienes, Zoltan, and Perner Josef. 2002. "A Theory of the Implicit Nature of Implicit Learning." In *Implicit Learning and Consciousness: An Empirical, Philosophical, and Computational Consensus in the Making*, edited by R. M. French and Axel Cleeremans, 68–92. Hove: Psychology Press.

Dijksterhuis, Ap, Henk Aarts, and Pamela K. Smith. 2005. "The Power of the Subliminal: Perception and Possible Applications." In *The New Unconscious*, edited by Ran R. Hassin, James S. Uleman, and John A. Bargh, 77–106. Oxford: Oxford University Press.

Dunn, Barnaby D., Tim Dalgleish, and Andrew D. Lawrence. 2006. "The Somatic Marker Hypothesis: A Critical Evaluation." *Neuroscience and Biobehavioral Reviews* 30: 239–71.

Ercolani, Anna P., Alessandra Areni, and Luigi Leone. 2002a. *Statistica per la Psicologia. I. Fondamenti di psicometria e statistica descrittiva* (Statistics for psychologists. I. Foundations of psychometrics and descriptive statistics). Bologna: Il Mulino.

———. 2002b. *Statistica per la Psicologia. II. Statistica Inferenziale e Analisi dei Dati* (Statistics for psychologists. II. Inferential statistics and data analysis). Bologna: Il Mulino.

Ericsson, K. Anders, and Herbert A. Simon. 1980. "Verbal Reports as Data." *Psychological Review* 87: 215–51.

———. 1985. *Protocol Analysis: Verbal Reports as Data.* Cambridge: MIT Press.

Field, Andy P. 2005. *Discovering Statistics Using SPSS.* London: Sage Publications.

Fodor, Jerry A. 1968a. *Psychological Explanation.* New York: Random House.

———. 1968b. "The Appeal to Tacit Knowledge in Psychological Explanation." *The Journal of Philosophy* 65(20): 627–40.

———. 1981. "The Mind-Body Problem." *Scientific American* 244(1): 114–23.

———. 2001. *The Mind Doesn't Work This Way: The Scope and Limits of Computational Psychology.* Cambridge: MIT Press.

Frensch, Peter A., and Rünger, Dennis. 2003. "Implicit Learning." *Current Directions in Psychological Science* 12(1): 13–18.

Gaillard, Vinciane, Muriel Vandenberghe, Arnaud Destrebecqz, and Axel Cleeremans. 2006. “First and Third-Person Approaches in Implicit Learning Research.” *Consciousness and Cognition* 15: 709–22.

Gaj, Nicolò. 2016. *Unity and Fragmentation in Psychology: An Overview of the Philosophical and Methodological Roots of the Discipline*. New York: Psychology Press.

Gale, Richard M. 1997. “John Dewey’s Naturalization of William James.” In *The Cambridge Companion to William James*, edited by Ruth A. Putnam, 49–68. Cambridge: Cambridge University Press.

Gardner, Howard. 1985. *The Mind’s New Science. A History of Cognitive Revolution*. New York: Basic Books.

Gigerenzer, Gerd, Peter M. Todd, and the ABC Research Group. 1999. *Simple Heuristics That Make Us Smart*. Oxford: Oxford University Press.

Goodale, Melvyn A., and A. David Milner. 1992. “Separate Visual Pathways for Perception and Action.” In *Human Cognitive Neuropsychology. A Textbook with Readings*, edited by Andrew W. Ellis and Andrew W. Young, 395–407. Hove: Psychology Press, 1996.

———. 2004. *Sight Unseen: An Exploration of Conscious and Unconscious Vision*. Oxford: Oxford University Press.

Goodman, Russell. 2013. “William James.” *The Stanford Encyclopedia of Philosophy*. http://plato.stanford.edu/entries/james/.

Gozzano, Simone. 2007. *Pensieri Materiali* (Material thoughts). Turin: Utet.

Graham, Graham. 2015. “Behaviourism.” *The Stanford Encyclopedia of Philosophy*. http://plato.stanford.edu/entries/behaviorism/.

Gray, Jeffrey A. 1971. “The Mind-Brain Identity Theory as a Scientific Hypothesis.” *Philosophical Quarterly* 21(84): 247–54.

———. 2004. *Consciousness: Creeping Up on the Hard Problem*. Oxford: Oxford University Press.

Greenwald, Anthony G. 1992. “New Look 3: Unconscious Cognition Reclaimed.” *American Psychologist* 47(6): 766–79.

Greenwood, John D. 1999. “Understanding the ‘Cognitive Revolution’ in Psychology.” *Journal of the History of the Behavioral Sciences* 35(1): 1–22.

Hardcastle, Valerie G., and C. Matthew Stewart. 2005. “Localization in the Brain and Other Illusions.” In *Cognition and the Brain: the Philosophy and Neuroscience Movement*, edited by Andrew Brook and Kathleen Akins, 27–39. Cambridge: Cambridge University Press.

Hatfield, Gary. 1997. “Wundt and Psychology as Science: Disciplinary Transformations.” *Perspectives on Science* 5: 349–82.

———. 2002. “Psychology, Philosophy, and Cognitive Science: Reflections on the History and Philosophy of Experimental Psychology.” *Mind and Language* 17: 207–32.

Heidelberger, Michael. 2003. “The Mind-Body Problem in the Origin of Logical Empiricism: Herbert Feigl and Psychophysical Parallelism.” In *Logical Empiricism. Historical and Contemporary Perspective*, edited by Paolo Parrini, Wesley C. Salmon, and Merrilee H. Salmon, 233–62. Pittsburgh: University of Pittsburgh Press.

Hempel, Carl G. 1935. "The Logical Analysis of Psychology." In *Selected Philosophical Essays*, edited by Richard Jeffrey, 165–80. Cambridge: Cambridge University Press.

———. 1952. *Fundamentals of Concept Formation in Empirical Science*. Chicago: University of Chicago Press.

———. 1958. "The Theoretician's Dilemma: A Study." In *Minnesota Studies in the Philosophy of Science, vol. 2. Concepts, Theories, and the Mind-Body Problem*, edited by Herbert Feigl, Michael Scriven, and Grover Maxwell, 37–98. Minneapolis: University of Minnesota Press.

———. 1965. "Aspects of Scientific Explanation." In *Aspects of Scientific Explanation and Other Essays in Philosophy of Science*, 331–496. New York: Free Press.

Henson, Richard N. A. 2005. "What Can Functional Imaging Tell the Experimental Psychologist?" *Quarterly Journal of Experimental Psychology* 58: 193–233.

———. 2006. "What Has (Neuro)Psychology Told Us About the Mind (So Far)? A Reply to Coltheart (2006)." *Cortex* 42(3): 387–92.

Hilgard, Ernest R. 1958. "Intervening Variables, Hypothetical Constructs, Parameters, and Constants." *The American Journal of Psychology* 71(1): 238–46.

Hooker, Clifford A. 1999. "The Unity of Science." In *A Companion to the Philosophy of Science*, edited by William H. Newton-Smith, 540–49. Oxford: Blackwell.

Hugdahl, Kenneth. 1995. *Psychophysiology. The Mind-Body Perspective*. Harvard: Harvard University Press.

James, William. 1890/1918. *The Principles of Psychology*, vols. 1 and 2. New York: Dover Publications.

Johnson-Laird, Philip N. 1980. *Mental Models*. Harvard: Harvard University Press.

———. 2006. *How We Reason*. Oxford: Oxford University Press.

Käufer, Stephan, and Anthony Chemero. 2015. *Phenomenology. An Introduction*. Cambridge: Polity Press.

Kelly, Thomas. 2014. "Evidence." *The Stanford Encyclopedia of Philosophy*. http://plato.stanford.edu/entries/evidence/.

Kihlstrom, John F. 1987. "The Cognitive Unconscious." *Science* 237: 1445–52.

———. 1999. "Conscious and Unconscious Cognition." In *The Nature of Cognition*, edited by Robert J. Sternberg, 173–204. Boston: MIT Press.

Kim, Alan. 2006. "Wilhelm Maximilian Wundt." *The Stanford Encyclopedia of Philosophy*. http://plato.stanford.edu/entries/wilhelm-wundt/.

Kim, Jaegwon. 1998. *Philosophy of Mind*. Boulder: Westview Press.

Kosso, Peter. 1992. *Reading the Book of Nature: An Introduction to the Philosophy of Science*. Cambridge: Cambridge University Press.

Kukla, André. 1989. "Is AI an Empirical Science?" *Analysis* 49: 56–60.

———. 2001. *Methods of Theoretical Psychology*. Cambridge: MIT Press.

Lachman, Roy, Janet L. Lachman, and Earl C. Butterfield. 1979. *Cognitive Psychology and Information Processing. An Introduction*. Hillsdale, NJ: Lawrence Erlbaum.

Leahey, Thomas H. 1992. *A History of Psychology: Main Currents in Psychological Thought*. Englewood Cliffs, NJ: Prentice Hall.

Levin, Janet. 2013. "Functionalism." *The Stanford Encyclopedia of Philosophy*. http://plato.stanford.edu/entries/functionalism/.

Lewis, David K. 1966. "An Argument for the Identity Theory." *Journal of Philosophy* 63(2): 17–25.

Locke, Edwin A. 2009. "It's Time We Brought Introspection Out of the Closet." *Perspectives on Psychological Science* 4: 24–25.

Longuet-Higgings, Hugh C. 1981. "Artificial Intelligence—A New Theoretical Psychology?" *Cognition* 10: 197–200.

Lowe, E. Jonathan. 2000. *An Introduction to the Philosophy of Mind*. Cambridge: Cambridge University Press.

Lundin, Robert W. 1996. *Theories and Systems of Psychology*. Toronto: D. C. Heath.

Lycan, William G. 1994. "Functionalism (1)." In *A Companion to the Philosophy of Mind*, edited by Samuel Guttenplan, 317–23. Oxford: Blackwell.

Lyons, William E. 1986. *The Disappearance of Introspection*. Boston: MIT Press.

MacCorquodale, Kenneth, and Paul E. Meehl. 1948. "On a Distinction between Hypothetical Constructs and Intervening Variables." *Psychological Review* 55: 95–107.

Maia, Tiago V., and James L. McClelland. 2004. "A Re-Examination of the Evidence for the Somatic Marker Hypothesis: What Participants Know in the Iowa Gambling Task." *Proceedings of the National Academy of Sciences* 101: 16075–80.

Mandler, George. 2002. "Origins of the Cognitive (r)Evolution." *Journal of the History of the Behavioral Sciences* 38: 339–53.

———. 2007. *A History of Modern Experimental Psychology: From James and Wundt to Cognitive Science*. Cambridge: MIT Press.

Manson, Neil C. 2000. "A Tumbling-Ground for Whimsies? The History and Contemporary Role of the Conscious/Unconscious Contrast." In *History of the Mind-Body Problem*, edited by Tim Crane and Sarah A. Patterson, 148–68. London: Routledge.

Marcel, Anthony J. 2003. "Introspective Report: Trust, Self Knowledge and Science." *Journal of Consciousness Studies* 10(9): 167–86.

Marshall, Peter J. 2009. "Relating Psychology and Neuroscience. Taking Up the Challenges." *Perspectives on Psychological Science* 4(2): 113–25.

Marx, Melvin H. 1951. "Hypothesis and Construct." In *Psychological Theory. Contemporary Readings*, edited by Melvin H. Marx, 112–29. New York: Macmillan.

———. 1963. "The General Nature of Theory Construction." In *Theories in Contemporary Psychology*, edited by Melvin H. Marx, 4–46. New York: Macmillan.

Marx, Melvin H., and William A. Hillix. 1963. *Systems and Theories in Psychology*. New York: McGraw-Hill.

McBurney, Donald M., and Theresa L. White. 2010. *Research Methods*, 8th ed. Belmont: Wadsworth.

McCauley, Robert N., and Bechtel, William. 2001. "Explanatory Pluralism and the Heuristic Identity Theory." *Theory and Psychology* 11: 736–60.

McGinn, Colin. 1980. "Functionalism and Phenomenalism: A Critical Note." *Australasian Journal of Philosophy* 58(1): 35–46.

McLaughlin, Brian P. 1994. "Epiphenomenalism." In *A Companion to the Philosophy of Mind*, edited by Samuel Guttenplan, 277–88. Oxford: Blackwell.

Mehler, Jacques, John Morton, and Peter W. Jusczyk. 1984. "On Reducing Language to Biology." *Cognitive Neuropsychology* 1: 83–116.

Miller, George A. 1981. "Trends and Debates in Cognitive Psychology." *Cognition* 10: 215–25.

———. 2003. "The Cognitive Revolution: A Historical Perspective." *Trends in Cognitive Sciences* 7(3): 141–44.

Mischel, Theodore. 1970. "Wundt and the Conceptual Foundations of Psychology." *Philosophy and Phenomenological Research* 31(1): 1–26.

Mondini, Sara, Daniela Mapelli, Alec Vestri, and Patrizia S. Bisiacchi. 2003. *Esame neuropsicologico breve. Una batteria di test per lo screening neuropsicologico* (Short neuropsychological assessment. A neuropychological screening battery). Milan: Raffaello Cortina Editore.

Naqvi, Nasir H., Shiv Baba, and Antoine Bechara. 2006. "The Role of Emotion in Decision Making: A Cognitive Neuroscience Perspective." *Current Directions in Psychological Science* 15(5): 260–64.

Naqvi, Nasir H., and Antoine Bechara. 2006. "Skin Conductance: A Psychophysiological Approach to the Study of Decision Making." In *Methods in Mind*, edited by Carl Senior, Tamara Russell, and Michael S. Gazzaniga, 103–22. Cambridge: MIT Press.

Neisser, Ulric. 1967. *Cognitive Psychology*. New York: Meredith Publishing Company.

Newell, Allen, John C. Shaw, and Herbert A. Simon. 1958. "Elements of a Theory of Human Problem Solving." *Psychological Review* 65: 151–66.

Newell, Allen, and Herbert A. Simon. 1965. "Simulation of Human Processing of Information." *The American Mathematical Monthly* 72(2): 111–18.

———. 1976. "Computer Science as Empirical Inquiry: Symbols and Search." *Communications of the Association for Computing Machinery* 19(3): 113–26.

Newell, Ben R., and David R. Shanks. 2014. "Unconscious Influences on Decision Making: A Critical Review." *Behavioral and Brain Sciences* 37: 1–61.

Nickerson, Raymond S. 2003. "Cognitive Science: Experimental Methods." In *Encyclopedia of Cognitive Science*, vol. 1, edited by Lynn Nadel. Hoboken, NJ: Wiley and Sons.

Nisbett, Richard E., and Timothy D. Wilson. 1977. "Telling More Than We Can Know: Verbal Reports on Mental Processes." *Psychological Review* 84: 231–59.

Öhman, Arne, Alfons Hamm, and Kenneth Hugdahl. 2000. "Cognition and the Autonomic Nervous System. Orienting, Anticipation and Conditioning." In *Handbook of Psychophysiology*, 2nd ed., edited by John T. Cacioppo, Louis G. Tassinary, and Gary Bernstson, 522–75. Cambridge: Cambridge University Press.

Okasha, Samir. 2002. *Philosophy of Science. A Very Short Introduction*. Oxford: Oxford University Press.

Page, Mike P. A. 2006. "What Can't Functional Neuroimaging Tell the Cognitive Psychologist?" *Cortex* 42(3): 428–43.

Pedon, Arrigo, and Augusto Gnisi. 2004. *Metodologia della Ricerca in Psicologia* (Research methods in psychology). Bologna: Il Mulino.

Peek, Charles J. 2003. "A Primer of Biofeedback Instrumentation." In *Biofeedback. A Practitioner's Guide*, edited by Mark S. Schwartz and Frank Andrasik, 43–87. New York: Guilford Press.

Petersen, Steven E., Peter T. Fox, Michael I. Posner, Mark A. Mintun, and Marcus E. Raichle. 1988. "Positron Emission Tomographic Studies of the Cortical Anatomy of Single-Word Processing." *Nature* 331(6157): 585–89.

Phelps, Elizabeth A. 1999. "Brain vs. Behavioral Studies in Cognition." In *The Nature of Cognition*, edited by Robert J. Sternberg, 295–322. Cambridge: MIT Press.

Piattelli Palmarini, Massimo. 2005. *Psicologia ed Economia delle Scelte. Quattro Lezioni al Collège de France* (Psychology and Economics of Choices. Four Lectures at the College of France). Turin: Codice Edizioni.

Piccolo, Domenico. 1998. *Statistica* (Statistics). Bologna: Il Mulino.

Place, Ullin T. 1956. "Is Consciousness a Brain Process?" *British Journal of Psychology* 47: 44–50.

Polger, Thomas W. 2004. *Natural Minds.* Cambridge: MIT Press.

Previc, Fred H. 1996. "Occipital Lobe." In *The Blackwell Dictionary of Neuropsychology*, edited by J. Graham Beaumont, Pamela M. Kenealy, and Marcus J. C. Rogers, 540–47. Oxford: Blackwell.

Putnam, Hilary. 1960. "Minds and Machines." In *Dimensions of Mind*, edited by Sidney Hook, 148–78. New York: New York University Press.

———. 1975. 'The Nature of Mental States." In *Mind, Language, and Reality: Philosophical Papers*, vol. 2, 429–40. Cambridge: Cambridge University Press.

———. 1997. "Functionalism: Cognitive Science or Science Fiction?" In *The Future of Cognitive Revolution*, edited by David M. Johnson, and Christina E. Erneling, 32–44. New York: Oxford University Press.

Reber, Arthur S. 1989. "Implicit Learning and Tacit Knowledge." *Journal of Experimental Psychology: General* 118: 219–25.

Reber, Arthur S., and Emily Reber. 2001. *The Penguin Dictionary of Psychology.* London: Penguin.

Reed, Edward S. 1997. *From Soul to Mind: The Emergence of Psychology from Erasmus Darwin to William James.* New Haven: Yale University Press.

Rey, Georges. 1997. *Contemporary Philosophy of Mind: A Contentiously Classical Approach.* Oxford: Blackwell.

Robinson, Howard. 2011. "Dualism." *The Stanford Encyclopedia of Philosophy.* http://plato.stanford.edu/entries/dualism/.

Rosen, Gideon. 2012. "Abstract Objects." *The Stanford Encyclopedia of Philosophy.* http://plato.stanford.edu/entries/abstract-objects/.

Rosenthal, David M. 1994. "Identity Theories." In *A Companion to the Philosophy of Mind*, edited by Samuel Guttenplan, 348–55. Oxford: Blackwell.

Rossetti, Yves, and Antti Revonsuo, eds. 2000. *Beyond Dissociation: Interaction Between Implicit and Explicit Processing.* Amsterdam: John Benjamins.

Sarter, Martin, Gary G. Berntson, and John T. Cacioppo. 1996. "Brain Imaging and Cognitive Neuroscience: Toward Strong Inference in Attributing Function to Structure." *American Psychologist* 51: 13–21.

Schultz, Duane P., and Sydney E. Schultz. 1996. *History of Modern Psychology*. Fort Worth: Harcourt Brace.

Schwitzgebel, Eric. 2014. "Introspection." *The Stanford Encyclopedia of Philosophy*. http://plato.stanford.edu/entries/introspection/.

Shallice, Tim. 1988. *From Neuropsychology to Mental Structure*. Cambridge: Cambridge University Press.

Simon, Herbert A. 1993. "The Human Mind: The Symbolic Level." *Proceedings of the American Philosophical Society* 137(4): 638–47.

———. 1992. "What Is an 'Explanation' of Behavior?" *Psychological Science* 3: 150–61.

Smart, John J. C. 1959. "Sensations and Brain Processes." *The Philosophical Review* 68(2): 141–56.

———. 2007. "The Identity Theory of Mind." *The Stanford Encyclopedia of Philosophy*. http://plato.stanford.edu/entries/mind-identity/.

Smith, Edward E. 1997. "Infusing Cognitive Neuroscience into Cognitive Psychology." In *Mind and Brain Sciences in the 21st Century*, edited by Robert L. Solso, 71–90. Cambridge: MIT Press.

Smith, Eliot R., and Frederick D. Miller. 1978. "Limits on Perception of Cognitive Processes: A Reply to Nisbett and Wilson." *Psychological Review* 85(4): 355–62.

Sober, Elliott. 1998. "Black Box Inference: When Should Intervening Variables Be Postulated?" *British Journal of Philosophy of Science* 49: 469–98.

———. 1999. "The Multiple Realizability Argument Against Reductionism." *Philosophy of Science* 66(4): 542–64.

Solso, Robert L. 1991. *Cognitive Psychology*. Boston: Allyn and Bacon.

Spence, Kenneth W. 1951. "Types of Constructs in Psychology." In *Theories in Contemporary Psychology*, edited by Melvin H. Marx, 162–78. New York: Macmillan.

Sternberg, Robert J. 1996. *Cognitive Psychology*. Fort Worth: Harcourt Brace College Publishers.

Stevens, Stanley S. 1963. "Operationism and Logical Positivism." In *Theories in Contemporary Psychology*, edited by Melvin H. Marx, 47–76. New York: Macmillan.

Stich, Stephen. 1978. "Beliefs and Sub-Doxastic States." *Philosophy of Science* 45(4): 499–518.

St. Johns, Mark F., and David R. Shanks. 1997. "Implicit Learning from an Information Processing Standpoint." In *How Implicit Is Implicit Learning?*, edited by Dianne C. Berry, 162–94. Oxford: Oxford University Press.

Tassinary, Louis G., John T. Cacioppo, and Eric J. Vanman. 2000. "The Skeletomotor System: Surface Electromyography." In *Handbook of Psychophysiology*, 2nd ed., edited by John T. Cacioppo, Louis G. Tassinary, and Gary Bernstson, 267–99. Cambridge: Cambridge University Press.

Thagard, Paul. 2009. "Why Cognitive Science Needs Philosophy and Vice Versa." *Topics in Cognitive Science* 1: 237–54.

Tolman, Edward C. 1922. “A New Formula for Behaviourism.” In *Collected Papers in Psychology*, 1–8. Berkeley: University of California Press, 1951.

———. 1925a. “Purpose and Cognition: The Determiners of Animal Learning.” In *Collected Papers in Psychology,* 38–47. Berkeley: University of California Press, 1951.

———. 1925b. “Behaviourism and Purpose.” In *Collected Papers in Psychology*, 32–37. Berkeley: University of California Press, 1951.

———. 1935. “Psychology versus Immediate Experience.” *Philosophy of Science* 2(3): 356–80.

———. 1936. “Operational Behaviourism and Current Trends in Psychology.” In *Collected Papers in Psychology*, 115–29. Berkeley: University of California Press, 1951.

———. 1948. “Cognitive Maps in Rats and Men.” In *Collected Papers in Psychology*, 241–65. Berkeley: University of California Press, 1951.

Tranel, Daniel, and Antonio R. Damasio. 2000. “Neuropsychology and Behavioral Neurology.” In *Handbook of Psychophysiology*, 2nd ed., edited by John T. Cacioppo, Louis G. Tassinary, and Gary Bernstson, 119–41. Cambridge: Cambridge University Press.

Uttal, William R. 1998. *Toward a New Behaviourism: The Case against Perceptual Reductionism*. Mahwah, NJ: Lawrence Erlbaum.

Van Orden, Guy C., and Kenneth R. Papp. 1997. “Functional Neuroimages Fail to Discover Pieces of Mind in the Parts of the Brain.” *Philosophy of Science* 64 (Proceedings): S85–S94.

Van Orden, G. C., Bruce F. Pennington, and Gregory O. Stone. 2001. “What Do Double Dissociations Prove?” *Cognitive Science* 25: 111–72.

Von Eckdart, Barbara. 2003. “Cognitive Science: Philosophical Issues.” In *Encyclopedia of Cognitive Science*, vol. 1, edited by Lynn Nadel. Hoboken, NJ: Wiley and Sons.

Ward, Jamie. 2006. *The Student's Guide to Cognitive Neuroscience*. New York: Psychology Press.

Watson, John B. 1913. “Psychology as the Behaviorist Views It.” *Psychological Review* 20: 158–77.

———. 1925. *Behaviorism*. London: Kegan Paul.

Wegner, Daniel M. 2005. “Who Is the Controller of Controlled Processes?” In *The New Unconscious*, edited by Ran R. Hassin, James S. Uleman, and John A. Bargh, 19–36. Oxford: Oxford University Press.

White, Peter. 1980. “Limitations on Verbal Reports of Internal Events: A Refutation of Nisbett and Wilson and of Bem.” *Psychological Review* 87(1): 105–12.

Wilson, Timothy D. 2002. *Strangers to Ourselves*. Cambridge: Harvard University Press.

Wozniak, Robert H. 1997. “Behaviorism.” In *A Pictorial History of Psychology*, edited by Wolfgang G. Bringmann, Helmut F. Luck, Rudolf Miller, and Charles E. Early, 198–205. Chicago: Quintessence.

Wundt, Wilhelm M. 1897. *Outlines of Psychology*, translated by C. H. Judd. London: Williams and Norgate, 1902.

Index

About the Author

Giuseppe Lo Dico is a postdoctoral fellow in philosophy of the human sciences and psychological sciences and practice at Catholic University of Milan. His research interests focus on the empirical and epistemological foundations of psychology including the concept of mind as the basis for different psychological paradigms, the nature of psychological explanation, the sources of data for psychological research, and the intersection between psychology and other disciplines such as economics and neurobiology.

www.ingramcontent.com/pod-product-compliance
Lightning Source LLC
LaVergne TN
LVHW101448200926
848483LV00001B/87
* 9 7 8 1 4 9 8 5 1 6 6 0 0 *